Advance Praise for

Superbia!

Superbia! is a great read while you're stuck in traffic. It's full of practical ideas for moving from commuting to community. Whether you live in the city or in the 'burbs, it will help you connect with nature, with neighbors, and with yourself.

— JIM DIERS, Founding Director, Seattle Department of Neighborhoods

Chiras and Wann have not only visualized ways to create a higher quality of life, they provide real life examples of people who are doing it. I highly recommend this book as a model for action. Do it for yourselves; but most of all, do it for your children.

JUDY CORBETT, Executive Director, Local Government Commission

This is a book about connections: connecting with our neighbors, connecting our communities and the ecosystem, and connecting our everyday lives to our search for quality. Dan Chiras and Dave Wann show us that these connections aren't available only to those who live in new developments designed on the principles of new urbanism, smart communities or sustainability. With some thought and effort, we can establish these connections in our existing neighborhoods. Under the Chiras-Wann blueprint, sustainability in suburban America can grow from the exception to the rule.

— WILLIAM BECKER, founder of the U.S. Department of Energy's Center of Excellence for Sustainable Development.

31 ways to create
sustainable
neighborhoods

Superbia!

DAN CHIRAS & DAVE WANN

Sustainable Suburbs Project
The Sustainable Futures Society

NEW SOCIETY PUBLISHERS

Cataloguing in Publication Data:
A catalog record for this publication is available from the National Library of Canada.

Cover design by Diane McIntosh. Cover Image, background suburb: Photodisc Blue (RF).
Interior design by Jeremy Drought, Last Impresssion Publishing Service, Calgary, Alberta
Printed in Canada by Transcontinental Printing.

New Society Publishers acknowledges the support of the Government of Canada through the Book Publishing
Industry Development Program (BPIDP) for our publishing activities.

Paperback ISBN: 0–86571–490–8

Inquiries regarding requests to reprint all or part of *Superbia! 31 Ways to Create Sustainable Neighborhoods*
should be addressed to New Society Publishers at the address below.

To order directly from the publishers, please add $4.50 shipping to the price of the first copy, and $1.00 for
each additional copy (plus GST in Canada). Send check or money order to:

New Society Publishers
P.O. Box 189, Gabriola Island, BC V0R 1X0, Canada
1 (800) 567•6772

New Society Publishers' mission is to publish books that contribute in fundamental ways to building an
ecologically sustainable and just society, and to do so with the least possible impact on the environment, in a
manner that models this vision. We are committed to doing this not just through education, but through
action. We are acting on our commitment to the world's remaining ancient forests by phasing out our paper
supply from ancient forests worldwide. This book is one step towards ending global deforestation and climate
change. It is printed on acid-free paper that is 100% old growth forest-free (100% post-consumer recycled),
processed chlorine free, and printed with vegetable based, low VOC inks. For further information, or to
browse our full list of books and purchase securely, visit our website at www.newsociety.com

NEW SOCIETY PUBLISHERS   www.newsociety.com

Books for Wiser Living from *Mother Earth News*

Today, more than ever before, our society is seeking ways to live more conscientiously. To help bring you the very best inspiration and information about greener, more-sustainable lifestyles, New Society Publishers has joined forces with *Mother Earth News*. For more than 30 years, *Mother Earth* has been North America's "Original Guide to Living Wisely," creating books and magazines for people with a passion for self-reliance and a desire to live in harmony with nature. Across the countryside and in our cities, New Society Publishers and *Mother Earth News* are leading the way to a wiser, more sustainable world.

Contents

Acknowledgments

WE GRATEFULLY ACKNOWLEDGE THE MANY PEOPLE who contributed to this book and to our work on *Superbia!* To G. Winter, president of the Sustainable Futures Society, who played a pivotal role in the birth of this project, a world of thanks.

Interviews conducted several years ago with authors James Kunstler and Alan Durning, and with New Urbanists Peter Calthorpe, Andres Duany, Elizabeth Plater-Zyberk, Victor Dover, Elizabeth Moule, Harrison Rue, Dan Williams, Jonathan Rose, and others were extremely useful in launching this project. We would also like to thank the many people who recently responded to a stream of questions from the two of us: Lois Arkin (L.A. Eco-Village), Jim Diers (Seattle Neighborhoods), Judy Corbett (Local Government Commission, Sacramento), Doug Linkhart and Jane Hanley (Neighborhood Resource Center, Denver), Deb French (Denver), Brad Lancaster (Tucson), David Engwicht (Creative Communities International, Australia), Albert Bates (Ecovillage Training Center at The Farm), Jim Soules and Ross Chapin (The Cottage Company, Seattle), Val Oliver (Crystal Waters Ecovillage), Cherie Murphy (Elgin, Illinois), Jim Cowern (City of Boulder), Daniel Lerch (The City Repair Project, Portland, Oregon), Kim Hendess (Better Environmentally Sound Transportation, Vancouver, B.C.), Charles Ehrlich (Muir Commons, Davis, California, Kevin Wolf (N Street Cohousing, Davis, California), Penny Poyzer (Global Action Plan, London, England), Fred Olson (The Cohousing Network, Berkeley), Shay Salomon (Tucson), and Jon Schulz (Sustainable Futures Society). We also gratefully acknowledge the many people who provided photographs for this book.

Our many colleagues in the sustainable building and cohousing movements deserve some of the credit for this book's contents. As a concept, *Superbia!* has been coalescing in many minds. We are excited about giving it shape and grateful for the hard work and dedication of our friends and colleagues.

We'd like to express our extreme gratitude to our publisher, Chris Plant, of New Society Publications, for believing in this idea and taking a chance on it. It has been a pleasure working with you and your fine staff on this book.

We would also like to thank the directors of the Sustainable Futures Society for providing financial, intellectual, and moral support for this project. Their comments have shaped its contents and helped us understand both the obstacles we face in creating sustainable neighborhoods and the many benefits that will accrue to those who embark on this path. We and our SFS colleagues, a band of cutting-edge thinkers, are eager to help neighborhoods achieve Superbia! through workshops, consultation, and other means.

Dan Chiras   Dave Wann

We should seek the atmosphere and the surroundings that call forth the best that is in us.
COUNCILLOR

Introduction
From Suburbia to Superbia!

THIS IS A BOOK ABOUT REINVENTING *existing* neighborhoods — both suburban and urban — to make them livelier and more productive, a goal shared by many. For example, many residents of suburban neighborhoods, where the majority of the American population now lives, express a longing for a stronger sense of place, including stronger connections with people, local traditions, and nature. Urban residents express similar desires. This book offers specific ideas for social and physical changes to enrich the neighborhoods we already live in. It's intended as a book of possibilities for reconnecting people with both neighbors and nature.

We believe most neighborhoods have the raw ingredients and resources to become sustainable, resilient, and healthy. We want to help make that transition happen because the potential economic, environmental, and social benefits are huge! But it won't happen automatically — it will take cooperation, vision, and strategy. The truth is, many neighborhoods are currently programmed for dysfunction.

In this book we'll look at three major barriers that limit options in the suburbs:

- The physical layout of suburbs, which results in social isolation and resource consumption (for example, lots of driving and high fuel bills).

- The "mold" of suburban culture, which reinforces extravagant, private lifestyles that often disregard public values and require expensive, time-consuming maintenance.

- Government incentives, municipal zoning laws, and bank lending policies that shaped suburbia but have become obsolete. American culture has changed, but the rules haven't.

1

Superbia! presents 31 specific steps that neighborhood groups can take to overcome these barriers and bring their neighborhoods fully into bloom. The first steps involve the creation of a more active, neighborly culture — a "we" rather than "me" mentality. Later steps take advantage of neighborhood skills and strengths to create significant changes in landscape, architecture, resource use, traffic patterns, municipal landscaping and building policies, and overall functioning of the neighborhood. Instead of just remodeling our houses, we remodel our neighborhoods, using a powerful resource that is often untapped these days — cooperation.

Examples from dynamic neighborhoods on this continent and elsewhere demonstrate techniques for becoming more sustainable — meaning that essential needs are met closer to home and in more environmentally friendly ways. In a sustainable community, energy, health, elder care, day care, entertainment, water, employment and enterprise, transportation, and horticulture are all set up as efficiently and accessibly as possible to meet people's needs with the least amount of effort and resources. The compelling incentive is that a more efficient, supportive neighborhood will require less time, money, stress, and human effort from residents, increasing their quality of life.

What we propose here are refreshing changes in suburban and urban culture, one neighborhood at a time. With the empowerment of a neighborhood alliance, we can make small but significant changes in both architecture and landscape. Creating sustainable neighborhoods will require flexible thinking and a willingness to experiment, but it can be an adventure that adds purpose and excitement to our lives. The truth is, we need fresh ideas that will carry our neighborhoods through the challenges and transitions that lie ahead.

Compared to thousand-year-old villages throughout the world, our neighborhoods are very young indeed. Suburbs built in the last half-century have not yet faced major changes that occur over long periods of time — changes in resource availability, demographics, work patterns, and other "mega-trends" — but they will. Fortunately there's plenty of room for adaptation and improvement because many American suburbs, especially those built recently, were engineered for consumption, not efficiency. For cars, not people. They were built to provide housing, not community, even though Gallup, Fannie Mae, and Roper polls report that people value a good neighborhood over a trophy home by a margin of three to one. It hasn't occurred to most Americans to reinvent their suburban neighborhoods because many are relatively new, and because there aren't many roadmaps out there like this book, which presents alternatives.

If we begin to think outside the box of the individual home, we can move our neighborhoods beyond adolescence into maturity. It's a safe bet that no one else is going to do it for us. We urge you to use our ideas to get started, and then add your own customizations to bring your neighborhood into blossom. Write us and tell us what you're up to! (Our address is in the Appendix).

Spreading out means driving more to do the same.
F. KAID BENFIELD, MATTHEW D. RAIMI, DONALD D.T. CHEN, *Once There Were Greenfields*

1

The Changing Face of Suburbia

THE AMERICAN HOUSE-AND-CAR SUBURB was invented in Los Angeles in the 1920s, but after World War II it became an American institution. Following the war, 14 million military personnel with sudden family syndrome played a frantic game of musical chairs, living with extended family or friends or wherever else they could find, from converted boxcars to chicken coops and garages. Crowds lined up at funeral parlors to get the addresses of newly vacant apartments. One Omaha newspaper ad read, "Big Ice Box, 7 by 17 feet. Could be fixed up to live in."

In response to the emergency, the US government shifted gears and came up with a new plan of attack. We had open land and we knew how to access it strategically. You could say we declared war on American soil, deploying bulldozers instead of tanks to level hills, fill creeks, and yank trees out like weeds to build one subdivision after another. And the economy boomed![1]

Various factors shaped the suburbs, including the availability of open, affordable land, the embrace of the automobile; urban flight from the inner city; and the birth of a glitzy new American dream in which every family aspired to have its own house in the suburbs, filled with the latest new appliances as seen in programs like *The Donna Reed Show* and *Leave It To Beaver* on the new technology of television. Even fear played into the equation. These were the days of bomb shelters and elementary school kids obediently covering their heads in basement hallways during air-raid drills. Military experts warned that if a nuclear attack occurred, high-density developments would be more vulnerable, so we should spread development out. Highways would be needed to evacuate civilians after the bombs hit. President Dwight D. Eisenhower met that challenge by signing the Interstate Highway Act in 1956, which authorized and scheduled the construction of 41,000 miles of roads.

Economists loved what the new dream did for the Gross National Product, and the media loved the storyline: "GI Families Occupy Suburbia." Developer William Levitt, a five-star general on the tract home front, appeared on the cover of *Time* magazine, and stories about Levittown, the nation's first subdivision in New York, also ran in *Life* and *Reader's Digest.* How could we question this energetic, giddy, sexy dream? All the pieces seemed to fit together, and money flowed into the country's green fields like harvested grain through a combine, making subdivisions the last and most profitable crop. In battalions of brand-new Fords and Chevies, Americans rolled into the suburbs on highways and streets that now measure 4 million miles — enough to circle the planet 157 times. Just ten years earlier, only 44 percent of American homes were owned by residents, and fewer than half of the households had cars. But that was changing, quickly.

The ideal of the suburb was country homes for city people — nature without the mud. In the suburbs, a family could have it all: community, fresh air, proximity to the city, and convenience. "The most house for the money" was the mantra for both buyers and sellers. Naturally, people wanted the biggest and best piece of the dream they could get, and the best perceived value was in the suburbs. With the Federal Housing Administration (FHA) guaranteeing buyers' loans, the new American dream lay on the horizon — on the outskirts of Emerald City.

But there was a glitch.

A legal precedent, *Ambler v Euclid* (1926), in effect made it illegal to put houses, businesses, and stores together in suburban neighborhoods. Based on the dubious assumption that residences should be separate from commerce, civic life, and even recreation, planning departments throughout North America adopted boilerplate zoning codes. The result was look-alike neighborhoods that stretched from suburban Toronto to suburban San Diego. Rather than being custom designed to fit the needs of each piece of land, subdivisions were mass-produced like automobiles or metal mailboxes.

As Andres Duany, Elizabeth Plater-Zyberk, and Jeff Speck explain in *Suburban Nation,* "A typical contemporary zoning code has several land use designations; not only is housing

1.1: *The typical suburban house emphasizes private space but neglects public and community space. Credit: Dave Wann.*

separated (by code) from industry but low-density housing is separated from medium-density housing, which is separated from high-density housing. Medical offices are separated from general offices, which in turn are separated from restaurants and shopping." Americans took the habits of the past and technologies of the present and turned them into codes and laws for the future. Because it was assumed that we'd always love our cars, much of suburbia was built with a drive-in mentality. The result: you can't get anywhere on foot. The new template of suburban design housed fewer people per unit of land than ever before and required much more resource-intensive travel time.

Nevertheless, without much of a trial period, low-density, large-lot housing became the standard, prescribed and encoded in great detail in the planning manuals. The quality of "community" was somehow thought to be automatic or unnecessary — or was not thought about at all. Developers didn't worry about this intangible quality when the standard formula (code-driven mass production of houses) was very lucrative indeed.

1.2: About 38 million suburban homes were built in the United States between 1950 and 2000. Together, they represent an incredible opportunity for increasing efficiency, security, and quality of life. Credit: Dave Wann.

Suburban *villages* — subdivisions that looked more like small towns with all the amenities — were rarely an option, so the new homeowners bought what was available. They let the experts build new kinds of neighborhoods, not realizing their expertise had more to do with engineering than with the design of people-friendly communities. "We live today in cities and suburbs whose form and character we did not choose," write the authors of *Suburban Nation*. "They were imposed on us, by federal policy, local zoning laws, and the demands of the automobile. If these influences are reversed — and they can be — an environment designed around the true needs of individuals, conducive to the formation of community and preservation of the landscape, becomes possible."

That's the purpose of this book: to put us back in charge of our own neighborhoods. This is a non-partisan, participatory, and fundamentally patriotic endeavor. The potential for energy and water savings and reduced environmental impact is mind-boggling, and so are the social benefits. Imagine what suburbia would be like if we had new centers of business, recreation and art right in our neighborhoods; slower traffic, more

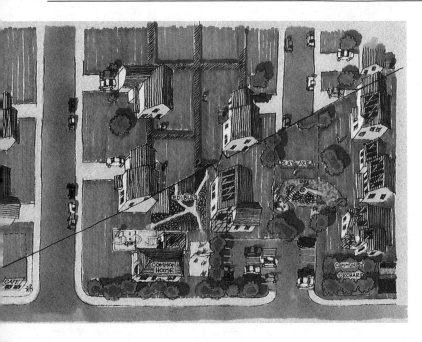

1.3: The transition from suburbia to Superbia! might include clustered parking to save space and get cars out of people's way, greater use of solar energy, community gardens, and a common house owned cooperatively by the neighbors. Credit: Dan Bohlan.

public space, and more opportunities for cooperation and support. These elements are within our grasp simply because we live somewhere and have neighbors. There's no shortage of ideas, either. We're in the right place at the right time.

The Booming Burbs

We want to make it clear up front that we aren't bashing the burbs. In fact, both of us were born in and currently live in variations of suburbs. Rather, we're looking for ways to make them better because, let's face it, we've already sunk trillions of dollars into the suburbs. There are 50 *million* suburban homes already built (three-quarters of them since 1950), along with millions of miles of roads, billions of square feet of malls and office parks, and 30 million acres of suburban lawn. We're talking about protecting and enhancing that investment, making it more enjoyable, less stressful, and more fulfilling. We think it's inevitable that 50 or 75 years from now we'll employ millions of people to upgrade building stock and rearrange metropolitan areas — including "constructive demolition" of chunks of suburbia — to make them more dense and efficient, like small towns. Many suburban developments were simply not built to last, and they weren't built to save energy, either. However, in the short term we need to appreciate and optimize what we have. Instead of judgment, we need creativity.

What I (Dave) call home is a "cohousing" community, Harmony Village, which I helped design, physically and socially, in 1994. The village's 27 households are in Golden, Colorado, a small suburban town with a great sense of place. From my experience with this project, I know firsthand that cooperative efforts can get things done. I'll describe Harmony in more detail in Chapter 4.

I was born right at the epicenter of the mid-century baby boom, in a prototype tract home development — Park Forest, Illinois — 30 miles south of the Loop in Chicago. I remember the abundance of dragonflies and toads by a stream only a short bike ride from my house — until the stream was channeled into a culvert and paved over. And I remember spending a whole morning with my dad about 50 years ago, transplanting a cottonwood sapling from the "swamp" near that stream. In those days there was still open land we kids could play on. Little did we know it was already slated for development.

When I was eight we moved to a classic 1890s vintage suburb, Larchmont, New York, where I spent my elementary through high school years. I went back there a few years ago, stepping into a time warp. Same cracks in the sidewalk (a kid would notice), same steel steps at the elementary school, same shortcut through my girlfriend's backyard under the dogwood trees, same sturdy homes, many made from stone or brick. Larchmont had strong bones and still does: great parks and landscaping, the ocean, proximity to the Big Apple, open areas near its borders with adjacent towns, and a great little downtown.

I tested town planner Peter Calthorpe's ideal walking distance from house to shops and parks, discovering that my old house was a perfect five minutes from downtown. I was also tempted to try architect Andres Duany's blindfold test, in which you assume that slow-moving cars will stop if you cross a commercial street blindfolded. I think the test would have worked, but I didn't feel like scaring the drivers. A commuter train, always on time, pulled up as I walked past the station, and 20 or 30 people climbed aboard. My visit to Larchmont made me realize that when certain

1.4: Dave's Park Forest, Illinois, tract house in 2003, with a half-century-old cottonwood tree that he and his dad planted in the front yard. Credit: Park Forest Public Library

1.5: Located west of Denver, in a mountain subdivision, Dan's house is heated and powered by the sun. Credit: Dan Chiras.

features are incorporated in the design phase, neighborhoods have a higher quality of life right from the start.

Dan also draws on his life experiences. He has lived in suburban and rural environments for more than 50 years and spent most of the last 25 years focusing on creating more environmentally friendly homes. First he retrofitted several conventional homes for greater energy efficiency and greater reliance on renewable energy. More recently he designed a house from the ground up to optimize environmental performance.

That house uses about a quarter of the electricity a conventionally built home does, and the electricity it does use comes from the sun via photovoltaic panels. The house was built using a variety of environmentally friendly building materials, including tile, carpeting, carpet pad, paint, and insulation made from recycled materials. It has been featured in *Solar Today*, *Mother Earth News*, and on NBC Nightly News. It is regularly included on the American Solar Energy Society's National Tour of Solar Homes.

Dan has also worked on other aspects of Superbia!, including water conservation, organic gardening, composting, recycling, alternative wastewater systems, and community development. He currently lives in a mountain subdivision in Evergreen, Colorado, where he participates in an organic food-buying co-op.

One of his earlier homes, in an inner ring suburb of Denver, is a good example of how suburban neighborhoods can mature and blossom. After Dan moved from the neighborhood, developers remodeled a shopping mall into a New Urbanist neighborhood — a small village that looks a lot like a traditional people-friendly town with a park, shops, and restaurants all within walking distance of residences.

The two of us have always had an interest in adapting the suburbs to meet more of our needs directly. We think suburban villages can work, even in the U.S. where too often, in Gertrude Stein's words, "There's no there there." Nor should readers living in older urban neighborhoods put this book down. Most, if not all, of what we have to say about the suburbs applies to urban settings as well. You can create Superbia! just about anywhere.

What Exactly is Suburbia — and What Is It Becoming?

For the purposes of this book, we define suburbia as car-dependent, land-hungry, strictly residential neighborhoods that are physically isolated from schools, workplaces and civic centers. Quite often suburbs don't have pedestrian access to neighborhood shopping; they don't have a center or a sense of community; elderly, young, and physically challenged residents are often isolated; populations are often ethnically homogeneous. In upscale suburbia, homeowners often feel the pinch of escalating bills for energy, water, and transportation. Consumption is finally unmasked as time-consuming because of all the driving and shopping that is necessary, and the joy of accumulating suburban *stuff* often seems to wear thin.

People in suburbia want a greater connection with nature. They want to be more productive and less competitive. Many are tired of getting by on less sleep than they need, and the thought of ever-longer commutes does not tickle anyone's funny bone either. Stress levels are high, and working in one's home, or at least closer to home, seems advantageous.

The transformation to something better — Superbia! — will require an understanding of where we are now, where we came from, and where we are going. The suburbs are changing so quickly that we need to stop, take a deep breath, and see how some of the changes will affect suburban lifestyles.

While the suburbs used to be satellites of the city — bedroom communities for commuting and consuming — most of them are now components of a metropolitan mosaic and are not necessarily dependent on the urban core. In fact, many of the early, first-ring suburbs have become part of the urban core and face inner-city challenges such as aging infrastructure, crime, and unemployment. Meanwhile, 25 minutes up the highway, second and third-ring suburbs have in recent years become financial strongholds, where the world headquarters of corporations like AOL, Dell, Cablevision, and Lockheed Martin are located. Where was the Computer Age born? In the suburbs — not San Francisco, but Silicon Valley.

In 1979, 74 percent of American office space was still located in cities, according to the Brookings Institution. A short 25 years later, the suburbs' share of total office space has risen to 42 percent and will soon pass 50 percent. Sociologist Bruce Katz calls it the "exit ramp economy," with commercial and retail facilities increasingly located along suburban freeways and commercial strips, providing tax benefits for solicitous suburban governments.[2]

The 2000 U.S. Census shows that the suburbs now contain more *non*-family houses — young singles and elderly couples — than traditional households of married couples with children. *A full quarter of the population now lives alone.* (With Ozzie gone, Harriet struggles to maintain both the house and her own health.) The aging of the U.S. population will present major challenges for the suburbs: half of the population is now 35 or older, and every eight seconds an American turns 50. The lack of eldercare, especially in the suburbs, has become an emergency.

More people are working at home than a decade ago. This is an environmental benefit because it reduces transportation costs and pollution, but it is also a potential social liability because the workplace community is lost.

1.6 & 1.7: In 1954, Fairview Gardens near Santa Barbara, California, was one farm among many, but 50 years later it's surrounded by suburban homes. At first the neighbors resented farmer Michael Ableman's operation, but eventually they adopted it as the neighborhood farm. Credit: Michael Ableman.

Fairview Gardens 1998

1.8: Two cars in each driveway, and how many more in the garages? There are now more cars in the U.S. than licensed drivers. Credit: Dave Wann.

The ethnic mix of the suburbs is changing, too. A recent study of metropolitan Washington DC demonstrated that in the 1990s, 87 percent of immigrants chose to live in the suburbs rather than the city. Far from being the Caucasian enclaves they once were, the suburbs are becoming intercultural. The majority of Asian Americans, half of Hispanics, and 40 percent of American blacks now live in the burbs.[3]

The legendary baby boom, which saw 76 million babies born between 1946 and 1964, is a primary reason the US population nearly doubled in the last 50 years, shooting from 150 million to 280 million. If you get the feeling that the familiar landscapes are disappearing quickly, population surge is one of the reasons why — and there's more on the way. The Census Bureau projects that by 2050 the U.S. will have as many people as India had in 1950 — 400 million.

The point is, as the available pieces of our enormous pie continue to shrink, we'll see the value of each morsel of land become more precious. Housing patterns will contract to reflect this new value. We'll build up rather than out, even in the suburbs, and we'll also build closer together. The car, public space-eater number one, will have to curb its appetite. Since each car requires a fifth of an acre for its share of roads and parking spaces, every additional five cars smothers another football field-sized chunk of America the size of a football field. Ponder this image for a moment: *38 million* football fields, already covered with pavement.[4]

One might compare the changes in suburbia with a jacket that doesn't fit anymore. Our central focus in this book is at the neighborhood scale, where both personal shape and the jacket can be altered.

A Place Apart: The Evolution of Suburban Culture

For millennia, people have looked for homes away from the city center. In a letter on a cuneiform tablet written in 539 BC, a suburbanite told the king of Persia, "Our property seems to me to be the most beautiful in the world. So close are we to Babylon that we enjoy all of the advantages of the City, yet when we come home we are away from all the noise and the dust." We can imagine the writer striding in sandals down the exit trail to the good life.

The word "suburb" was first used in 14th-century England to refer to a hamlet outside the walls or boundaries of the city. Within a few hundred years, suburbs moved farther out, becoming royal retreats from the hot and often stinky days of summer in the city. The new merchant class wanted a place apart, too. In Victorian-era Clapham, outside of London, merchants could be weekend aristocrats on their tiny estates, retreating from the noise, smoke, and congestion they had to tolerate during their workweeks.

> *The old suburban dream is increasingly out of sync with today's culture. Our suburbs are designed around a stereotypical household that is no longer predominant. But we continue to build suburbs as if families were large and had only one breadwinner, as if the jobs were all downtown, as if land and energy were endless, and as if another lane on the freeway would end congestion.*
>
> PETER CALTHORPE, *The Next American Metropolis*

The first American suburbs were built in the 19th century along streetcar and train lines that radiated from central cities like spokes on a bicycle wheel. Development occurred linearly, typically within a five-minute walk of the transit station. The streetcar suburb was apart from the city, yet still a satellite.

In the 1920s the idea of the automobile suburb spread outward from Los Angeles with enthusiastic endorsement from city leaders.

Throughout those early years, when L.A. sprawl was gobbling farmland and converting it into freeways and subdivisions, there were advocates for comprehensive planning, but they were largely unnoticed as the flash flood of large-lot ranch houses smothered the city. Regional planner Catherine Bauer Wurster, for example, insisted that the preoccupation with individual homes must go, to be replaced by strategies for building integrated communities capable of meeting their own needs. Maybe the car engines were too loud — few people heard what she and colleagues like architectural scholar Lewis Mumford had to say.

Individual homes and auto dependence were also the themes of suburbs like Levittown, forerunner of a "suburban-industrial complex" that ultimately built hundreds of thousands of subdivisions. In Levittown, New York, developers mass-produced 30 four-bedroom houses a day by dividing the construction process into 27 different steps. Every piece of lumber was numbered, every nail accounted for, and every task in the house-building process was given to a different team.

Each home came with one willow tree and three fruit trees in addition to 28 to 30 flowers and shrubs. Interestingly, in the sales agreement signed by each new homeowner, Levitt mandated one of this book's 31 steps: no fences were allowed around the properties. The result was that the backyards formed a large

1.9: When the prototype suburban tract development, Levittown, was built in the late 1940s, William Levitt specified "no fences" in the contract. Though that mandate was gradually forgotten, many early residents recall how pleasant it was. Credit: Charles Tekula.

common area. Early residents have fond memories of the big backyard — the kids played together safely, there was room for parties, and everyone knew everyone else.

But in the 1960s the world changed rapidly, and the quality of community suffered. Robert Putnam, author of *Bowling Alone*, writes, "It's as though the postwar generations were exposed to some mysterious X-ray that permanently and increasingly rendered them less likely to connect with the community." The X-ray (or was it the TV-ray?) blanketed all age groups. One celebrant at Levittown's 50th anniversary recalled that the adults began to go out to dinner more often in the 1960s, a rare event a decade earlier. The kids, bored by neighborhoods where there was "nothing to do," began to inhabit the shopping centers.

The one-time Levittowner put his finger on a primary reason why backyard fences eventually went up in defiance of Levitt's original mandate. The consumer culture propelled more suburbanites into the workforce, leaving the abandoned neighborhoods less lively and less neighborly. When the workers came home, they were tired. The private life of consumption and convenience was steadily winning out over a public life that was rich in social, natural, and cultural connections. PTA participation was inversely proportional to rising incomes. The hurry-up mindset of postwar housing shortages had become the law of the land, scripted into thick tomes of municipal code that often specified resource-exhausting, time-consuming patterns of development.

Unrestrained consumption became a patriotic duty, even the basis of governmental policy. In 1950, marketing analyst Victor Lebow wrote, "Our enormously productive economy demands that we make consumption a way of life, that we convert the buying and use of goods into rituals, that we seek our spiritual satisfaction, our ego satisfaction, in consumption…. We need things consumed, burned up, worn out, replaced, and discarded at an ever-increasing rate." The American dream, a dizzying composite of cars, houses, appliances, lawns, frozen food, and all the rest, was the cultural mechanism that made Lebow's imperative a reality.

Steadily, suburbanites retreated inside, morphing into a sub-nation of housecats, lazy and content. We quickly learned to consume 120 pounds of stuff every day — a total that includes all the materials that went into the stuff. We had everything we needed; it rarely occurred to us that what we consumed in our houses was leaving scars somewhere else, that the wood in each house represented harvested forest, and that the manufacture and operation of each car required the energy equivalent of many railcars of coal and barrels of oil. Mining the coal, oil, and steel left lifeless holes in the earth, and burning the fossil fuels created a blanket of carbon dioxide into the atmosphere, making the planet feverish.

Simply put, the suburbs — where houses have on average doubled in size and miles driven annually has tripled since the 1950s — are the best possible invention for mindless consumption. They may well be the single largest environmental impact the world has ever known.

To the Bureau of Labor Statistics, the American home is not a household but a "consumer unit" that spends disposable income (or is that "disposes of spendable income"?). While many insist that people should be allowed to consume at whatever level their paycheck permits, we respectfully disagree. Dan and I have spent decades researching the need for sustainable production and consumption. We believe the American dream has reached the point of diminishing returns. The costs of high living are out of control and are disrupting personal health, family closeness, community vigor, and economic and environmental stability.

The environmental impact of suburban sprawl has been relentless. Peter Calthorpe, a veteran designer and re-inventor of the suburbs, recalls his early years in Silicon Valley in the 1960s. "I moved from London to Palo Alto just in time to watch how Silicon Valley basically grew and wiped out one of the most productive agricultural valleys in the world," he told me in a video interview. "Gorgeous citrus groves and orchards disappeared before my eyes. And I would often go up in the hills and mountains above the peninsula and look down, back when there was a view. You could see the smog rolling and watch the sprawl moving across the land. I was a teenager at the time, but I had an overwhelming sense there was something wrong here."

The Public Costs of Privacy

Suburban culture intrigues novelists, playwrights, and movie producers. They use the suburbs as a setting where things are not quite as they seem. Suburbia appears to be a place of leisure, abundance, and propriety, but there are secrets behind the fences and front doors, and many more repercussions than meet the eye. For example, chronic family friction is hidden from view. A friend of ours who is a police dispatcher observes that a high percentage of suburban police calls these days are responses to domestic violence. A household may have the highest net income on the block, but the "joy-to-stuff ratio" is at low tide.

Environmental quality is also hidden from view. A private landscape might be picture-perfect, but we don't perceive the cumulative health effects downstream — cancer, endocrine system disruption, or fish mortality — from lawn chemicals that wash into waterways after a heavy rain.

Other indicators of dysfunction or "unsustainability" are swept under the welcome mat — for example, the negative consequences of suburban privacy. Private mobility cascades into public congestion and public expenditures for new highway lanes. (The average time lost in gridlock is now 36 hours per year.) Private consumption results in public environmental impacts as resources are stripped to meet the demands of the dream. But we don't see the slash piles or mine tailings, so their existence rarely occurs to us. The demand to live on large lots, closer to nature, often destroys the nature we hoped to be near. But we don't notice when a chorus of cricket chirps is reduced to a sparse, desperate quartet.

Since 1950 the amount of public space — parks, civic buildings, schools, churches, and so on — in our communities decreased by one-fifth, while the average amount of square footage in new homes roughly doubled. In roughly the same time period, the percentage of income spent for house mortgages and rental payments — our private realm — increased from one-fifth to half, according to the American Planning Association.

What this all means is that we're turning our backs on the commons and letting it degrade. As we continue to disinvest in public spaces, funneling resources, time, and money into our private lives instead, we get tunnel vision. The time we spend in the privacy of our cars and homes reduces the time we have for active involvement in public decision making and community building. We look for a sense of community in the media world of events and opinions, but we're unfamiliar with how to create it in our own neighborhoods.

"Privacy is the most important thing to me," said one participant in a focus group study called *Choices Between Asphalt and Nature: Americans Discuss Sprawl* (available on line at www.biodiversityproject.org). "I want a spacious yard and a large house. The lack of convenience doesn't really bother me." But does she choose privacy, or is she retreating to safety?

A poll conducted by the Pew School of Journalism in 2000 reflects a collective queasiness in America. This was heightened by the events of September 11, 2001. Compared to the 96 percent who felt safe in their homes, 20 percent did not feel safe in their own neighborhoods and 30 percent did not feel safe at the mall. What do these results say about the world "out there?" Has our attitude become: "Grab the take-out dinner, survive the commute, just get home"?

The pollsters asked a wide sample of Americans: "What do you think is the most important problem facing the community where you live?" Crime and violence scored the highest, but, surprisingly, they shared top ranking with suburban problems like development, sprawl, and traffic. Perhaps as the quality and vitality of our public world declines, both urban and suburban cultures are "cocooning."

We asked James Kunstler, outspoken author of *The Geography of Nowhere*, to critique the quality of America's public spaces. Walking in front of a post office building with no windows on one very long side, he commented, "Our towns and neighborhoods are full of these blank walls, which are really a form of civic vandalism. The public realm is a physical manifestation of the common good, and when we degrade it, we also degrade our ability to think about the public interest."

Another kind of public space, nature, has been neglected in the resettling of America. A handful of species now dominates our backyards and parks — bluegrass, robins, English sparrows, nursery-grown trees and shrubs, squirrels, mice, sometimes a deer or fox — because insensitive development and uninspired landscaping smother diversity and wipe out natural vistas. While the build-out of suburbia continues to destroy and displace wildlife, a population explosion of cuddly yet highly dependent dogs and cats has taken over our lawns and living rooms — currently there are about 60 million cats and 55 million dogs in the country. We value "private" animals but allow the public habitats of native species to be eradicated.

Even our glimpses of nature are being lost. Jane Kirschner, a resident of Highlands Ranch, a mega-subdivision west of Denver, told us how she moved into this development with an understanding that her house would front on open space facing the mountains. When the developer's plans changed, her family had front row seats for the big, blank screens of the new neighbors' garage doors — all three of them.

In an interview, New Urbanist architect Victor Dover recalled his childhood explorations of public spaces that were rich in natural settings. "Growing up in Hickory Grove, North Carolina," he told us, "we could walk or ride our bikes to the woods, and experience the natural resources. Now, because nature, including farmland, has been pushed so far away from where we live, we have to get in the car and drive our kids to see something natural."

It's Later Than We Think

Besides being unhealthy and often very stressful, life in the suburbs, with its high levels of transportation and consumption, and its orientation toward private values, is simply not sustainable. There aren't enough resources on the environmental "shelves" to maintain suburbia's life-support systems, nor is there enough uncontaminated nature to absorb all the waste this lifestyle generates. We can't afford the suburbs as they currently function.

Table 1.1: Land Required to Meet the Needs of One Suburban Resident

CATEGORY	ACRES/PERSON
Energy	18.9
Timber	3.5
Food	6.2
Accommodating roads, houses, and other infrastructure	2.5
Total	31.1

Source: "A Step Ahead," University of Wisconsin website: <www.madisonfootprint.org/sustain/action.html>.

Here's why: Reliable supplies of energy and clean water are not limitless, and the cost of each resource will rise as supplies fall. We need to change the way we use them. Groundwater supplies are being pumped at much higher than recharge rates in many parts of the country, and the contamination of water supplies has already resulted in an 800 percent increase in sales of bottled water in the last few decades.

As for oil, experts at the U.S. Geological Survey predict that petroleum production will peak in the next 20 years and then begin a long and very expensive decline. Natural gas production is expected to peak even sooner. When oil, natural gas, and water prices go up, so will food prices. And don't forget consumer waste. As costs of waste disposal continue to rise, more waste handlers will go to "pay as you throw" services, in which households pay for waste by the pound.

The bottom line is that the typical suburban lifestyle requires 31 acres of prime, productive land — farms, mines, fields, and forests — to meet just one person's needs (see Table 1.1).

The problem with this equation is that there are fewer than five acres available to each person in the world, and those five acres per capita must also feed and shelter millions of other species whose health and stability we rely on. If the rest of the human race catches the affluenza that infected America's suburbs, we'll need four or five more planets. (Let's see, who delivers?)

The environmental, social, and economic impacts of the suburban lifestyle are both a crisis and an opportunity. While the construction and maintenance of America's suburbs may have hit the Earth's ecological systems like a planeload of nuclear bombs, many opportunities remain for us to rethink the streets, yards, and houses that now occupy so much of our landscape. Our purpose is not to put the brakes on sprawl (although we do support that) or even to lament all the impacts. The goal in this book is to start where we are and do what we can to revitalize existing suburban neighborhoods and reduce their impact on people and the planet.

Waking Up From the American Dream

If you look at suburban behavior from the perspective of a baby or an extraterrestrial, you start noticing some of the crazy things we do. For example, we spend hundreds of dollars and dozens of hours every year to maintain a lush, spacious green lawn, much of which is unused, and then we mow and throw away the final product.

Or take an ET-look at the way we get energy to provide warmth, mobility, and power. We spend billions of dollars every year and risk the lives of loved ones to protect oil supplies; then we burn the oil to create pollution that contributes to global warming. Wouldn't it make more sense to use great design to capture warmth directly from the sun, mobility from our legs, and industrial power from renewable flows that we won't use up — like wind power, heat and cooling stored in the ground and accessible with readily available heat pumps, and hydrogen?

Transportation in America is another dysfunctional system. We've forgotten that the best way to go somewhere is to already be there. Sociologist Ivan Illich calculated in the book *Toward a History of Needs* that when we add time spent in a car to the time spent purchasing, pampering, and maintaining the car, we're going less than five miles an hour. Compare this to the average human pace of three to four miles per hour, which also gives the walker free exercise.

The essential question of our time is: If our lifestyles are dysfunctional, why don't we change them? Why, for example, don't we get back in tune with what we are biologically — a species that cooperates and takes care of each other? To psychologist Erich Fromm, the American dream is another term for crazy. In *To Have or To Be* he wrote, "That millions share the same forms of mental pathology does not make those people sane."

The TV documentary *Escape from Affluenza* opens with the Joneses standing on their suburban front porch, surrendering. News cameras roll as Mrs. Jones pleads with her neighbors not to try to keep up with them anymore. Junior waves a white flag as Mom says, with great relief, "We're just going to try to live our lives more simply." *Superbia!* is about surrendering, too. We urge suburban readers to turn off their TVs, come out of their houses, and begin to work cooperatively with neighbors rather than escalating the Cold War of competition that results in Mutually Assured Debt, long workweeks, stress overload, and prescription drugs.

Cooperation creates social contracts and helps the environment at the same time. Neighbors who get to know each other begin changing their priorities: they need less private entertainment; less traveling to be with friends; less time shopping for tools, food, and equipment the neighborhood can already provide. There is less eating out, since potlucks, yard parties, and common meals — one of the suggestions we make for creating Superbia! — become a neighborhood norm. The good news is that cooperative efforts can save time and money as well as reduce stress.

Humankind has so much become one family that we cannot ensure our own security unless we ensure the security of all others.
BERTRAND RUSSELL

Reinventing Our Neighborhoods for Health, Profit, and Community

ALTHOUGH SUBURBS *at their best* do offer a world of wonderful benefits like quietness, green spaces, privacy, and large houses, the social, economic, and environmental impacts of the conventional suburb are significant. As outlined in Chapter 1, finite supplies of energy, water, land, raw materials, and social stamina (for long commutes and long working hours to pay for the lifestyle) mean we won't be able to finance suburbia for much longer in its current form. Other costs include social isolation, little provision for low-income people or for people who can't drive, air pollution and traffic fatalities because of our total dependency on the automobile, poor health, loss of farmland and natural areas, and added expense for longer runs of pipes, wires, cables, roads, and their maintenance. While we emphasize opportunities in this book, we feel strongly that the costs need to be evaluated, too, because unless the costs are perceived, we won't feel the need to make beneficial changes.

These first two chapters provide a cost-benefit analysis. In Chapter 1 we showed some of the environmental costs. In this chapter, we'll look at some of the social costs of suburban life, then show you how you can turn them around so they become benefits. Often suburban liabilities present key opportunities for achieving a higher quality of life in existing neighborhoods.

The Social Cost of Suburbia

Isolation and loneliness are what suburbanites complain about most. These two shortcomings arise largely from the fact that modern suburbs were not designed to enhance community life. They were designed for exclusivity and separation. The trillions of dollars that went into creating suburban America were channeled

There is a fantasy abroad. Simply stated, it goes like this: "If we can resolve our conflicts, then someday we shall be able to live together in community." Could it be that we have it totally backward, and that the real dream should be, "If we can live together in community, then someday we shall be able to resolve our conflicts"?

M. SCOTT PECK, *The Road Less Traveled.*

toward the private residence, a retreat from the perceived harshness of urban crime, congestion, and industrialism. Herbert Gans writes in *The Levittowners*, "People moved to Levittown for the good or comfortable life for themselves and their families, and the anticipated peacefulness of outdoor living, but mainly they came for a house and not a social environment."[1]

Certainly, in terms of floor space, convenient appliances, climate control, and home entertainment, even the *average* suburban home is unparalleled in human history. But while convenience and privacy are important, so are community and social interaction.

For example, a recent newspaper headline read "Elderly Tennessee Woman Runs Over School Kids." An 86-year-old woman on medication was driving to pick up her granddaughter after school, lost control of the car, and pinned nine children against a stone wall, killing several of them. This suburban grandmother and her car were forced to be a single, codependent organism. (Town planner Andres Duany compares the car to a prosthesis.) In the suburbs, there is no public transportation to fall back on, and usually there is too little support from neighbors. Result: people who shouldn't be driving are driving, and car accidents — the leading cause of death in children — occur three times as often in suburbs as in cities.

Opportunities, Lost and Found

"I was amazed when my neighbor waved to me," one of Dave's suburban friends confided to him. "She's lived a few houses down for three or four years now, and she's never waved before."

She still hasn't.

As it turns out, she wasn't waving; she was just reaching for the garage door opener on the sun visor.

What the two neighbors know about each other is still limited to superficial things like the appearance of their front lawns. Despite the fact they live only four large shade trees apart, they don't even know each other's names.

There are many things the two neighbors have in common, and many of the daily challenges they face individually might be easier and more fun if they did know each other. Although they don't yet realize it, they work in the same suburban office park (a 35-minute commute). They both enjoy growing flowers and vegetables, and they're both interested in amateur theater. One has a young child who sometimes needs a baby-sitter, while the other's kids are grown up and live hundreds of miles away. In other words, one has a need that the other could very effectively fill. But they have no idea about these mutual interests because they've never spoken.

Up and down the street there are hundreds of potential links between people — links that could reduce time, human energy, and money spent by individuals on tight schedules and equally tight budgets. But few of these connections are being made, partly because the collective lifestyle — the neighborhood culture — doesn't encourage it or empower it. "It's just not the way we do it; we value our privacy," we say, a privacy created by hedges and fences, gates, walls, security locks, surveillance cameras, and burglar alarms. When we add the 8 or 10 million living in gated communities, the 12 million or so in elaborately secured apartment

2.1: Credit: David Horsey, Seattle Post-Intelligencer.

buildings, 2 million in prison, and uncountable millions of deadbolt and security alarm fanatics, a significant percentage of America is now living behind bars. Is this a reasonable way to create community?

When minor challenges or major emergencies come up, each person's options are narrower than they might be if the neighborhood culture were richer. If a tool is needed, each household immediately sends a designated shopper to the mega-hardware store, even if the next-door neighbor already has the tool. When a water pipe breaks or a tree needs trimming, a panel truck appears magically on each driveway, even if someone on the block is a plumber or knows how to trim trees.

Some household budgets are stretched several zeros beyond the comfort zone, while in other households it's not money but a shortage of time that creates stress. In either case, the support and cooperation of neighbors can help. For example, three-quarters of all jobs are found by networking, not by studying the want ads. Neighbors can help us find work. And when we need emergency help getting the backyard cleaned up for a wedding or family reunion, wouldn't it be great if we could hire the teenagers who live next door?

The first barrier to creating a living community is the lack of a vibrant neighborhood culture in which everyone knows each other. The second barrier is the physical design of a typical neighborhood. Wide streets

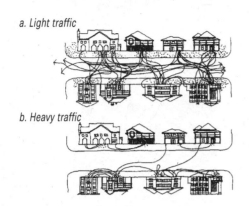

a. Light traffic

b. Heavy traffic

2.2: *The private convenience of cars often creates social isolation because it separates one neighbor from another. Lines show where people said they had friends or acquaintances. Credit: David Engwicht.*

2.3: *How traffic reduces home territory: When traffic is light, the whole neighborhood is considered "home territory," but when traffic is heavy, neighbors tend to stay inside. Credit: David Engwicht.*

prescribed by codes, privacy fences, bland garage door facades, and the lack of public open space all tend to isolate neighbors rather than bring them together.

Suburban streets are typically a neighborhood's largest public area, but they often divide rather than unite a neighborhood. Studies have shown that the speed and volume of street traffic often determine how many people we know on the other side of the street. Sociologist Donald Appleyard discovered that on a street with light traffic (2,000 vehicles a day), residents had, on average, 3 friends and 6.3 acquaintances in the neighborhood, as compared to the street with heavy traffic (16,000 vehicles a day), where residents had 0.9 friends (what kind of a friend is that?) and 3.1 acquaintances.[2]

Linkages with people on the other side of the street were understandably reduced, but Appleyard found out that relationships on the same side of the street also failed to mature. "Home territory," including perceived public space, was dramatically reduced on the street with heavy traffic, whose residents retreated inside. However, as we show in Chapter 7, there are effective techniques we can use to reduce traffic speeds and volumes and reclaim the street as public space.

Health, Social Capital, and other Forms of Wealth

The Centers for Disease Control (CDC) has done valuable research on how the physical structure of a neighborhood affects residents' health. Says CDC director Richard Jackson, M.D., "The diseases of the 21st century will be chronic diseases like diabetes, obesity, asthma, and depression that steal vitality and productivity, and consume time and money. These diseases can be moderated by how we design, build, and maintain our human environment."

Jackson points to the connection between suburban sprawl design, which makes fewer sidewalks and bike paths available, and the recent surge in adult-onset diabetes. "Obesity increases the risk of this type of diabetes as much as 34-fold," he told us, "which in turn increases the incidence of amputations, blindness, kidney failure, and heart disease." Since 1975, childhood obesity doubled and adult obesity shot from 47 percent to 61 percent of the population. Other health impacts related to the design of suburban neighborhoods include high blood pressure, colon cancer, high levels of teenage suicide, bicycle and pedestrian accidents, and less mobility for the elderly and disabled.[3]

The good news is that weight loss and physical activity control diabetes more effectively and cheaply than medication. The same is true for other sprawl-related diseases. For example, physical activity is as effective as prescription drugs for treating relatively mild cases of anxiety and depression, according to Jackson.

A recent issue of *Shape* magazine, read by a million and a half health-conscious readers, points out that people who live in either urban or suburban homes built before 1974 are 50 percent more likely than those who live in newer homes to walk a mile or more at least 20 times a month. These older neighborhoods were built for people as well as cars. "There's a growing body of evidence that your environment can influence your behavior and your health," says National Cancer Institute researcher David Berrigan, who conducted the study.

2.4: To accommodate the automobile in America, we've paved over an area equivalent to 38 million football fields. Credit: INSERT MISSING CREDIT.

However, if our neighborhoods aren't interesting or even safe to walk in, and if there are no stores, parks, and other destinations near our homes that give walking a sense of purpose, we won't leave our houses. We'll stay inside, snacking in front of the TV or computer, adding on the 10 or 12 pounds beyond fitness that has become the national average. Many resolute Americans do climb in their cars and drive to the gym, but they have to pay for the exercise, and the driving creates other health risks, as Jackson points out. "Respiratory disease, especially asthma, is increasing yearly in the U.S., and poor quality air makes it worse. In 1997, smog pollution was responsible for more than 6 million asthma attacks and 160,000 emergency room visits."

The connection between asthma and the ground-level ozone caused by cars was as clear as the air was clean in a 1996 CDC study at the Olympics in Atlanta. Because vehicular traffic was kept at artificially low levels by city authorities, ozone concentrations decreased by 30 percent and desperate trips to emergency rooms for asthma attacks dropped by 42 percent.

Besides contributing to asthma and other pollution-related diseases, our car use can produce stress as we find ourselves wasting time driving from home to work to store. With 214 million vehicles now on American roads, each logging three times as many miles a year as in 1950, a short list of errands can eat up a whole afternoon. One of the biggest incentives for the steady evolution of neighborhoods is the reclamation of time, and there's good news to report: Many municipal zoning departments are making codes more flexible to increase the possibility of "mixed uses," such as convenience stores and shops in residential areas, so we can meet some of our needs in our own neighborhoods. New strategies for land preservation are being used to create public spaces on vacant lots, on overly wide streets, and even on common greens assembled from donated chunks of private yard.

Imagine a remodeled neighborhood, partly funded by government, partly by the neighbors themselves, with new bike trails, better street access for the disabled, homes that each have better indoor air quality because of the efforts of a cooperative "eco-team," schoolyards with butterfly habitats, and gardeners' markets on the weekend. By working together to create such things, suburban neighbors can create a strong sense of community, which doctors tell us is one of the strongest promoters of good health.

In one 2002 experiment, psychiatric and behavioral researchers at Emory University ran MRIs on volunteers and discovered that when pairs of participants behaved cooperatively, regions of the brain known as *reward circuits* showed elevated readings. It was more beneficial, individually and socially, to trust and cooperate with one's partner than to betray her. Other research reveals that in a closely knit community, levels of serotonin (a natural anti-depressant) are higher, so the neighborhood is collectively more optimistic and energetic. We've been so busy competing in the workplace, cocooning at home, and commuting between the two that we've forgotten a basic biological truth: humans have survived as a species because we're *cooperative* by nature.

In a book titled *The Power of Clan*, Dr. Stewart Wolf and John Bruhn examine a multi-decade study of Roseto, a small town near Philadelphia, where longevity was legendary. They attribute the town's remarkable health to three-generation bonding in families, neighborliness, devoted churchgoing, and membership in social organizations. Back in 1961, anthropologist Margaret Mead estimated in *Cooperation and Competition Among Primitive Peoples* that for 99 percent of the time humans have been on the planet, we've lived in clans of 12 to 36 people. Only under stress do we revert to the nuclear family, the hallmark of urban and suburban neighborhoods in modern times.

In a healthy community, young and old know and relate to each other. Educator Richard Kordesh observes that the bond between ages builds an attachment to history in the young and renews in the old their attachment to the future.[4] Think about it — when we create "social capital" in the form of bonds, networks, and support systems, the more we "spend," the more we have. Why wouldn't any neighborhood want to create wealth such as this?

Suburban Feudalism: Strangers in our Own Neighborhoods

Sadly, the residents in a typical suburb don't make time for building social capital. They spend far more time in the car and at the mall (six hours or more a week) than they do communicating with family members. Friendships among neighbors fall off the schedule altogether. Everyone in the typical neighborhood has at times felt deprived by the lack of local public space when there's not even a vacant lot-sized park in which to sit and read a book, throw a Frisbee, or walk the dog.

A deficiency of open space may have been a contributing factor in the ongoing skirmish between the Reeses and the Silvas. Far from being friendly and supportive, these neighbors resorted to psychological warfare and guerilla tactics on the home front, complete with surveillance cameras to document the noise, late hours, alleged invasions of privacy, and other offenses that fan the flames of neighborhood feudalism.

The feud began when the Reeses' Airedale left one too many artifacts on the Silvas' meticulous front lawn. The deposit became a trowel-launched grenade that landed unceremoniously on the windshield of the Reeses' brand-new SUV. In retaliation, Jim Reese felled his own apple tree rather than let the Silvas harvest fruit from its overhanging branches. (That'll teach 'em.) The Silvas cranked their stereo all the way up to drown out the growl of the chain saw, and the houses on the corner became known as a "war zone."

A year into the campaign, evidence-gathering cameras rolled whenever garbage cans scraped on driveways or a teenager jumped a fence to retrieve a stray basketball shot.

2.5: Suburban Feudalism Credit: David Horsey, Seattle Post-Intelligencer.

Readers take note: This is a true story, though the names have been changed to protect the innocent. In a neighborhood near Denver, two households admitted to news reporters that they've collectively invested close to $100,000 in mutually unsuccessful campaigns to oust their evil enemy neighbors. Both families are still there, fortifying their yards and houses.

Further evidence of suburban unrest comes from Highlands Ranch, a Colorado mega-subdivision that grew from zero to 70,000 people in a few short decades — and continues to grow by a thousand homes every year. The largest of the country's 240,000 or so community associations, Highlands Ranch has a full-time staff of "covenant cops" who patrol the streets looking for illegal dandelions and house trim colors that aren't listed in the association code book.[5]

One resident, Vicki Stevens, had the audacity to display modern art sculptures in her backyard, which the neighborhood kids loved, but the rent-a-cops and the community association's architectural technician did not. "During a recent neighborhood survey," an official letter warned, "it was noted that you have installed ornament(s) that are not in compliance with the guidelines." Stevens isn't the only Highlands resident in the hot seat for dangerous infractions such as this. Every day the covenant cops receive about ten complaints from vigilant defenders of propriety. So it goes on many streets in the land of suburbia: Reality seldom matches expectation. We expect village life at Chester Village, and butterflies in Butterfly Gulch, but we rarely get them.

Let's imagine for a moment that neighbors begin to think outside the boxes of their suburban homes. The Reeses, Silvas, and 22 other households between the drainage culvert and Western Avenue decide to have a block party, though some neighbors participate only grudgingly at first. At the party, one resident mentions a book he's reading (this one, of course) and proposes a neighborhood newsletter and e-mail listserv as a way to exchange telephone numbers and present brief biographies of everyone in the neighborhood. It's a simple but very effective step beyond isolation and toward community. Other steps quickly follow.

In the fictitious neighborhood you'll encounter in Chapters 5 to 7 of this book, neighbors decide to empower themselves. A lackluster, divided neighborhood is transformed into a lively and productive "butterfly neighborhood" — a place many of us would give our eyeteeth to live in.

How Community Adds Value

What if creating community could save your household $3,000 or more annually in utility, health, and food bills; transportation costs; childcare; entertainment costs; and lawn care expenses? What if you also gained 200 hours — five workweeks — every year by changing your priorities? Savings like these are completely realistic if neighbors form an alliance and set strategic goals to reinvent the way the neighborhood functions. Once a neighborhood begins to create "social capital" (trust and support) and, in turn, designs ways to become more sustainable, chances are that property values on the block will increase proportionally, yet the number of home sales will decrease because people will want to stay put. This has already happened in many of the neighborhoods described in this book, such as Village Homes and Harmony Village.

We're not proposing you make personal sacrifices to create a livelier neighborhood; all you need is a change in priorities and an interest in working cooperatively. We know you're busy. In our current culture, we all are, partly because "keeping up with the Joneses" takes time. We may be able to help you slow down, turn off the TV, and create your own life. Tangible rewards — such as savings of time, money, and human effort, along with improvements in health — can result from basic cultural changes accessible to anyone. By working with our neighbors we can have a less competitive, less judgmental neighborhood and a more fulfilling "Net Neighborhood Product," or quality of life.

For example, how much do we work to pay for a flawless landscape? The care and feeding of a lawn covering a third of an acre typically costs $500 or more a year, including lawn equipment, 10 pounds of pesticides, 20 pounds of fertilizer, 170,000 gallons of water, and 40 hours of mowing labor. According to the Audubon Society, the pollution generated by a gas-powered lawn mower for that mowing is equivalent to driving a car 14,000 miles — more than halfway around the world.

A water meter reader told us about three homes that consistently consume twice as much water as others on the street, apparently to outdo their neighbors in lawn appearance. How many such competitions are going on across the continent? Instead of

2.6: Family life is important at Pioneer Valley Cohousing in Massachusetts. Credit: Mike April.

2.7: Researchers have demonstrated that a feeling of community reduces suburban depression. Credit: Mike April.

watering and fertilizing to the richest shade of green, no matter how much it costs, why don't we just develop an informal, mutually beneficial agreement with our neighbors? Why not change the rules, with a neighborhood "mission statement" to make front lawns more productive and less consumptive? Why not plant low-maintenance strawberries as ground cover and a few dwarf fruit trees in sections of our front lawns, then set up a neighborhood consulting enterprise — call it Lawnbusters — to show other neighborhoods how to do it?

There are support organizations for alcoholics, gamblers, and drug abusers — why not create a neighborhood support group to battle suburban affluenza? If members of each household evaluated the size and shape of their Household Domestic Product (HDP), they would find many ways to eliminate consumer debt in their own homes and then could help neighbors do the same. Many cost-saving synergies occur in a healthy neighborhood, not the least of which is that when a person's self-esteem rises, less money is spent to fill the emptiness. Being active in a "we" culture rather than passive in a "me"/TV culture can elevate self-esteem and calm the costly storms of consumer splurges and binges. In a nutshell, our neighbors can help us redefine the term "wealth."

It might be useful to look at how much money is spent on specific purchases in an average household, and then examine opportunities to get more value from less money. In a recent report the U.S. Bureau of Labor Statistics tracked the consumer spending patterns of an average Milwaukee family with a $37,000 income. This family spends about 35 percent of its income ($12,950) on housing, which includes the house, utilities, furniture, and supplies; 20 percent ($7,400) on transportation; and 12 percent ($4,400) on food. Each of these categories represents huge opportunities for reducing waste, stress, and "disposable" income with the physical and social support of the neighborhood. If family members reevaluate and redistribute their expenditures, making spending decisions based on an item's ability to meet their needs precisely, they will discover they maybe don't need such a large income, and leisure time will become more abundant and enjoyable. If purchases (and decisions not to purchase) bring more durability, greater intellectual growth, and more laughter into their house, a family's quality of life expands.

For example, rather than spending nearly $13,000 a year on housing, the family could win back time, money, and human energy by living in a house with efficient appliances and good natural lighting, buying well-built furniture that doesn't need constant replacing, and having a different attitude about what a house is for. If they consider it mostly a display unit, they'll spend hours a week decorating and redecorating it, cleaning it, or paying someone else to clean it. If they simply consider it a home, they'll be more interested in comfort than in impressing the neighbors.

Table 2.1: Potential Savings from Community Cooperation and Household Efficiency

CURRENT EXPENSE/TIME COMMITMENT	NEIGHBORHOOD ACTION	POTENTIAL SAVINGS IN MONEY & TIME
• *Food bought to eat at home:* 7.9% of Household Domestic Product (HDP)	• Community garden, community-supported agriculture (CSA), community meals	• $200 a year
• *Food eaten away from home:* 5.7% of HDP	• Lifestyle changes, garden, CSA, job closer to home	• $200 a year, 10 hours saved
• *Utilities, fuels, and public services:* 6.4% of HDP	• Upgrades in home efficiency and water conservation, improvements in neighborhood micro-climate, neighborhood-produced energy	• $200 to $900 a year
• *Housekeeping supplies, equipment, and furnishings:* 4.1% of HDP	• Cooperative buying, equipment sharing, availability of used items, de-emphasis on consumer goods	• $300 a year, 40 hours shopping saved
• *Apparel and related services:* 4.7% of HDP	• More casual wardrobe, second life for clothes	• $200 a year, 6 hours shopping saved
• *Transportation:* 19% of HDP	• Carpooling, car-sharing, lifestyle changes that reduce need to travel, elimination of second car	• $1,000 a year, 120 hours saved
• *Health care:* 5.3% of HDP	• Healthier diet from community garden, more exercise, health benefits of community, elimination of prescription drugs, reduction of insurance costs (higher deductible)	• $200 to $600 a year, 20 hours of sickness avoided
• *Entertainment:* 5.1% of HDP	• More social time spent in neighborhood activities, less entertainment required	• $300 a year
• *Tobacco, alcohol:*	• Elimination of tobacco, reduction of alcohol use	• $50 to $200 a year
• *Job searching:*	• Neighborhood networking helps find job, or neighborhood enterprise provides income	• Time and expense saved
• *Waste disposal:*	• Neighborhood composting, recycling	• $100 a year
• *Overtime work:*	• Lifestyle changes and money saved reduces overtime worked	• 30 hours a year saved
• *Lawn Maintenance:*	• Changes in neighborhood culture, edible landscaping	• $150 a year saved, $200 a year generated

Source of data on expenditures: Bureau of Labor Statistics, Consumer Expenditure Survey, as compiled by Segal, J. (2001) *What We Work for Now.* Redefining Progress. Available from: http://redefiningprogress.org/

By working with their neighbors to research and implement improvements that will make houses more efficient, households can save money and enhance the comfort of their homes. One example of neighborhood cooperation to make individual homes more efficient is the "EcoTeam." Global Action Plan, an international group that organizes EcoTeams, reports that average savings from such improvements are in the range of $265 to $389 per year, including a 45 percent reduction in garbage costs, 30 percent reduction in water costs, and 15 percent reduction in gasoline and other energy costs.

If the house is located near work, school, friends, groceries, banks, and other amenities, the Milwaukee family can reduce transportation costs by at least 10 percent, or about $750 per year. Getting rid of a second car would yield even greater benefits.

The family spends 12 percent of its income on food, which is down from the 30 percent their grandparents spent in the 1930s. However, since 43 percent of that is for food eaten away from home, the family could save $500 a year by eating out less frequently. More important, if the food they eat delivers energy rather than lethargy, they'll exercise more and participate in sports rather than buying season tickets and cable sports channels. We spend billions every year for exercise tapes, drugs, tummy tucks, and "thick, delicious diet shakes," partly because we don't exercise enough and partly because a strict regimen of packaged food delivers about 50 teaspoons of sugar daily. If we eat more from the garden and from local growers, health care costs will be lower and weight-loss equipment and programs won't be necessary. With better food in our lives, we'll go to the doctor less and require less insurance. We'll spend more social time eating quality food, reducing our entertainment costs. And almost certainly, we'll feel a greater sense of contentment and wellness.

By slowing down the speed of life and getting to know *who* their neighbors are rather than just what they seem to have, the Milwaukee family can become more than just an "average" family. They can be an exceptional family. Instead of *disposing* of their income, they could save it, share it, eat it, and live it. Table 2.1 shows how much time and money they can save through cooperation and efficiency.

As a final example of cost-saving synergies in the neighborhood, imagine a creative group of neighbors pooling their expertise and aspirations and starting a computer-based business in a well-designed, remodeled, triple-bay garage. Each ex-commuter would now save expenses for driving, work-related clothes, childcare, and food, since they'll eat at home more.

After running this chapter's cost-benefit analysis, readers may agree that the appropriate question isn't "Where will we find the time and money to create synergistic, sustainable neighborhoods?" The more pressing question is "How can we afford not to?"

You have to love the area you're trying to improve.
JANE JACOBS

3

Imagining a Sustainable Neighborhood

IT'S TIME TO REDEFINE THE AMERICAN DREAM," insists neighborhood designer Peter Calthorpe. "Certain traditional values — diversity, community, frugality, and human scale — should be the foundation of a new direction."

Many suburban residents agree, and they're emerging one by one from their cocoons to create a bright new lifestyle that can make suburbs more vibrant and sustainable. Deb French, a long-time suburban resident, believes coordination among neighbors will help her neighborhood, and any other, become more lively. "If we find a way to tap into the expertise, talents, and skills of all the people in my neighborhood, we can create a little utopia," she says. "I'm a public health specialist and could help with safety issues and environmental concerns. Up and down the block there are engineers, architects, accountants, bankers, attorneys, builders.... We need to come together and pool our energies." Deb finds that neighborhood reinvention happens best when a group works on a specific project together — such as the Neighborhood Watch project she and her neighbors launched eight years ago — then uses their momentum to work on another project.

Says Ed Fendley, a resident of Arlington, Virginia, "We need to remember that the primary reason communities exist is for interdependence. If we look at what works, compact development that links transportation options — such as cars, bikes, walking, trains, buses — is high on the list. We need to create these links in the suburbs."

For Michele Donel, who lives in a Chicago suburb, one word says it all: "Time." More than anything else, she doesn't want to feel in a hurry. The ideal neighborhood for her would be a place that allowed her to feel less frantic.

3.1: A sustainable suburb is full of human activity, with cars assuming a place of secondary importance. Credit: Lyle Grant.

Better-Tasting Suburbs

An infant may think pureed squash is the greatest taste in the universe … until she gets a nibble of chocolate, and maybe it's the same with suburban neighborhoods. Many people don't know there's anything else out there. And the lenders who finance new developments aren't looking very hard either. They approve the kind of projects that have worked before and that don't present financial risks. Innovative designers and builders have to work overtime to find financial support for neighborhoods-by-design.

Polls repeatedly show that we want a better version of suburbia. When the 1997 Fannie Mae National Housing Survey asked people where they wanted to live, 44 percent of the respondents chose medium (20 percent) to small (24 percent) towns, and 24 percent chose the suburbs. Of course, many small towns are in suburban territory, but the key word is "towns." If these figures are valid, reinvention of suburban subdivisions seems to be about creating housing with all of the amenities of villages and small towns.[1]

The 1995 New Urbanism Survey, produced by market research firm American Lives (www.americanlives.com), offered further evidence of a trend away from exclusivity and privacy and toward community. Only 18 percent of respondents indicated they wanted to live in a "private country club," while 64 percent preferred a "small cluster of convenience stores nearby." A dramatic entrance appealed to only 8 percent of respondents, while 64 percent preferred a "small neighborhood library." Only 12 percent requested walls around the subdivision, compared to 46 percent who wanted little parks nearby. In question after question, respondents expressed a greater desire for the conveniences of neighborhood life than for the amenities of middle-class suburbia.[2]

Lovers of suburbia will ask, "If suburbs are so bad, why do so many choose to live there?" The apparent answer is: "To get the most house for the money," but obviously there's more to it than that. We value suburbs for good schools; for less congestion, crime, and noise; for perceived access to work (despite the reality of longer commutes); for a sense of being closer to nature; and for a chance to fit the mold of upward mobility. We look to the suburbs to find certain values, identified in the Biodiversity Project's *Choices Between Asphalt and Nature* (www.biodiversityproject.org) as responsibility to family, freedom of choice, expression of individuality, a sense of community, and appreciation of nature.

The question is, speaking generically, how well do suburbs fulfill these requirements? For example, do they supply freedom of choice in housing? In a *Scientific American* article, Donald Chen shows why he doesn't think so. Mandated by law to be low-density, the suburbs offer "a limited range of choices in the style and location of new housing — typically, single-family homes in automobile-oriented neighborhoods built on what was once forest or farmland."[3]

Certainly New Urbanist designers are putting choice into the market with high-quality, community-oriented, new developments like Mashpee Commons, The Crossings, and Kentlands, which offer the amenities of small towns. The cohousing model, imported from Denmark, is another choice coming into the market. We will discuss it in detail in Chapter 4, but briefly, cohousing provides many of the conveniences and comforts of small town living and is an American mini-movement. More

3.2: (above) Would you rather have this behind your house ...
Credit: Community Greens.

3.3: (below) ... or this, a common area with a pathway that leads to shops and parks? Credit: Community Greens.

3.4: A New Urbanist neighborhood in Longmont, Colorado, includes a restaurant, antique shop, mortgage broker, barber, yoga studio and other small businesses, by design. Credit: Mark Sofield.

than 70 neighborhoods have already been co-designed and built — by future residents — throughout North America, and a hundred more are in the pipeline. Who knows, maybe readers of this book and others will create dozens (or hundreds!) of *New Suburbanist* neighborhoods to give homebuyers a wider menu of options.

Even developers, an often-maligned species, are buzzing about the marketability of community. In a 1998 speech to the National Association of Home Builders, developer Vince Graham said, "If what you are selling is privacy and exclusivity, then every new house is a degradation of the amenity. However, if what you are selling is community, then every new house is an enhancement of the asset."

Redefining the American Dream

In the timeless words of the Sioux spiritual leader Sitting Bull, "Let us now put our heads together and see what life we will make for our children." Let us see, in other words, if we can make the suburbs superb. When a higher proportion of kids chooses to remain in, or return to, neighborhoods they grew up in, we'll know we're doing something right. And that's the key issue in this chapter: How exactly do we know what's *right*? If a neighborhood is worth staying in and improving, it needs to be safe, healthy, economically stable, diverse, accessible to nature and culture, friendly, and supportive.

If it's built (or rebuilt) to last, it needs to be "sustainable." Because that word tends to induce slumber even among the energetic, let's work with the idea a little. Essentially, it means that we can't take more than nature can replenish on a continuing basis. To use a biological example, fishing technologies now exist that are capable of locating schools of fish with sonar and then casting huge draglines to harvest them. These technologies can completely deplete whole sections of the ocean in a single season. Instead of leaving enough fish to keep the population stable, the fishing industry continues to harvest until there are no fish left. The same concept applies when we draw down a bank account or an aquifer, when we deplete the soil in a farm

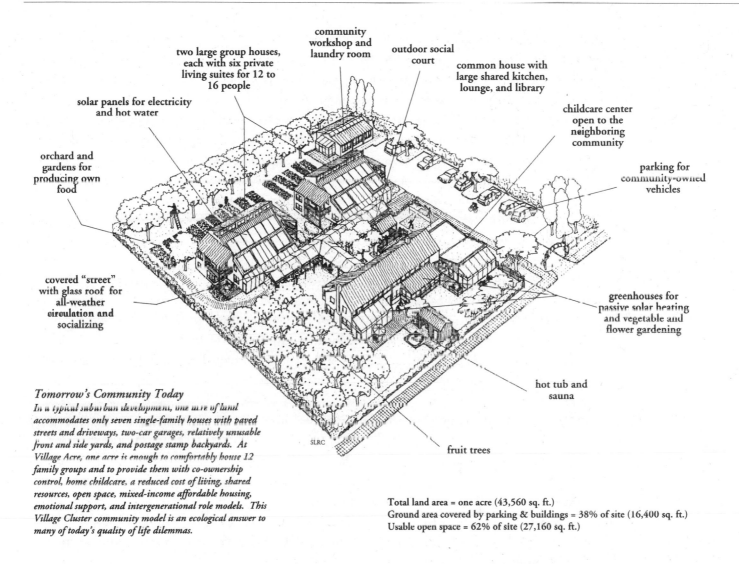

two large group houses, each with six private living suites for 12 to 16 people

community workshop and laundry room

outdoor social court

common house with large shared kitchen, lounge, and library

solar panels for electricity and hot water

childcare center open to the neighboring community

orchard and gardens for producing own food

parking for community-owned vehicles

covered "street" with glass roof for all-weather circulation and socializing

greenhouses for passive solar heating and vegetable and flower gardening

hot tub and sauna

SLRC

fruit trees

Tomorrow's Community Today

In a typical suburban development, one acre of land accommodates only seven single-family houses with paved streets and driveways, two-car garages, relatively unusable front and side yards, and postage stamp backyards. At Village Acre, one acre is enough to comfortably house 12 family groups and to provide them with co-ownership control, home childcare, a reduced cost of living, shared resources, open space, mixed-income affordable housing, emotional support, and intergenerational role models. This Village Cluster community model is an ecological answer to many of today's quality of life dilemmas.

Total land area = one acre (43,560 sq. ft.)
Ground area covered by parking & buildings = 38% of site (16,400 sq. ft.)
Usable open space = 62% of site (27,160 sq. ft.)

3.5: A sustainable neighborhood meets many of its own needs. More than that, it's a place that makes people glad to be alive!

Credit: Shared Living Resource Center, Berkeley, California.

field or allow a neighborhood — and its hinterland supplies of resources — to be "drawn down." The authors of *Sustainable Communities*, Sim Van der Ryn and Peter Calthorpe, offer an extremely simple and concise definition for our purposes: "A sustainable community exacts less of its inhabitants in time, wealth and maintenance, and demands less of its environment in land, water, soil, and fuel."

These two designers are strong advocates for public values such as energy efficiency, restoration of nature, and significant reductions in miles traveled by private vehicles. They acknowledge that citizens must protect resources that are common to all because, really, who else will? Looking into the near future, they predict we will see "more compact housing patterns interspersed with productive areas to collect energy, grow crops for food, fiber and energy, and recycle wastes." They forecast that the suburban lifestyle of the future "will rely more on information and a careful integration with biological processes. This will mean far greater design diversity than we have today, with each region developing unique forms based on regional characteristics that have long been overridden by cheap energy."[4]

In a paper for the Sustainable Futures Society, systems engineer Jon Schulz examines what it will take to make our suburbs truly sustainable, emphasizing that the suburb needs to be perceived as a whole system that can provide a higher quality of life and can actually enhance, rather than degrade, the environment.[5] Looking at flows and fates of resources like money, food, water, energy, wastewater, solid wastes, communication, and people, Schulz concludes that suburbs are places of tremendous unrealized benefit and opportunity that can best be tapped by gradually implementing the following ideas:

1. Develop a way of learning and acting together to deliberately redevelop the suburb to serve the common good.
2. Celebrate diversity and actively promote inclusion of all people.
3. Implement a community-wide energy conservation program including homes and appliances and using renewable sources of electricity and heat where possible.
4. Implement a community-wide water conservation program inside and outside the house; know where the water is coming from and protect the source and watershed; use rain and storm water to create urban forests and edible landscapes.
5. Create paths, pocket parks, picnic areas, bike storage areas, community gardens, and other public spaces that are safe for children and wonderful gathering places for adults.

6. Create income-generating community businesses by thinking about all wastes as resources, whether they are solid waste, yard waste, or even wastewater.
7. Value the capacity for individual and collective learning and adaptation.
8. Evaluate ways of reducing transportation and its impacts.

To determine if your neighborhood is becoming more sustainable, the most useful trends to track are such things as vehicle miles traveled per capita, energy and water consumed per capita, significant relationships in the neighborhood, number of houses per acre, number of jobs per acre. A sustainable neighborhood aims for a high ratio of parks to pavement. It also aims for a high "signal to noise" ratio, meaning that neighbors are interested in filling their brains with useful and interesting information as opposed to commercial static. They are increasingly aware that the human mind is the territory in which nature will be saved or lost. Consequently, they're more interested in the natural history of the neighborhood than they are in finding out which "survivor" was voted off the "reality" show's Pacific island. They can give answers to the following questions and exercises, adapted from *Deep Ecology* by Bill Devall and George Sessions:

1. Trace the water you drink from precipitation to tap.
2. Describe the soil around your home.
3. Name the primary subsistence techniques of the cultures that lived in your area before you.
4. Name five native edible plants in your bioregion and their seasons of availability.
5. Where does your garbage go?
6. Name five resident and any migratory birds in your area.
7. What animal species have become extinct in your area?
8. What spring wildflower is consistently among the first to bloom where you live?
9. What kinds of rocks and minerals are found in your bioregion?
10. What is the largest wilderness area in your bioregion?

Unlike a polled 62 percent of the American population, who believe that fuel efficiency in cars is up or holding steady in the past decade, they know that gas mileage is down, and they even know why: because of the recent popularity of gas-guzzling sports utility vehicles and light trucks that roam the streets and cul-de-sacs of suburbia, and because of the dramatic increase in travel resulting from suburban sprawl. They have a pretty

3.6: Scheduling events such as this bicycling trip brings neighbors together and creates something in common. Credit: Mike April.

good idea that 80 percent of our oil is consumed by cars and trucks and that about a third of the carbon dioxide implicated in global warming comes from our massive fleet of vehicles. They suspect, though most haven't quantified it, that members of their household are making a dozen auto trips a day on average, and that the location and design of their neighborhoods are primary reasons why.

They're also interested in knowing about "commercial ecology," that is, the origins and impacts of the products they buy and use in their homes and yards. They know that each product is the main character in a story with a beginning, middle, and end. Extracting the raw materials that go into a gadget or an article of clothing may have disrupted biological habitats at the mine site, farm field, or forest. Then product manufacture, distribution, advertising, and packaging take their toll. At the end of the tale, our use of the product may cause further impacts to health, air, water, and land. Only if efficient, sustainable technologies are used throughout the story can there be a happy ending.

These people include sustainability in their neighborhood mission statements, partly because it's "the right thing to do," but also because of enlightened self-interest. To these heads-up residents, sustainability isn't just an abstract word; it's right in their faces. It's about blisteringly hot afternoons and summer-long droughts due to global climate change caused by excessive use of fossil fuel; it's about kids with asthma and adults with plugged sinuses from breathing polluted air; it's about lakes that are now off-limits to swimmers and anglers because they are so contaminated. Sustainability is about the rising cost of drinking water due to falling groundwater levels, and about whether or not we can see the stars from our backyards, smell the native sage and wildflowers, or hear the nocturnal call of an endangered species of owl.

Residents of Superbia!-to-be came to the suburbs for a better quality of life, and they want to preserve it. Some are among the growing number of Americans that sociologist Paul Ray and Sherry Ruth Anderson, authors of the book *The Cultural Creatives*, think can change the world for the better — 50 million or more Americans in the environmental, civil rights, gay rights, peace, and voluntary simplicity movements who aren't satisfied with the status quo. And they are part of a swelling population sector whose work schedules have shifted radically in the last decade — self-employed, part-time, temporary, and contract workers who now number about one-fifth of the workforce.

"The new economy makes possible the reintegration of work and home," says Kim Walesh, coauthor of "Linking the New Economy to the Livable Community," a report funded by the James Irvine Foundation (available on-line at www.irvine.org/pdfs/). "In half a century's time," he writes, "it may seem extraordinary that millions of people once trooped from one building (their home) to another (their office) each morning, only to reverse the procedure at evening."

This much is certain: the baby boomers are well represented in today's suburban population. The baby boomers: 66 million individuals whose retirement will be the biggest social movement of all. Who made health food a mainstream industry that's growing by 20 percent a year — an industry that now occupies at least one aisle in each mainstream supermarket and *all* the aisles in whole foods markets. Who like to try crazy things like ecotourism and car-free vacations. Who like to start discussion groups and community gardens. The baby boomers, who grew up with the car and TV and are now losing interest in each. Choices made by the boomers will likely determine the shape of suburbia in the near future.

Creating a Neighborhood Vision

"Nothing happens unless first a dream," wrote poet Carl Sandburg, and his sentiments are echoed by a legion of community activists and municipal neighborhood liaisons who help neighbors get organized and imagine better neighborhoods. Jon Clarke, who works with the city of Longmont, Colorado, is one of those liaisons. His division has just issued a $100,000 grant to one of the city's neighborhoods to bring neighbors together and let them dream. "We hope to see a workable plan emerge, spelling out what they want their neighborhood to be," he told us.

While it's great to have financial support and a local government that understands the importance of having a vision, the tools in this section can be used by neighborhoods with or without the involvement of local government. "Visioning" is a process that takes account of where a neighborhood is now, then projects into the future to imagine a preferred scenario. As planner Steven Ames explains, "Through visioning, citizens come together to create a shared image of their preferred future; once this image has been created, they can begin working to achieve their goal."

In the first step, they ask, "Where are we now?" They identify the neighborhood's background and important features through the lenses of current issues and shared values.

In the second step they ask, "Where are we going?" They develop a scenario showing what the neighborhood might look like in the future if it continues on its current course with no major changes in direction.

In the third step they ask the critical question "Where do we *want* to be?" This step is the core of the visioning process, in which participants develop a "preferred" scenario showing what the neighborhood could look like if it chooses to honor its core values. Ultimately, this "realistically idealistic" picture becomes the basis of a formal vision statement, which is always open to revision.

The fourth step asks, "How do we get there?" Neighbors begin to formulate an action plan, identifying short-term strategies and actions needed to move the neighborhood toward its long-term vision. This step also identifies people responsible for implementing specific actions, timetables for completion of these activities, and "benchmarks" for monitoring progress. In the visioning process for an inner-ring suburban neighborhood of Kansas City, the Westside, residents voiced concern about the neglect of neighborhood parks, which were becoming crime scenes. (One park had actually been there before Kansas City became a city, but had been bisected by a large highway.) They agreed that parks were necessary for the well-being of both kids and adults, and they imagined how the parks would function if they were better maintained. The process ultimately led them to an action plan for restoring the parks.

Tools for Creating the Vision

Since 1979, planner Anton Nelessen has used the Visual Preference Survey (VPS) to help residents identify features they like and don't like about their neighborhoods. In his work to identify what makes a community sustainable, he began to see how people felt about specific features. "What did they feel was positive? What didn't they like? What type and density of new development would they find acceptable? We photographed the town and picked other scenes from our slide library. The slides were then shown to townspeople at a large public meeting. We asked them to give us a positive sign if they liked the picture, and a negative one if they didn't."[6]

Typical results of a VPS tend to favor narrow, tree-lined streets with sidewalks and lights; open spaces that are visually interesting; and houses that don't have prominent garage doors. "Everybody will call for a green open space in the middle — that's automatic," says Nelessen. "They will put the major community buildings

3.7 & 3.8: Besides making a neighborhood much prettier, trees provide shade and purify the air. Credit: Urban Advantage, Berkeley, California.

3.9: In an exercise called Box City, residents make a replica of their neighborhood, then agree on changes that will improve it. Often their suggestions result in valuable changes in zoning and building codes. Credit: Ginny Graves, CUBE.

around the plaza, then group the houses on relatively narrow streets. Ninety-nine percent don't want streets that are more than two lanes wide. At the edges of the village they leave open space."[7] In short, survey participants favor neighborhoods that emphasize people and nature, rather than cars. In many cases, VPS results have been used to guide changes in zoning and building regulations.

The Center for Understanding the Built Environment (CUBE) in Kansas City also provides great hands-on strategies to help people understand and discuss their own neighborhoods. One of their most effective tools is Box City, an exercise in which 3-D models of neighborhoods are built out of cardboard boxes and construction paper. With help from CUBE facilitators, residents go through a visioning process on potential neighborhood improvements. Box City is not intimidating to young or old — in fact it's fun. It helps get the ball rolling in the process of identifying what features neighbors want to keep and what they would like to change. In many cases a town's mayor and officials from the planning department are elbow-to-elbow with residents — scissors and glue in hand.

Another great tool for helping residents focus on livability is an index of indicators that are carefully tracked to show how a neighborhood or a community is doing. The prototype index is Sustainable Seattle, created by Seattle residents who identified key indicators for measuring quality of life. Although these indicators were compiled with a whole city in mind, most of them are also relevant at the neighborhood level. Physician John Neff, a physician at the Seattle Children's Hospital, uses indicators such as Asthma Hospitalization to gauge the medical health and vitality of the community. "It helps focus local attention on what improvements need to be made," he says. For Seattle resident Linda Storm, the indicators have personal significance. "For me, sustainability means living in a place where the air is fresh and clean, where there are green places where I can take my kids to enjoy nature, where I know and trust my neighbors...."

In the anthology *Ecopsychology: Restoring the Earth, Healing the Mind*, Seattle resident Alan Durning offers his take on the meaning of sustainability: "In the final analysis, accepting and living by sufficiency rather than

Sustainable Seattle's 40 Indicators

- Wetlands
- Biodiversity
- Soil Erosion
- Air Quality
- Pedestrian-Friendly Streets
- Open Space in Urban Villages
- Impervious Surfaces
- Population
- Residential Water Consumption
- Solid Waste Generated and Recycled
- Pollution Prevention and Renewable Resource Use
- Wild Salmon
- Farm Acreage
- Vehicle Miles Traveled and Fuel Consumption
- Renewable and Nonrenewable Energy Use
- Employment Concentration
- Real Unemployment
- Distribution of Personal Income
- Health Care Expenditures
- Work Required for Basic Needs

- Housing Affordability Ratio
- Children Living in Poverty
- Emergency Room Use
- Community Capital
- Adult Literacy
- High School Graduation
- Ethnic Diversity of Teachers
- Arts Instruction
- Volunteer Involvement in Schools
- Juvenile Crime
- Youth Involvement in Community Service
- Equity in Justice
- Low Birthrate Infants
- Asthma Hospitalization Rate for Children
- Voter Participation
- Library and Community Center Usage
- Public Participation in the Arts
- Gardening Activity
- Neighborliness
- Perceived Quality of Life

excess offers a return to what is, culturally speaking, the human home: to the ancient order of family, community, good work and good life; to a reverence for skill, creativity, and creation; to a daily cadence slow enough to let us watch the sunset and stroll by the water's edge; to communities worth spending a lifetime in; and to local places pregnant with the memories of generations."

There's no reason a suburban neighborhood can't come up with its own system for tracking quality-of-life indicators. For example, neighbors can track indicators such as:

• Wheelbarrows of compost used in the community garden per season
• Reductions in energy usage in homes
• Area of underused private spaces converted to public spaces
• Renewable energy systems installed
• Jobs created in the neighborhood
• Trash diverted to recycling facilities
• Area of impervious surfaces converted to landscaping and public spaces
• Number of trees planted
• Number of potlucks and community meals per year

Because people are busy, a typical reaction to the idea of "extra" activities seems intimidating. We want to make it clear that we are talking about activities that can be fun and that ultimately give more than they take. Some of these actions can replace current unproductive activities in our lives — they are substitutes rather than "add-on" activities, so they won't take up additional time. For example, if you go to a play put on by people in your neighborhood rather than to a professional performance, it may cost $100 less, yet provide more enjoyment overall.

Another typical reaction from suburban residents reflects the mythology of the American dream. "I've worked hard to get where I am," goes the myth, "and it's okay for me to do whatever I want."

One of the primary reasons we wrote this book was to help establish an everyday ethic that challenges that myth — we can't have everything we want, because there's a limit to the resources the Earth can provide. In the context of a family, when a rebellious teenager has the "whatever I want" attitude, isn't he or she requested to think again?

The design of a neighborhood seems like something that's out of our control — somebody else does it. But our personal experiences in cohousing, natural house building, and other sustainability projects tell us differently. All we really have to do is step outside the box. In one of our favorite children's books, *The Big Orange Splot*, Mr. Plumbean leads the way to a more colorful neighborhood. After a bird drops a can of paint on his roof, he begins to reinvent his house and landscape. His neighbors, outraged at first, begin to see the possibilities of reinventing their own houses and the neighborhood as a whole. One by one they sit with him in his transformed yard — complete with alligators on leashes and palm trees — and a fanciful piece of Superbia! is born. The same thing can happen in thousands of neighborhoods all over America.

When a subdivision is first constructed, the landscape is bare and then the trees begin to mature. Now it's time for neighborhoods to mature — or to blossom, if you will. The suburbs aren't done yet, it's that simple.

We must be the change we wish to see in the world.
MOHANDAS GANDHI

4

How to Remodel a Neighborhood

WHEN YOU REMODEL A HOUSE, you have certain goals in mind — to make the kitchen bigger, for example, while at the same time providing a place for people to take off muddy shoes and boots when coming in the back door. We propose a similar strategy for remodeling a suburban neighborhood: set your goals before you start. These goals might be to create a sense of community, provide more public spaces, and meet more individual needs right in the neighborhood.

After building the neighborhood's social capital to create a functional network (Chapter 2) and identifying common values like community and sustainability (Chapter 3), the next step is to agree on basic design principles and building blocks that can guide a long-range neighborhood remodeling program. This, in turn, can make streets, sidewalks, and backyards more valuable, and neighborhoods less dependent on costly, imported resources. By thinking outside the box, we can gradually upgrade the *performance* of our neighborhoods, making them more desirable places to live. Really, our only other option is to keep looking for those elusive neighborhoods where "the grass is greener." In other words, to participate in the huge game of musical chairs that sees one-sixth of the U.S. population moving every year.

Neighborhoods and communities have five basic types of features: paths, edges, nodes, landmarks, and districts. As we think about remodeling our neighborhoods, we need to look at how these components interact. At the end of this chapter we'll look at two neighborhoods that were built with these components in mind.

Paths, or corridors of movement, give a neighborhood form. These include streets, sidewalks, bike paths, alleys, wildlife corridors, canals, and railroads. As we will see, there are many opportunities to upgrade paths in suburban neighborhoods, despite the fact that many were really engineered to serve machines, not people.

4.1: Having a place where neighbors can gather is fundamental in creating a sense of community. Credit: Shared Living Resource Center, Berkeley, California.

In successful communities, *edges* are physical/visual boundaries or transitions between distinct districts or neighborhoods. They could be creeks, open spaces, or higher-volume avenues.

Nodes are places within a neighborhood that are accessible by paths. People often travel to and from them for specific activities. They range from a well-used basketball hoop in a driveway to a local park or community building. Because they are centers of activity, they help create a neighborhood sense of place.

Landmarks are icons that create a sense of familiarity in a neighborhood. A large, stately tree, like a giant oak planted in a median strip, is a landmark. A sculpture situated on a piece of donated front lawn could be a great neighborhood landmark, as could a community garden, an old schoolhouse, or a church.

A *district* is a distinctly identifiable region, a concept that is more familiar in urban settings. However, districts may also be developed in suburban neighborhoods. For example, imagine a neighborhood that has a well-landscaped, common parking area for both residents and visitors, several shops that specialize in musical instruments, and facilities for small-stage concerts. Streets could be "slowed down" with county-funded landscape features such as traffic circles, and trees might line either side of the street, creating a people-friendly atmosphere. A neighborhood like this, with its own focus and identity, would be thought of as "the music district."

Ten Basic Design Principles for Remodeling Neighborhoods

The following are some key principles of neighborhood design to help you think about how a neighborhood can be remodeled.

1. *Human Scale.* There are some basic physical relationships that can create resonance in a neighborhood, including focal points, a sense of transition, and a sense of enclosure in key places. An ideal distance between elements of a neighborhood with its own sense of community is 450 feet, because at that distance it's still possible to recognize individuals. Cohousing research indicates that

an optimum neighborhood scale is 25 to 40 houses, because that number of families can successfully share a common building and get to know each other well.

2. *Resource Responsibility*. If a neighborhood develops an everyday ethic that includes efficient household resource use, recycling, community gardening, shared transportation, and energy generation at the neighborhood level, it stands a better chance of being economically and socially viable. Individual efforts to be sustainable can be greatly augmented by cooperation within the neighborhood.

3. *Walkability*. We've got legs, we just need good sidewalks, bike paths, and parks to use them. The five-minute walk is considered a good measurement of "walkability." What destinations should lie within five minutes of the typical suburban front door?

4. *Open Spaces*. Whether they are common backyards, vacant lots, or areas reclaimed from the car, open spaces can be used for picnics, for community gardens, and as places for conversation, reading, and relaxation.

5. *Public Facilities*. A neighborhood that becomes a "we" rather than a string of "me's" will probably want to create a place where neighbors can gather. Such a place could be a neighborhood church or school, or it could be a cooperatively purchased home that becomes a common building.

6. *Streetscapes*. By working with the city or county, neighborhoods can create well-landscaped, people-friendly public areas in and around streets. The best time to plant a shade tree is 15 years ago. The second best time is now.

7. *Variety*. Landscaping and house decoration have typically been the only tools for creating variety in subdivision neighborhoods. At Fox Run, featured in the next three chapters, residents create variation and neighborhood color by adapting garages, planting a community garden and orchard, removing driveways, creating gardens and pathways, and taking down fences.

8. *Mixed Uses*. Home businesses are becoming a large sector of the American economy. In Superbia!, shops and neighborhood enterprises like composting, energy generation, and daycare will begin to make suburban neighborhoods more lively and productive.

9. *Coordination*. This refers to how "architectural style," including walls and fences, streetscapes, colors, and materials work together. A neighborhood should co-design features to create a sense of harmony and resonance.

10. *Maintenance*. Public features should be designed with the future in mind by using materials, technologies, and plant species that won't require large amounts of capital or time for maintenance.

Adapting the Building Blocks of Suburbia to Create Superbia!

It takes vision to see the many possibilities for giving your neighborhood a new look and feel. In the book *Yard Street Park*, Cynthia Girling and Kenneth Helphand picture "driveways used as patios, backyards as playgrounds, streets as squares, and parks as refuges. Streets are more than thoroughfares; with imagination, they can become public gardens, linear parks, or urban forests. Similarly, storm sewers need not be pipes underground. They can be swales, streams, and wetlands." Indeed, there are intriguing possibilities for re-creating waterfalls and ponds. In Seattle's Madrona neighborhood, residents dug up a pipe that was channeling spring water from the hillside into a storm drain below. Rather than replacing the pipe, the group installed boulders where the pipe had been to create a spectacular urban waterfall.

We need to consider applying the lessons of a Dutch experiment, the *woonerf* (in Dutch, *woon* means "residential" and *erf* means "yard."), in which cars, people, and landscapes share space that used to be strictly a street, to our own cul-de-sacs. Why shouldn't low-traffic cul-de-sacs have pervious, grassy surfaces (still solid enough to support fire trucks), with benches and flowerbeds? This would promote the objective of a higher ratio of parks to pavement.

To create great neighborhoods we need to think about suburban components in fresh new ways. We need to ask, "What's the *meaning* and *purpose* of these components?" For example, the car-street has competed with the house-yard for space and importance throughout the era of the postwar suburb. The car-street represents the world "out there," carrying the occupant to and from places dominated by things largely out of our control: rules, prices, and deadlines. The house-yard, where we don't have to punch the time clock or fight traffic, has traditionally been a retreat from a dizzying, often discordant

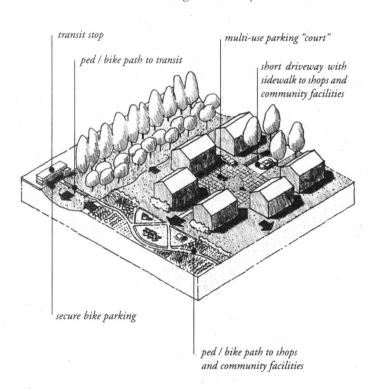

transit stop

ped / bike path to transit

multi-use parking "court"

short driveway with sidewalk to shops and community facilities

secure bike parking

ped / bike path to shops and community facilities

4.2: By adapting the existing features of a neighborhood, we can create community-by-design. Why shouldn't a cul-de-sac also be a green space? Porous pavers offer this opportunity. Credit: Tom Richman, Richman Associates.

world. At home we perceive ourselves as masters and ladies of the manor. We can express our individuality and read the paper in the backyard in our pajamas. That is, until the grass cutters arrive or the boss calls to announce a weekend meeting....

The typical suburban climate-controlled house also demonstrates a tension between public and private values. As the suburban empire expanded, we abandoned basic design principles of traditional architecture that had kept houses cool in summer and warm in winter. Instead, initial costs became the dominant consideration: both the cost of construction and the cost of purchase. Because energy was cheap, suburban house design was more responsive to private comfort and aesthetics than to public values such as the environment. For example, in Denver, streets were often laid out so houses would face the mountains rather than the sun. This emphasis on aesthetics has resulted in a lot of unnecessary energy consumption and unnecessary discomfort.

These tensions between public and private priorities leave an indelible signature on the suburban landscape. The battle between car and house has caused the disappearance of shade trees along the street, since traffic engineers regard them as "hazardous obstacles." The walkway from the house to the front sidewalk is disappearing, too, and often the front sidewalk itself — all victories for the car-street. Once parked in the vestigial carriage house on the alley, the car now typically assumes a dominant architectural position. Really, it has become a member of the family, with its own sometimes-heated room in the front part of the house.

Many of the familiar features of suburbia — the yards, streets, sidewalks, and parks — were first seen in the coach and streetcar suburbs of the 19th century, but in a more grandiose, humanized form. Llewellyn Park, for example, an 1850s New Jersey suburb with a spectacular view of Manhattan, introduced the curvilinear street, the setback house, and the idea of a green open space at the center of a *suburban* development. In Riverside, an 1860s Chicago suburb, Frederick Law Olmstead incorporated "generous spaces and the absence of sharp corners, to suggest and imply leisure, contemplativeness and happy tranquility."[1] The streets were depressed two or three feet to minimize their visual impact, and in strategic locations they broadened into open spaces for small groves of trees, croquet lawns, picnic areas, and drinking fountains. An impressive 44 percent of Riverside's acreage was retained for public use.

In Radburn, New Jersey, influenced by the British idea of the Garden City, several basic concepts were introduced to rehumanize the Motor Age of the 1920s. Radburn designer Clarence Stein's goal was to create a place where people "could live peacefully with the car — or in spite of it."[2] Neighborhoods were designed

4.3: A solar house can dramatically reduce fuel bills. Credit: Dan Chiras.

as distinct units or "superblocks," each with its own central courtyard, school, and nearby shopping area. Each house had two faces, with the living room facing pedestrian walkways and a common green, and the kitchen facing the cul-de-sac and street. About half of the houses were multifamily dwellings, allowing more open space per living unit.

Networks of walkways and streets were separate, with overpasses and underpasses enabling pedestrians to walk through the community without having to cross a single street. Each pathway led to a centrally located park, making the community a haven for kids. At the same time, streets were narrow, traffic was slow, and kids could use scooters and bicycles on the pavements.

While many of these prototype suburban components survived into the 1950s, the typical Federal Housing Administration-backed, postwar subdivision was a pale imitation of its forerunners. Both planning departments and lenders encouraged an emphasis on private space, issuing permits and loans only for familiar-looking projects. Public areas were referred to in planning and lending guidelines, but the perceived need for speed in traffic flow made streets — traditionally a public space — unsafe for people, who also lost public parks and green spaces because developers maximized the number of houses and yards per development. Public space was often limited to utility rights-of-way, highway exits, and steep unusable hillsides.

Sunrise Over Superbia!

As we take an inventory of the typical suburban neighborhood, we find many of the raw materials necessary for creating a more vital, secure, and friendly neighborhood. Using the ten principles described above, we begin to see possibilities for improving the performance of our houses, streets, and yards. For example, we see the potential for installing solar panels to heat water, providing dependable energy that doesn't require coal mines, nuclear power plants, or wars in the Middle East. Interestingly, the installation of state-of-the-art solar water heaters would effectively take our homes "back to the future," since the solar water heater was first patented in the 1890s.

Solar space heating and solar electrical generation are also good bets for remodeling a neighborhood. Picture a courtyard solar greenhouse that supplies heat as well as food for several houses in the neighborhood. It could even connect two houses. Another possibility for suburban homes is the solar attic, described by Sim Van der Ryn in *Sustainable Communities*: "The rafters and ceiling are superinsulated and lined with black plastic. Double-glazing panels are installed in the south slope of the roof, together with 'heat rods': plastic tubes filled with high-tech salts to retain heat. The heat captured in the attic is then distributed through a conventional duct and fan system to other parts of the house." During the summer, the solar attic can be covered for the season or continuously vented to prevent the house from overheating, or it may be used to preheat water before it goes into the water heater.

Solar energy has been used for thousands of years in the architecture of advanced cultures, but it seems to suffer in the current market because the sun's energy is free. As a result, the profit-motivated suppliers of conventional energy often portray solar technologies as "unproven." The industry almost overcame that perceptual barrier in the energy-conscious years following World War II. "One way for America to hedge against future fuel shortages," announced a 1943 *Newsweek* feature, "would be to build more solar homes like that of Mr. and Mrs. Hugh Duncan in Homewood, a Chicago suburb." A *Reader's Digest* article the following year called the work of solar architect George Keck "probably the most exciting architectural news in decades."[3] Research teams from MIT to Stanford worked overtime with an energy conservation ethic that had become gospel during the war years. "It is time," concluded a 1952 presidential commission report, "for aggressive research in the field of solar energy — an effort in which the United States could make an immense contribution to the welfare of the free world."[4]

But instead of taking the road toward sustainability, America quickly took a step backward to resource-consuming, air-conditioned electric homes that people believed would soon be powered by "atomic energy too cheap to meter," as one enthusiastic 1950s politician put it. Energy conservation was thought to be necessary only in wartime. Yet as we write this book, we are once again in wartime. Renewable energy sources and efficiency upgrades can be essential strategies in our campaign for homeland security, not only because they conserve fossil fuels, but also because they are decentralized and less vulnerable to terrorism — and they reduce our dependence on fossil fuels from a politically unstable part of the world.

4.4: *LA Ecovillage; people eating lunch in street, as part of their street calming efforts.*
Credit: Lois Arkin.

Reforesting our suburban neighborhoods is another essential step in the creation of Superbia! In *The Bulldozer in the Countryside*, Adam Rome writes, "To speed the work of site preparation, the typical subdivision builder cleared away every tree in the tract, so millions of new homes had no shelter against bitter winter winds and brutal summer sun."

According to the National Academy of Sciences (NAS), there are more than 100 million spaces for new trees available in metropolitan America. NAS estimates that planting trees in these spaces — less than one tree per adult — and lightening the color of dark paved surfaces would save 25 percent of the kilowatt-hours consumed every year by air conditioners in the United States. Tree planting is something we can do as a neighborhood alliance to add shade, clean air, and public character to our parks and streets. There are many opportunities to buy young trees for a few dollars apiece through extension offices and city agencies.

Adapting the streets themselves — and widening the sidewalks — will be more of a challenge, yet municipal momentum may be on our side. In many metropolitan areas such as Portland (Oregon), Minneapolis, Seattle, and Santa Barbara, street redesign has become standard practice. Street narrowing, median strips, roundabouts, and islands are being installed to reclaim public space for residents — and slow traffic. In Seattle, one-way streets called *chicanes* narrow short sections of street from two lanes to one. Western Europe has converted many streets into multiuse *woonerfs*, in which slowly moving cars share public space with pedestrians. Some municipal governments in Germany actually provide grants to subsidize the de-paving of specified sections of street. Their rationale is that the less pavement there is, the more rainwater can soak into the ground instead of carrying pollution into waterways and causing flooding.

How did streets become so wide to begin with? Again, we go back to postwar thinking. Part of the formula that became generic suburbia was streets that were wide enough to evacuate populations in the event of a nuclear attack. Local fire departments supported the construction of these wide streets because they saw it would improve access and response time for their trucks. However, as perceptive architects and planners have pointed out, wider streets have resulted in higher speeds through suburban neighborhoods and higher incidences of traffic-related accidents and deaths.

Town designer Andres Duany told us, "An eight-year study in Longmont, Colorado, recorded no increased fire injury risk from narrow streets, but in the same eight years, there were 227 automotive accidents resulting in injuries, 10 of them fatal. These accidents correlated most closely to street width, with new 36-foot-wide streets being about four times as dangerous as traditional 24-foot-wide streets."

We can already see glimpses of the suburban future, and wide neighborhood streets are not part of it because they absorb heat, are energy intensive, socially divisive, unsafe, and require high maintenance. Architect Sim Van der Ryn has even designed a fanciful asphalt-eating machine that chisels up sections of pavement, converts them to fuel, plows the soil underneath, and plants trees, all in one smooth operation.

Another look into the future reveals smaller yet more productive lawns. We'll be less victimized by what *Timelock* author Ralph Keyes calls the convenience catch. "Gasoline-powered mowers made it possible to mow lawns neatly and often — once a week or more. The easier it became to cut grass, the higher our standards rose. By now many homeowners consider any lawn a failure that doesn't look like it could sustain a few holes of golf." Yet is the perfect lawn ever really attainable?

F. Herbert Bormann, Diana Balmori, and Gordon T. Geballe, in *Redesigning the American Lawn*, suggest an eminently sensible alternative — the Freedom Lawn, a domesticated variant of the prairies and meadows that preceded the Industrial Lawn. The logic is simple: the Freedom Lawn absorbs the enemy rather than eradicating it. As wildflower, herb, and weed seeds germinate in the lawn, they are incorporated into the landscape as long as they can tolerate the occasional whirring blades of the lawnmower in areas that are mowed. The resident gains freedom from all the lawn care and all the lawn care products. By being in tune with its natural surroundings, the Freedom Lawn goes cold turkey on chemicals. In Milford, Connecticut, up to five local residents are recognized every year for having the best Freedom Lawns. The judges look for chemical-free lawns that contain a diversity of plant species, patches of forest or meadow, bird feeders and birdbaths, and the presence of gravel driveways that allow rainwater to sink into the soil rather than run off into the street.[5]

You can surf the web for dozens of other ideas on how to create alternative landscapes: hedges with edible berries; perennial gardens with native wildflowers; brick courtyards; and mini-orchards with dwarf fruit trees. Once you declare independence from the Industrial Lawn, a new neighborhood ethic could elevate landscaping to higher levels. Think about it — would you rather fill your environment with pesticides or eat a bowlful of Bing cherries? Would you rather mow the lawn or go hiking with good friends?

Village Homes: A Time-tested Glimpse of Superbia

Let's look at two examples of Superbia!, where the principles of this chapter have been well applied and the building blocks correctly assembled. My (Dave's) favorite neighborhoods-by-design are Village Homes in Davis, California, and Harmony Village, in Golden, Colorado, where I live. In fact, seeing and experiencing the "inside out" shape of Village Homes was a primary stimulant for my joining the cohousing group that later became Harmony Village.

Rather than facing the street, the houses at Village Homes face greens, gardens, and walkways, as in many suburban prototypes built in the early 1900s. There is a small private space in between each house and the low-volume street. Because private yards are comparatively small, there are almost twice as many houses per acre at Village Homes as in surrounding neighborhoods, but residents are content to trade private space for public: each house opens onto common areas where people can meet one another informally. There are many spontaneous potlucks that happen when someone posts an orange flag in the common area and those interested in joining the group gather for dinner.

Close to 30 years into its life as a livable suburban community, Village Homes attracts builders from all over the world. Designer-resident Michael Corbett maintains, "We don't view Village Homes as an ideal. We just see it as a step in the right direction." Nothing's perfect, but there are many indications that Village Homes must be creating a sense of community and resident satisfaction. Although the houses are smaller than average, the value per square foot is higher. Turnover is much lower than average, but when homes do go on the market, they sell immediately. Crime is much lower in the neighborhood, too; Davis police estimate it's only ten percent of the city's average.[6]

When Michael and Judy Corbett decided to develop Village Homes, their primary focus was to build community. To do that, they arranged for shared ownership of common areas and common spaces, shared laundry space for some units,

4.5: In Village Homes, many different kinds of public space are connected by pedestrian and bike paths. Credit: Michael and Judy Corbett.

community gardens, and community fruit and nut trees and vineyards. They made people more important than cars. The neighborhood's extensive network of walkways makes it easy to bike to work and walk for exercise and access to neighbors. When the city of Davis commissioned a study comparing Village Homes with surrounding developments, it found that residents of Village Homes, on average, knew 42 of the people in their neighborhood well (there are 240 houses in Village Homes), while in other developments, the average was only 17.

Village Homes combines energy conservation with solar energy. All of the houses have 60 percent or more of their windows on the south side. Throughout the neighborhood, solar energy satisfies about two-thirds of heat needs, and bills average about half those of surrounding developments.

Each house has basic solar features such as an overhang on the south facade (which shades the house in the summer, but allows sun in during the winter), concrete slab construction to store and release solar heat, and extra insulation in the roof.

4.6: Most of the homes and common buildings at Village Homes have good solar orientation. Credit: Bill Browning, Rocky Mountain Institute.

Many homes have solar hot-water systems with collector panels on the roof, and some homes have unique designs to collect the sun's heat. For example, the Corbetts' house has a sliding panel under a skylight that's manually opened with a pulley in the daytime and closed at night.[7]

What really struck a positive chord with me was the edible landscape. I visited the community when the cherries were in season and walked on the village paths with a smile on my face and cherry juice on my fingers. The Corbetts planted a vineyard and several orchards that have now matured, producing almonds, cherries, peaches, pears, persimmons, and plums. The fruit that is not harvested by residents (free of charge) is sold to local markets. Profits go into the maintenance fund, which pays for several full-time, live-in gardeners.

Houses are laid out in clusters of eight to create a feeling of neighborliness. Residents choose the features they want in their common areas, typically putting in grass, shrubbery, sandboxes, fire pits, gardens, and benches. All the common areas initially included fruit-bearing trees and shrubs. According to Michael, "All

4.7: *Within the larger neighborhood at Village Homes, there are smaller sub-neighborhoods created intentionally by clustering eight homes around a common area. Credit: Bill Browning, Rocky Mountain Institute.*

these years, we've only had one disagreement among neighbors about how the common space in a cluster should be used. In that case, since seven other households wanted garden space, the eighth household went along."[8]

The Corbetts went to bat to protect two design concepts that have really paid off in quality of life: narrow streets and natural, on-the-surface, storm water collection.

The city planning department was not enthusiastic about streets that would be 20 to 26 feet wide, rather than the standard 44 to 52 feet, because it just wasn't *normal*. A thorough job of researching and presenting the benefits of narrow roads finally won approval from the planning department. The Corbetts and their colleagues brought many European examples to the table, arguing that narrow roads are safer, cheaper, quieter, and measurably cooler. The air temperature over a narrow street is 10 to 15 degrees Fahrenheit lower than that in surrounding neighborhoods during the hot summer months because the narrower streets have less heat-absorbing mass, and trees shade more of the street area than they would in a typical development.

The fire department also balked until a member of city council suggested there be a three-foot easement on either side of the road that could be landscaped but driven over in an emergency. Judy told us, "We asked the fire department to bring their trucks out and show us what they needed to do. They wanted two trucks to be able to get past each other, with doors open. But we arranged an easement that finally satisfied them. If a fire occurs, they can drive over the landscaped area on either side of the narrow road."

It wasn't easy to get aboveground storm water drainage approved either, but persistence paid dividends. In place of storm sewers, a network of drainage "swales" or ditches runs throughout the neighborhood, capable of handling even the heaviest downpours. In the typical subdivision, lots are graded toward the street, but at Village Homes, water actually runs off both house roofs and streets into the ditches and then into retention ponds.

Avoiding the installation of sewers saved hundreds of dollars per house, and valuable rainwater is absorbed for use in the landscape. The rock-lined ditches irrigate trees and shrubs that provide shade, food, and habitat for muskrats, ducks, and many other species of birds. In fact, the city of Davis has sometimes diverted floodwaters *into* Village Homes because the system works so well.

At Village Homes, an experiment in changing the shape of a neighborhood has been extremely successful. You can apply many of the lessons learned there in the creation of Superbia!

4.8: Developers Michael and Judy Corbett created drainage "swales" to capture rainwater and use it on-site, rather than channeling it into storm sewers. Credit: Michael and Judy Corbett.

Designing it Ourselves in Cohousing

A bumper sticker distributed by the Cohousing Network reads, "Cohousing: Creating a better society one neighborhood at a time." That's an ambitious goal, but cultural change has to start somewhere.

So what is cohousing?

Wonderland Hill Development Company, a Colorado company that specializes in cohousing communities, describes it on their website (www.whdc.com) as:

> Small-scale neighborhoods created with resident participation which provide a balance between personal privacy and life in a close-knit community of neighbors. Individual homes enjoy convenient access to shared space, including a "common house" with facilities such as a kitchen, dining room, play room for children, workshops, guest rooms, office space, a sitting area and laundry. Each home is self-sufficient with a complete kitchen, but typically, optional resident-cooked meals in the common house are offered several times a week.

Cohousing was imported from Denmark in the 1980s by architects Chuck Durrett and Katie McCamant, the pioneers of the American cohousing community. The first cohousing community in the U.S., Muir Commons in Davis, California, was completed in 1991. Since then, growth has been exponential. There are already more than 70 cohousing neighborhoods built in the US, with 100 or more in process. Within a few years, at least 10,000 Americans will be living in these "do-it-ourselves" neighborhoods, experimenting with both physical and social innovations.

What Makes Cohousing Unique?

1. Resident participation in the creation of the neighborhood
2. A design that encourages community interaction
3. Extensive common facilities supplementing private homes
4. Resident management of the community
5. Nonhierarchical decision making (most decisions are made by consensus)

Source: *Cohousing: A Contemporary Approach to Housing Ourselves* by Katie McCamant, Charles Durrett, and Ellen Hertzman.

4.9: At Harmony Village, a common green creates the comfortable feeling of an outdoor room. Credit: Dave Wann.

Cohousing creates a sense of community because residents focus on projects and issues that everyone has in common. My neighbor, Linda Worswick, comments, "You can have all the architects, planners, and engineers in the world try to design 'community,' but how do you engineer the social fabric? It's the underlying intent and shared experience that does it."

By creating a social network that focuses on common goals — whether it's opposition to a new mall or creation of a community garden — suburban neighborhoods can also create social fabric. Even in the private realms of suburbia, elder neighbors may look out the door after a snowstorm and discover that an anonymous shoveler has cleaned and sanded their walks, as frequently happens in cohousing. When neighborhood kids are skateboarding in a dangerous place, they'll hear about it from any of us.

Partly because of a demonstrated ability to fulfill a desire for community, cohousing is achieving mainstream acceptance. A friend called not too long ago to tell me he'd seen a short video about Harmony Village on a United Airlines in-flight program. Maybe the best indicator of cohousing's hard-won legitimacy is that my mother tells her bridge and church buddies what's going on at Harmony Village — a departure from my early years in the community when she was afraid they'd ask how many wives I had.

Virtually all of the ideas and approaches we propose in this book have been used in one cohousing community or another to create neighborhoods-by-design. While most cohousing involves new construction, there are a handful of cohousing communities that have adapted existing neighborhoods, such as OnGoing Concerns Cohousing in Oregon and N Street Cohousing in California. They're referred to as *retrofit cohousing.*

4.10: Harmony Village has 27 private residences as well as community assets like a common house, workshop, and community garden. Credit: Dave Wann.

The Design Process at Harmony Village

Harmony Village began as a dream of architect Matt Worswick and his wife, Linda, in the early 1990s. By the time I joined the group in 1993, a lot of ideas as well as prospective members had come and gone. Six or seven core households continued to meet every month, even though we hadn't yet found the perfect piece of land on which to build the dream neighborhood. The longer we were members, the more of a financial commitment we had to make. From an initial $25 a household — essentially petty cash to mail information to potential new members — we stair-stepped up to the $1,000 a household that would reserve a house in the community.

Many of the early meetings were visioning sessions. We got to know each other through exercises in which we described what we liked to do or imagined how the new neighborhood's facilities could accommodate our passions, skills, and physical needs. One member wanted an open field big enough for throwing a Frisbee; another wanted the common house kitchen to be equipped with built-in recycling bins. I couldn't stop thinking and talking about a garden where we could work together growing healthy food.

These sessions made even a slow-moving process exciting. At one brainstorming retreat we imagined how the pieces would fit together: pedestrian walkways, community garden, playgrounds, and various rooms in the

Harmony Design Criteria

Homes

- Quality construction/Low maintenance
- Energy efficiency/Passive solar architecture
- Affordability
- Open, spacious feel to houses
- Southwestern architecture
- Public/Private balance
- Marketability, or resale value
- Flexibility of functions for different spaces
- Quality daylighting
- Expandability
- Environmentally responsible materials
- Simplicity

- Production construction
- Warmth
- Good views

Landscapes

- Looks great
- Integrates/Unifies physical and social aspects of the community
- Provides interface with the natural environment
- Affordability
- Low maintenance
- Environmentally conscious

common house. Since we had already agreed the architecture would be southwestern, we imagined the tolling of a mission bell in a Santa Fe-style bell tower. Seven or eight years later, that imaginary bell has a very real clang, and kids love to pull the rope and ring it. Salvaged from an old farm where one of the members grew up, the massive bell calls neighbors together for meals, meetings, and celebrations.

Our initial search for land was somewhat frustrating, but one day, as two of us were driving around the group's primary "areas of interest," I got the idea of going to the City of Golden's planning department to ask about open parcels of land within city limits. I'd spent 20 years commuting from a rural, bedroom community, and I wanted to live within walking distance of things I needed. The property we found that day was a gift from the cohousing gods because it had a rural feel (complete with coyotes and great horned owls), but was only eight blocks away from a great little downtown. We could hop on a bicycle to avoid burning a quart of gasoline to pick up a quart of milk. On this piece of land we could create a small community within a larger one.

After spending a full meeting at the site, we began our design process in earnest. New members joined enthusiastically now that we had a beautiful piece of ground. Step-by-step we created a list of design criteria for homes and landscapes to guide our thinking as we co-created the features of our community.

We listed "production construction" — which refers to the ability to use conventional, economical building techniques — as a criterion because, after running the numbers, we realized that our members could not afford customized suburban castles. However, that stipulation also ruled out houses built from adobe because they would take too long to build and cost too much. We focused instead on designs and approaches that pushed the envelope of conventional construction. We used energy-efficient, low heat-emissivity ("low-E") windows, efficient appliances, cellulose insulation made from recycled newspapers, compact fluorescent bulbs, water-conserving plumbing fixtures, non-toxic paints and carpets, tiles made from recycled materials, and other readily available products. Although we didn't install solar hot-water heating in the homes at this point, we brought the plumbing for it to the roofs so it would be easy to install solar panels later.

4.11: Six years after Harmony's co-designers moved in, the landscape is maturing. Residents pick up mail at the common house, shown in the background.
Credit: Dave Wann

Before we moved in we formed a "tiling cooperative," in the spirit of an old fashioned barn raising, to help each other lay floor tiles. Dressed in kneepads and mortar-spattered clothing, we were often still up at midnight, washing out grout buckets. We laid thousands of heat-retaining southwestern tiles before we hung up our trowels. Partly to honor our hard work, a community custom was born in those early days — we remove our shoes when entering a neighbor's house or the common house.

With chain saws in hand, a small band of future neighbors carried out another cooperative project: thinning a mountain forest owned by the project superintendent in order to harvest logs for the rustic front porches. While we were out having fun, we also saved the project at least $6,000.

After seeing what a big chunk of the budget was going to landscaping, we formed a landscaping team to design water-conserving turf and flower beds and to specify trees and shrubs that were hardy enough to

4.12: It took most of the summer of 2001 to overlay 60,000 bricks to make Harmony's concrete pathway come to life. It was literally a community sweat equity project, as temperatures often soared above 95 degrees. Credit: Dave Wann.

survive Colorado's unpredictable weather. We saved the project another $6,000 by doing the landscaping plan ourselves, giving us a sense of responsibility for the landscape.

We deliberated for many hours about the design of the pedestrian walkway. We wanted it to look and feel more "quaint" than poured concrete, but building codes required that the materials be able to accommodate fire trucks and other emergency vehicles. We formed subgroups to research road base and paving alternatives, and finally reached a workable decision: we would lay concrete walkways at first, but later would lay bricks on top. Six years later we worked together for 10 or 12 very hot summer weekends to lay 60,000 bricks. What a difference! It was like a flower's blooming.

Typically, developers approach a project with a "clean-slate" mentality that leaves few natural features on site, but we took extra care to preserve a row of huge cottonwoods that reduced the need for air conditioning and provided habitat for birds, squirrels, and adventurous cats.

We kept cars out of the village center, instead parking them in common parking lots, carports, and garages. Although it's a radical departure from the suburban norm, this has been one of the most pleasant features of all. There's a sense of calmness in the center of the neighborhood, like a tranquil courtyard in a college campus — except, of course, when a soccer game or a wedding reception is in progress.

We quickly became accustomed to carrying groceries to the house and purchased several durable carts for that chore. We often cross paths with neighbors as we walk from the car to our home; spontaneous conversations lead to baby-sitting arrangements or agreements to cook a common meal together the following week. In addition to a very noticeable reduction in car noise and in land required for individual parking, we've also improved the air quality in our homes because we're not living above or next to vehicle-related fumes.

When guests come from out of town, they can stay in the guest room at the common house, which makes better use of the space in each house. We have a hot tub on the flat roof of the common house, a large-screen

TV in the basement recreation area, and a few rooms for kids. If you want to hold a business meeting or a party in the common house, you just schedule it on the calendar. The roof deck is a resource that I'm very excited about, though so far it hasn't really been used much. I can imagine small concerts and lectures up there, and common meals, too.

A neighborhood newsletter keeps community members up-to-date on one another's activities, convictions, and aspirations. One memorable article detailed the findings of senior citizen and retired clergyman Macon Cowles, who has spent a lifetime advocating positive changes. Macon carefully made note of the amount of electricity consumed when his interior lights were not dimmed, consulting the meter outside his front door. Then he went inside, dimmed the lights that had rheostats on them, and observed a significant difference in unwasted watts. After presenting the potential savings in money, fuel, and carbon dioxide emissions, Macon urged his neighbors to "Dim it, damn it."

When the community was completed in May 1997, it immediately received the National Building Innovation Award, presented by the assistant secretary for Housing. Superior insulation (R19-23 walls and R38-50 ceilings) and advanced air-sealing techniques help Harmony achieve an average Energy Star rating of 91 — a solid five-star rating that saves each household an average of $250 per year over conventional homes.

4.13 & 4.14: *The community green, planted in water-conservative fescue grass, is a great place to have outdoor meetings. In the first picture, a neighbor announces he's going to have his wedding reception at Harmony. A few months later (below), the reception is in high gear. Credit: Dave Wann.*

Obviously the "hardware" fosters sustainability, but so does the "software." One idea we are actively discussing is an effective, businesslike, car-sharing cooperative. In an era with high percentages of at-home workers and retired people, and a gradual re-emergence of public transportation, some Harmony residents wonder why we can't get around in fewer cars. We already have an informal network of car and pickup truck lending, and a very supportive approach to transportation. "When you need to pick your car up from the shop, just walk around the neighborhood and see who's around to get you there," says Jonathan Daniel, a renter in the community.

I've never been a great fan of the term "cohousing," preferring a more literal translation from Danish, "living community." At its best, a sustainable neighborhood resembles a living system in which all resources — human, natural, and economic — are interdependent and draw strength from each other. Like nature, most cohousing communities are diverse and flexible, though the collective decision-making process is at times cumbersome.

Yet each meeting, each hour of volunteered work, is another stitch in the neighborhood fabric because we're working on projects that are mutually beneficial. We believe that with a little determination and a lot of patience the typical suburban neighborhood could also become a living community. In the next three chapters, Dan will show you how your dreams might unfold.

Even the longest journey is begun with a single step.
CONFUCIOUS

5

Germination: First Steps

THROUGHOUT THE WORLD, people like you are building neighborhoods that are helping them achieve what they truly want: connection, responsibility, and closeness. Cohousing, described in Chapter 4, is one of the best examples of this exciting movement. However, not all of us can sell our homes and form a cohousing community — and not all of us want to! For one reason or another, we are tied to our homes in suburbia. Although our neighborhoods may be less than optimal, we can still enjoy the good life cohousers and others like them are creating for themselves.

How?

By reinventing the urban and suburban neighborhoods where we live in ways that foster more socially, economically, and environmentally sustainable lifestyles. By transforming our neighborhoods with ideas that are key to the success of cohousing communities.

Although some of the steps for remaking urban and suburban neighborhoods may appear unlikely or impossible — for example, tearing down backyard fences to create a common area — if you start small, are patient, and work cooperatively, you can succeed. You may find that many ideas we share with you lead naturally to other ideas. Once you start the process, a natural momentum should develop that will carry you and your neighbors along an evolutionary path toward a new and more fulfilling existence.

A Journey of the Imagination

In the next three chapters we take you on a journey of the imagination, a voyage of possibility, in a fictitious neighborhood inhabited by people like you, who yearn for a better life yet aren't aware that the answer lies at their fingertips, or more precisely, in their own hearts and minds. We hope this journey will open your mind to the possibilities of urban and suburban transformation — and will be more fun than a dry and detailed recitation of the steps involved in moving toward a more sustainable neighborhood. We hope that it will also show you how plausible these ideas are.

So let's begin.

"Fox Run" is a relatively new suburb with hundreds upon hundreds of homes lined along a maze of pavement that connects garages to feeder highways that merge with superhighways. The superhighways that were built to accommodate the new growth already show signs of overuse; each day they are clogged with traffic as commuters make their way to and from their places of work, or as parents shuttle to and from their homes, local schools, playing fields, or the grocery store.

The homes in Fox Run are attractive, but there is a monotonous sameness to them. One neighbor joked that, after he moved in, he could only find his house by pressing the garage door opener as he drove down the street to see which door opened. In Fox Run you will find wide streets, expansive green lawns, and tall wooden fences that cordon off backyards for maximum privacy.

The subdivision is peaceful enough most of the time, but there's little connection among residents. Sure, some neighbors know one another, but by and large the interactions are perfunctory. Then one day...

Sponsor Community Dinners

Tired of the loneliness and isolation in her new Fox Run home, Marion Remsted, a stay-at-home mother of two, has an idea. What if she organized a community dinner — actually a picnic — and invited all her neighbors? She calls her husband, Jack, at work and then phones Julie, one of her only friends in the neighborhood, and asks them their opinions. Both like the idea. "What do we have to lose?" Jack says. Without any more deliberation, the three of them set a date that works for them.

Before doubts can creep in, Marion sits down at her computer and prepares a flyer announcing the date and time for the dinner. With the paper still warm from her printer, she goes to each of the houses that line their street, introducing herself and handing out flyers. If no one is home, which is often the case, she wedges a flyer in the front door.

That evening, Marion and Jack's phone begins to ring as neighbors call up, eager to join in. Before she and her accomplices know it, half the families in the neighborhood (12, to be exact) have signed up and committed to bringing a dish. You and your family decide to join in. You've only lived in the neighborhood a year or so, and you've been longing to meet your neighbors, but there never seems to be enough time. This seems like a perfect opportunity to get out and meet the people you see driving off to work as you drink your coffee at the breakfast table.

Community dinners are a great first step in creating community. Food draws people like a magnet. (Interestingly, the word *companion* literally means "with bread.") Besides bringing people together, potluck meals and neighborhood picnics usually introduce participants to a wonderful assortment of new foods. Even more important from the standpoint of community development, friendships often emerge from casual conversations. Even something as innocent as recipe swapping may cook up new relationships.

Over dinner, neighbors explore common interests; new bonds begin to form with each bite. After dinner, as adults mingle, children gather to play. Following rules that remain a mystery to adults, they soon scatter to the four corners in a flurry of activity. With new play relationships comes additional community cohesion.

Inevitably, as the event winds down, someone expresses a desire to have another community dinner, maybe every month or so ... and before you know it, a neighborhood is off and running.

The next day you notice neighbors knocking on neighbors' doors, following up on conversations, dropping off recipes. Pretty soon community members begin to help one another out. Your family, for example, agrees to keep an eye on the Jenkins' home — and their pet guinea pig and ferret — over Christmas

Benefits of Community Dinners

- *Get to know your neighbors personally*
- *Discover common interests and concerns*
- *Develop a sense of community and a sense of belonging*
- *Make contact with others and gain closeness and friendship*
- *Develop allies among your neighbors*
- *Learn new recipes*
- *Eat exciting new foods*

5.1: *Community meals bring people together for food, conversation, and networking. In the process, they help build community one bite at a time.*
Credit: Mike April.

in exchange for caring for your black Lab, Ben, during spring break, while you're away with the kids, skiing in Colorado. This transaction saves each family on costly pet care. Neighbors begin to swap tools, for example, occasional use of a chain saw for access to a neighbor's table saw. And parents soon begin sharing in the incessant chauffeuring of children. Cutting a few trips out of your schedule each week yields a considerable amount of free time.

Besides the sharing that the community-building initiates, over time you find that monthly dinners begin to foster a sense of belonging. Out of disparate lives, a web of closeness and friendship is woven. And each month you get to try new dishes and learn some delicious new recipes!

Establish a Community Newsletter, Bulletin Board, and Roster

With the free time she's acquired by sharing in the chauffeuring of children to and from school events, Marion comes up with another idea — or set of ideas, to be precise.

First she suggests a community newsletter. "Nothing fancy, just a monthly neighborhood newsletter that anyone can submit to for any reason," she remarks. Whether you want to advertise your need for help on a household repair project, borrow a tool, tell friends and neighbors about an upcoming vacation, or announce that your teenager is looking for baby-sitting opportunities, the newsletter is your voice. It's a forum for political announcements, where you can alert neighbors to upcoming meetings sponsored by the planning department in your town that they might find instructive. It could be a place for promoting school productions or for selling used furniture. In addition, the newsletter is a way to keep track of exciting events in your lives and to share important happenings. In conversation with others at a community dinner, a newsletter committee emerges.

Marion also puts forward the idea of a community roster: a list of names and phone numbers for easy access. But she has another wild idea. "Why not include short bios in the roster so neighbors can get to know one another even better?" In the next newsletter, Marion asks each member of the neighborhood to submit a 500-word "essay" that tells something significant, something personal, and something humorous about themselves. She even has the foresight to ask everyone to list practical skills they possess — like carpentry skills — which starts an assets inventory. The results are remarkable. Who would have known that your neighbors were so creative and so funny? And who would have imagined there were so many useful skills so close at hand?

As you start the second year of your brave new adventure in community living, someone suggests that the neighborhood could use a community bulletin board. It doesn't take long for a couple of the men — Jack Remsted and Julie's husband, Tom — to build a board and install it near the mailboxes at the end of the street. Protected from rain and snow, the bulletin board provides a location for people to post announcements or alert neighbors of important events. Ads for used furniture, electronic equipment, musical instruments, music lessons, and used cars soon fill the board. Residents of neighboring streets are frequently seen combing the ads for treasures.

> ### Benefits of Community Newsletters, Bulletin Boards, and Rosters
>
> • *Help to create a closer-knit community*
> • *Provide vital personal information*
> • *Provide updates on important events*

Newsletters, rosters, biographical sketches, and community bulletin boards offer many obvious benefits. They help you keep track of events in your neighbors' lives and give you space to share important events in your own life as well. Most of all, they give you an opportunity to become better acquainted with the people you live near, to intertwine lives, to create friendship, interdependency, and love. They are simple ideas that plant vital seeds for the community-building process.

Establish a Neighborhood Watch Program

In the middle of the second year of your neighborhood's grand adventure, you come home to find a police car parked in a neighbor's driveway — two doors down. The next day you learn through the grapevine that someone broke into the home while the owners, Matt and Marcy, were away on a short business trip. The thieves made off with a houseful of valuables: two computers and printers, a couple of television sets, a stereo, two VCRs, a DVD player, a camera, a camcorder, jewelry, and silverware — a $10,000 loss. Like most people who experience similar circumstances, you are alarmed by the proximity of this crime. After all, you moved to the suburbs to avoid such occurrences.

While neighbors comfort the family, you and a few others brainstorm ways to prevent this from happening again. The answer comes quickly: Why not set up a neighborhood crime watch program?

With help from the local police, you and your neighbors join forces to establish a program. Matt and Marcy volunteer to serve as the neighborhood coordinators, who will act as liaisons with the local police station. Damion Knight, a single man who's been coming to community dinners since the outset, volunteers

Benefits of a Neighborhood Watch Program

• *Creates greater security*

• *Reduces crime*

• *Helps to create stronger community ties*

• *Creates greater interdependence*

to serve as block captain and goes door-to-door, encouraging neighbors to become block watchers. He passes out crime prevention information to each household.

Most people in the neighborhood join the block watch and receive training from the police department on identifying suspicious activities. You and your neighbors become the eyes and ears of the police and the neighborhood.

Neighborhood crime watch programs offer benefits far beyond personal security. They create a bond among neighbors. In a matter of weeks, one more strand in the growing community web has been woven.

Start Neighborhood Clubs

In Year Two, other people begin to proffer ideas at the monthly community dinners. "Why not form an investment club?" Julie asks. You've been hearing about these clubs on television for a while now. In an investment club, friends or coworkers unite to invest jointly in stocks. They meet regularly to talk about investment possibilities. Relying on the group's research abilities, they select stocks they think are worth investing their hard-earned money in. To spread the risk, members of an investment club typically pool their money, buying various stocks collectively and sharing gains or losses collectively as well.

Enriched by the insights, knowledge, research abilities, and experience of neighbors, your community's investment club turns out to be profitable and enjoyable. One member says, "Participating in our club showed me that I didn't have to leave the neighborhood to have fun."

During the second year, other clubs form in the neighborhood. Several couples get together to form an exercise club to trim off a few pounds. Well, let's be honest — to trim off quite a few pounds. Over the first six months, most experience dramatic decreases in blood cholesterol and substantial gains in cardiovascular fitness.

With a boatload of kids in the neighborhood, one dad organizes a weekly softball game after school lets out, providing an outlet for that boundless energy children possess.

A few avid gardeners in your neighborhood form a gardening club. "It's not much really," says Susan, the club's semi-official president. "Just an excuse to socialize and share gardening tips." Over time, however, members find themselves helping one another with daily gardening chores — pulling weeds or digging potatoes. "It's always more fun to work with someone," says Susan. Soon one gardener's surpluses start to end up in the hands of others, traded for their surpluses. "There's a zucchini economy emerging in the neighborhood!" quips Macon, Susan's husband.

In Year Three, one neighbor, JR, who has a passion for gardening and wildlife, joins the National Wildlife Federation's backyard wildlife program. He decides to start a club to enlist others. A good-natured mischief maker, JR publicizes the first meeting of the backyard wildlife club by announcing a meeting to "Create wildlife habitat right in our own backyards!"

With visions of coyotes and foxes wandering through the neighborhood, feeding on cats and small dogs, dozens of your neighbors show up ... only to learn that JR is proposing the creation of butterfly gardens in your backyards. A half dozen neighbors join in, creating small but colorful gardens that are now graced with the silent wing beats of delicate butterflies.

Form Discussion Groups

Not all gatherings in the neighborhood focus on food or investments or butterfly gardens. Martin McMann, a young college professor with a love of fiction, moved in last year. He picked this community in large part because of an advertisement Marion placed in the newspaper when one of the neighbors' homes went on the market. In it, she described the opportunity to buy a new home in a growing community.

Martin decides to start a book club. After he places an announcement in the newsletter, readers come out of the woodwork, even a few teenagers who are looking to widen their horizons.

> **Benefits of Neighborhood Clubs**
>
> - *Gain from the wisdom of others*
> - *Have fun without leaving the neighborhood*
> - *Get more exercise*
> - *Provide safe, fun activities for kids*

5.2: *Wildlife habitat in a neighborhood might consist of a bird-friendly garden enjoyed by both birds and people. You may even be lucky enough to have an occasional visit from the Elks Club, right before mating season. Credit: Dave Wann.*

Benefits of Discussion Groups

• *Enliven your intellectual life*
• *Develop close contacts with neighbors*
• *Discover common interests and concerns*
• *Expand your knowledge base*
• *Learn from others and share what you know*

5.3: Discussion groups let neighbors keep up with local, regional, and even global affairs. They also open our minds to new points of view and help satisfy our thirst for knowledge. And they can be great fun! Credit: Dave Wann.

Once a month now, Martin's living room is filled with people — you and your neighbors — eager to talk books. To accommodate the wide range of interests, participants nominate books from a wide range of genres from historical fiction to contemporary mainstream fiction, and from world politics to self-help. At some meetings members discuss and debate local political issues based on readings from newspapers and magazines. Many residents find it helpful to discuss the plethora of ballot issues before the election, and they vote to increase the frequency of meetings in the month prior to voting day. "We were all better informed as a result," comments Martin. "I felt as if I really understood the ballot issues and referenda after our discussions."

Neighborhood discussion groups enliven the intellectual life of a community and help neighbors develop a deeper understanding of contemporary issues, themselves, others, and the complex world around them. Differences of opinion will inevitably emerge. Far from being divisive, exposure to differences helps us understand and appreciate other viewpoints. It helps us become more compassionate and caring individuals.

Like other interactions in a community, discussion groups help us develop close contacts with neighbors, discover common interests and concerns, learn from others, and share what we know. As a community, we grow in many ways.

Establish a Neighborhood Baby-sitting Co-op

With teenagers' busy schedules, many modern suburbanites will tell you that a good baby-sitter is a premium commodity. Those who do babysit are often booked weeks in advance. Finding a sitter at the last minute can be a nightmare.

Early in the first year of Fox Run's evolution toward Superbia!, several parents in the neighborhood tackled the problem by creating a baby-sitting co-op. Those who were interested in participating — that is, serving as sitters in trade for baby-sitting by other community members — met after a monthly dinner. After a short discussion, people filled out a sign-up sheet, giving their names, phone numbers, and other pertinent information — for example, how many children they had. After the first year, the list was put on the neighborhood website for easy access and updating. (The website was established to provide electronic access to the newsletter and to help increase communication between neighbors after Year One.)

> ### Benefits of a Neighborhood Baby-sitting Co-op
>
> - *Save time and avoid the hassle of searching for a baby-sitter*
> - *Have someone you trust taking care of your children*
> - *Have children (the ones you are sitting) to play with your children*
> - *Provide a means for older adults who don't have children to be with kids*

Now when someone needs a sitter, even at the last minute, they call a member of the co-op. If available, that person takes the children for the evening, earning one point per hour per child. Points accumulate as credit for baby-sitting hours. Individuals enter points they accumulate for baby-sitting hours on an on-line tally sheet based on the honor system. Childless adults gather points they can use to get help with chores or household projects, part of the community work-share program described below.

A baby-sitting co-op requires little management and offers an essential service free of charge or in exchange for other services. Moreover, your children's care is entrusted to neighbors you know, not someone who lives halfway across town and was recommended by a friend of a friend. The children you baby-sit often play with your own children, so it's more fun for the kids and a lot less work for the adults.

Form an Organic Food Co-op

Although gardeners in the neighborhood are now producing copious amounts of food for themselves and others, the four-month growing season limits their production. One day, one of the gardeners calls a meeting to start an organic food co-op. Before the meeting he contacts a local health food outlet, part of a retail chain, and works out a deal. The supplier agrees to sell your group case quantities of fruits and vegetables year-round at ten percent over cost. In return, it asks that someone from the co-op call on Monday morning before 11 a.m. to place the order. The food will be ready and waiting for the co-op by noon on Tuesday.

Benefits of an Organic Food Co-op
• *Obtain a variety of healthy fruits and vegetables for you and your family*
• *Save money on organic produce by buying in bulk*
• *Reduce the weekly burden of vegetable shopping*
• *Develop community cooperation*

The project coordinator presents this arrangement to the neighbors who gather for the meeting. Not all families like the idea, but many sign up to give it a whirl.

Each week, one member from the committee places an order, taking suggestions from other members of the co-op. On Tuesday, that individual picks up the produce, then sorts it and divides it evenly among participating members of the community. The person in charge each week receives his or her order free, as partial compensation for coordinating the week's order.

Over time, some members drop out of the program, finding it too unpredictable. They like having more control over their groceries. Most of the others find it a delightful way to get pesticide-free fruits and vegetables at a huge discount over grocery store prices. Besides reducing shopping time, the system delivers a variety of healthful fruits and vegetables and further strengthens the growing bonds in the community.

Create Car or Van Pools

One day toward the end of Year Two, one of your neighbors (an accountant) reads through the community roster and makes a startling discovery: Most adults in the neighborhood work at the tech center, a sprawling office park that has grown up in your city in the past decade. After spending a little time on the phone and at his computer, he realizes that, each day, 22 cars leave the neighborhood and over half of them arrive within a mile or so of each other. "Why not organize a car pool?" he asks his wife. "We could easily cut down the number of vehicles on the road by half!"

He dives into the task, first writing an article for the newsletter that groups neighbors into car pools based on destination to minimize travel time. The day after the report hits the streets, he signs up a quarter of the potential carpoolers. Over the next week he contacts the rest, reeling in several more participants.

Carpooling isn't for everyone, but those who participate enjoy many benefits. Besides reducing wear and tear on vehicles, it can make the daily commute much more pleasant. Like other activities, it knits the community together as people have time to talk about world affairs, local politics, problems at work, and personal challenges. Carpooling can also save money and may cut down on travel time, as many cities have high-occupancy-vehicle lanes for cars carrying two or more passengers during the misnamed "rush hour." Carpooling cuts down on traffic and can make a small but significant dent in local, regional, and global air pollution. We all breathe a little easier when a group of office workers piles into a car or van for a trip to work.

Create a Neighborhood Work-share Program

"How many times have you and your spouse struggled with a home repair project, trying to fix drywall or wire a basement remodel with little or no knowledge of what you're doing?" Matt asks at the February community dinner. Most people nod knowingly. "What about setting up a co-op to help one another out?" he continues. "We've launched so many vital projects in the last couple of years. This one is sure to be a success."

"How do you propose making such a thing work?" someone asks.

"We can model it after the baby-sitting co-op."

Over the next few months, Matt and other neighbors go to work on a program to create a work-share program. Each member of the community who wishes to join submits a list of specific skills and knowledge he or she possesses, from dry walling to painting to plumbing to electrical wiring to tile installation. Individuals list their level of competency on their trade-for-work resumes as well. Matt, for instance, worked his way through college doing tile work and carpeting, but he also dabbled in electrical wiring. He lists himself as a master tiler and carpet installer but an "apprentice electrician." Clearly, though, you don't have to be a skilled home builder to participate — even cooks and cleanup crews are welcome on a work-share project.

Members also list projects they'd like to complete over the next year, along with project dates, the number of people they think they will need, and the skills they will require. As in the baby-sitting co-op, each hour a member donates earns credits for his or her projects.

Besides providing skilled help on home fix-it and remodeling projects, work-share programs can save money and bond a community more tightly together. Projects that may drag on for months, even years, when we are working on our own, can be completed in a weekend as a cooperative venture. Individuals also learn

> **Benefits of Car or Van Pools**
>
> • Cut down on expenses for gas, wear and tear, etc.
> • Make the daily commute more enjoyable
> • Meet your neighbors
> • Develop deeper friendships
> • Develop allies and contacts you may be able to help from time to time and vice versa

Benefits of a Neighborhood Work-share Program

- Get help on difficult projects
- Benefit from the skills of others
- Provide assistance to neighbors
- Complete difficult projects more quickly by working cooperatively
- Enhance community spirit/sharing
- Develop deeper friendships

5.4: Imagine how much more fun a weekend home project would be if neighbors chipped in to assist your family. Credit: Mike April.

from one another, broadening their skills. And, of course, there's the sense of community that grows even stronger with every hammered nail.

Create a Neighborhood Mission Statement

Sometime during the third year of Fox Run's new life, Marion suggests that you and your neighbors draft a mission statement, a declaration of interdependence and vision.

"It seems we're going somewhere," she says. "Maybe we ought to clarify where."

The group agrees. You've already developed a "we" mentality, but perhaps it is time to create a vision of where you are going.

"How will we know what direction we're going if we don't create some kind of vision?" one neighbor chimes in.

"How will we be able to tell others about our neighborhood and recruit new families when a house goes up for sale?" another adds.

Over the next few months the group tosses ideas around informally over the internet. Eventually, a statement emerges: "The aim of Fox Run is to create a cooperative neighborhood of diverse individuals sharing human resources within an ecologically responsible community."

While you are working on the vision statement, the group decides to establish a process for making decisions. You've found that getting the entire group to agree can take some time. While the community wanted to use consensus decision making, no one knew exactly how that worked.

To solve this, you and your neighbors rent two adjoining condos at a nearby lake resort and hold your first "neighborhood retreat." You meet for a weekend in the summer, hiring a facilitator who teaches you about the process of making decisions through consensus.

Create a Neighborhood Asset Inventory

With the mission statement nailed down and consensus decision making now your "formal" agreement process, Brad suggests creating an asset inventory.

"A what?" someone asks.

"An inventory of what we have — for example, personal skills and opportunities for saving resources and money," Brad responds. "It's standard practice in the community visioning work I'm doing." (Brad works in rural community development, helping citizens of small towns develop their community in ways that make sense from the standpoint of residents, their economy, and the environment.)

The asset inventory builds on earlier work, notably the community roster and the work-share program. From these projects you've developed a fairly comprehensive list of community members' personal and professional skills, including specialized knowledge and experience in gardening, landscaping, construction, and energy efficiency. You also prepare a list of tools that are available in the community. If you live in an older community you might assess other resources — for example, historic sites. In rural settings you may want to identify environmental assets, such as a nearby meadow worth preserving or a hiking trail.

• • •

At the outset of this chapter you may have been skeptical that a neighborhood could be transformed into a more closely knit, cooperative, and environmentally friendly community. Things won't always go smoothly. Some people may never want to join in. Disagreements may arise and some folks may drop out of the process. However difficult the path may seem at times, neighborhood re-inventors we've talked to say that the efforts pay huge dividends.

Despite all of the benefits your community is now enjoying, though, you are only part way to Superbia!

Benefits of a Neighborhood Mission Statement

- *Helps knit the community together*
- *Crystallizes thinking about the community*
- *Helps generate consensus on future projects*

The great thing in this world is not so much where we stand as in what direction.
OLIVER WENDELL HOLMES

6

Leafing Out: Bolder Ideas

YOU'VE ACHIEVED MANY THINGS in your neighborhood over the past three years through hard work and the dedication of a small, highly motivated core group — a key to the success of any neighborhood transformation. Neighbors who once greeted each other with automatic, sometimes forced, smiles now stop and chat with one another, catching up on the latest news. Community dinners and the community newsletter have been instrumental in this change. Because of them, the neighbor two doors down is no longer just the man who drives an energy-miserly Toyota Prius, but Damion, a 25-year-old musician who was born in Louisiana. You've learned that although he is currently writing copy for an advertising agency, he secretly dreams of becoming a songwriter. You've also learned that he plants an enormous vegetable garden in his backyard every year and shares tomatoes and, oh yes, bushels of zucchinis with you and other families "on the block." When you went for a hike with him and his fiancee in a nearby state park, he introduced you and your family to a little-known waterfall. Your children have noticed his love for kids, and they now join you on hikes and are often found helping Damion in the garden on weekends (and you can't even get them to pick up their rooms!).

Last week, the neighborhood watch program established after Matt and Marcy were robbed paid off. Two burglars broke into a neighbor's house. They were just getting into their car, ready to speed off, when the police car arrived, thanks to a phone call from one of your block watchers. The thieves would have made off with a couple of television sets, a stereo, a computer, and a new digital camera — not to mention $350 in cash they found stashed in a bedroom drawer.

This week marks the beginning of the third year of the investment club. Many members of the community continue to attend monthly meetings of the book club. The baby-sitting co-op has saved families in the neighborhood hundreds of dollars and countless hours of hassle. The organic food co-op continues to be a success, and some neighbors report that they feel better because of it, primarily because they're eating a lot more fruits and vegetables. The carpool is running smoothly. Work sharing is becoming a regular happening.

Like a garden, the soil of your community has been tilled and the seeds for a sustainable community — for Superbia! — have been planted. Over a period of three years the community has begun to transform into a community — a more genuine, caring ensemble. For the most part, people feel a sense of closeness, belonging, creativity, and excitement. There's a growing sense of interdependence and a strong feeling of pride, and many neighbors are benefiting economically — saving money by carpooling, work sharing, gardening, and participating in the baby-sitting co-op.

At times you've had doubts about your success. The process has not always been easy and not all seeds have germinated. For example, plans to start a neighborhood band never sprouted, but as in any good garden, that's to be expected. Despite these minor setbacks, your neighborhood is on the verge of even more promising development. Neighbors are beginning to think that there's more they can do. Where do you go from here?

Tear Down "De-fences"

In the middle of the fourth year, Marion and two of her neighbors take an even bolder step. As they prepare for a neighborhood picnic, Marion suggests that they remove a few sections of the fence that separates their yards. "This measure will make room for all the families who now gather for the monthly community picnics," she tells her husband. "It's just temporary," she adds.

But during the picnic, the open backyard becomes the center of discussion. Most adults are surprised at how spacious the yard feels with the fence down. "More elbow room," one neighbor notes. After the picnic, the children, with their usual enthusiasm for new ideas that ease restrictions on their movement, beg their parents to leave the fences down.

Marion and her next-door neighbor agree.

"Fences close us in, block our views, limit our play space, and isolate us from one another," another neighbor chimes in at the next meeting.

"Sooner or later, 'de-fences' are going to have to come down if we want to create community!" another adds.

Marion, the sparkplug of this community, simply smiles.

In the neighborhood, the "backyard green" grows slowly. The next summer, two more neighbors join in. A year later, five more families remove the tall wooden barriers. By then the backyard looks like a small park that has been mysteriously placed in your lives by a benevolent god of green spaces.

To maintain privacy, some neighbors build patios protected by shrubs and arbors. Fountains and bright flowers attract butterflies, songbirds, and hummingbirds, those delightful hovercrafts of the avian world that friends in the country are always talking about.

If they have dogs they don't want wandering through the conjoined backyards, some neighbors install kennels or leave a portion of their yards fenced.

The children soon forget that they were once boxed in. As you look out, you see a luxuriant green. Where a game of catch was possible, there's suddenly room for a game of touch football or soccer. And there's always a watchful parental eye monitoring the safety of neighborhood children. When you are in need of a nap, you don't worry. You can crash on the couch for a half hour to recharge your batteries. A less weary neighbor is always willing to watch the kids.

Plant a Community Garden and Orchard

As the backyard in your neighborhood transforms into a park, some of your neighbors begin talking about planting a community garden and a small orchard.

Benefits of Opening Up Backyards

- *Creates more room to garden*
- *Provides more room and more opportunities for children to play*
- *Increases supervision of children*
- *Creates a friendly, parklike atmosphere*
- *Ends isolation*
- *Allows you to share resources, such as lawn mowers, and work, such as lawn mowing*

6.1: Backyard privacy fences, one of the hallmarks of modern urban and suburban neighborhoods, can be barriers to social interaction, creating isolation as an unhealthy by-product of privacy. Taking them down opens up a world of possibilities!
Credit: Dave Wann.

> ## Benefits of Community Gardens and Orchards
>
> - *Provides healthy, locally grown fruits and vegetables in your own backyard*
> - *Allows you to work together and develop closer relationships and friendships*
> - *Provides meaningful work for children and older adults*
> - *Turns a grass-dominated landscape into a productive one*
> - *Reduces dependence on food from other countries or distant sources*
> - *Increases sense of self-reliance*
> - *Saves money*

And what a garden it becomes! This sprawling plot is every gardener's dream, yielding basket after basket of fresh vegetables — first spinach, radishes, and lettuce, then zucchinis, tomatoes, and potatoes. The carrots are pulled after the first frost to increase their sweetness.

The food in your garden is organically grown — no artificial fertilizer or synthetic pesticides to creep up the food chain into your bodies or the bodies of birds. The gardeners who manage "the farm," as it is called, occasionally recruit "non-gardeners" to assist in the planting, cultivating, and reaping. There have been a few converts, too. Once you have planted seeds, watched them grow, and then consumed the fruits of your labor, it is hard to resist the gently nurturing art of gardening.

Along the north side of the garden in Year Six, several gardeners clear a piece of land for an orchard. They plant a few apple trees, a cherry tree, and a couple of peach trees. The gardeners hope that when the trees mature and begin to bear fruit, they will produce enough for a year-round supply of applesauce, peaches, and cherries for everyone. You can almost smell the pies cooking! The gardening coalition's next step is to expand the orchard so they can sell some produce locally — to nearby neighborhoods.

As you work in the garden, your dog, Ben, adopted as the "block dog," lolls in the sun. On any given afternoon he can be found hanging out with gardeners; sleeping on a neighbor's patio, soaking up the sun; or romping with the children in the grass, stealing balls or chasing Frisbees. He's become the neighborhood pet, and because he's shared, some people have opted not to buy dogs. They've always got old Ben to pet or take for a walk, and he's accommodating, offering up his velvet-smooth fur for a friendly pat.

Because projects like the garden you are undertaking will require money, one member of your community suggests setting up a joint checking account.

Soon you have opened a bank account for your community. Each member makes an initial $100 deposit to start the ball rolling. Annual contributions will replenish the cash, if necessary. But who controls it? Who monitors the account and writes checks? Who decides how the money is to be spent?

The neighbors quickly agree on a neighborhood treasurer and a protocol for issuing checks. Decisions to spend the money, however, are made by the community each time a project is officially adopted at monthly meetings, which follow the monthly potluck dinners.

The neighborhood decides to start small, choosing simple projects like installing a few park benches in the commons for people to sit on while they chat, or building a bus stop to shelter children from rain and snow as they wait for the school bus that picks them up at the end of the block on school days. You also decide to use some of the money for a catered community picnic, to reward yourselves for all of the hard work and celebrate your successes.

For projects that benefit only a few people, Fox Run follows the example of Cobb Hill Cohousing in Vermont, setting up special accounts for activities such as a community art studio. Active participants donate to the fund. This means that those who benefit don't have to seek approval from the entire community. Others can join the venture at a later date.

Establish Neighborhood Composting and Recycling

Gardens need rich, organic soil and what better source is there in urban and suburban neighborhoods than food scraps and yard waste that are typically hauled away to a local landfill? Inspired by the gardeners, most of your neighbors soon begin to collect their organic waste, placing it in secure containers on their back steps each Wednesday to be hauled to the community compost bins. One bin is filled at a time. When it is full, another begins receiving waste. When that one reaches capacity, the first bin is fully composted, magically transformed from a motley mixture of carrot peelings, leaves, and discarded apple cores into a dark brown material called humus. The humus is shoveled into wheelbarrows and delivered to the nearby garden. Every year the soil gets better and the fruits and vegetables grow tastier.

"If we're composting as a community," one neighbor announces, "we might as well recycle as a community, too." In the fifth year

6.2: Composting kitchen and yard waste recycles an important, relatively nutrient-rich material back into soils, making our gardens more productive and reducing waste that goes to the landfills. Credit: Dave Wann.

Benefits of Neighborhood Composting and Recycling

- *Reduces trash and cuts garbage disposal fees*
- *Puts waste to good use*
- *Composting produces nutrients for enriching garden soils*
- *Provides useful work for children and others*
- *Helps those who don't want to bother with composting get involved in this important activity*

of your community's venture, Rick, a retired business executive who loves to build things, erects a shed to house the neighborhood's recyclable newspapers, cans, bottles, and plastic. Donations are hauled to a local recycling company every other month, and the proceeds go to gas and trailer maintenance. Rick, who also trucks the stuff over, gets a small stipend for his efforts. But that's not all. Rick talked the local trash hauler into slashing trash bills by 50 percent because of your recycling and composting efforts, which divert 80 percent of the neighborhood's trash from the landfill. It took Rick a year to convince him, but now you and your neighbors are reaping quintuple benefits from composting and recycling: lower trash bills, cash income, a cleaner environment, healthy soil for growing food, and a more secure source of resources (the recyclables) for future generations.

Plant Trees to Produce a Favorable Microclimate and Wildlife Habitat

With summer temperatures consistently breaking records, and cooling costs rising, caused in large part by the accumulation of greenhouse gases in the atmosphere, your community decides to take action — by planting trees.

Benefits of Planting Trees

- *Increases summertime comfort*
- *Reduces cooling bills*
- *Reduces pollution, including greenhouse gas production*
- *Creates habitat for songbirds*
- *Enhances play opportunities for children*
- *Beautifies the neighborhood*
- *Enhances property values*

Trees add to the beauty of a home, but they also block the sun, providing shade that keeps homes cooler. In addition, water evaporates from tiny openings in leaves — a process known as transpiration — which draws enormous amounts of heat out of the air around a home. Combined, these benefits help to reduce air-conditioning costs and provide far greater comfort. Trees can also be planted to shelter homes from the wind. Although more commonly used in rural settings, dense plantings called windbreaks can effectively reduce heat loss during cold winter months.

As your community develops, you buy trees in bulk, saving huge amounts, to create a cooler neighborhood. Besides supplying shade, the trees provide habitat for birds. Their songs brighten your days, and the birds are frequently seen snatching insects that invade the garden and orchard. It's a win-win-win situation: your houses are cooler and it costs less to maintain comfort; the birds are happy; and carbon-dioxide emissions fall, helping combat global warming.

Replace Asphalt and Concrete with Porous Pavers

In addition to your efforts to cool the neighborhood by planting trees, one of your neighbors decides he can contribute by reducing pavement. Pavement in streets, sidewalks, and driveways absorbs sunlight, which is then converted to heat, making neighborhoods considerably warmer than surrounding countryside. One day, Jonathan Markley and his wife rent a compressor and a jackhammer and take out their driveway, replacing it with concrete pavers — open blocks that form a solid, yet porous surface perfectly fine for parking cars. Grass often grows in the openings of the pavers.

Concrete pavers not only reduce heat absorption on hot days, keeping houses and the people in them cooler, but they also help to reduce surface runoff and flooding. When rain falls or snow on them melts, water percolates into the ground, replenishing groundwater supplies. Rather than rushing down driveways, onto streets, and into storm sewers, to be released in a huge gush into streams, causing flooding downstream, water goes where it should go: into the Earth. Your neighborhood becomes a little more like it was before the bulldozers moved in to level the site for construction.

Benefits of Replacing Asphalt and Concrete

- *Reduces heat absorption*
- *Cools a neighborhood*
- *Reduces fuel bills*
- *Reduces flooding*
- *Replenishes groundwater supplies*
- *Beautifies a neighborhood*

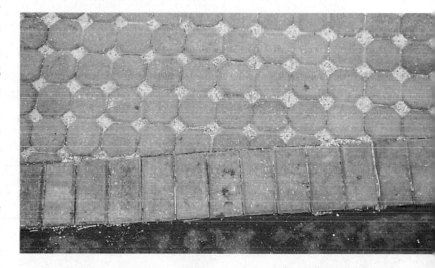

6.3: Porous pavers like these let moisture seep into the ground, reducing surface runoff, flooding, and nonpoint source water pollution. Porous pavers and other similar strategies reduce heat-absorbing pavement, making homes much cooler in the summer while reducing utility bills. Credit: Turfstone Company.

Benefits of an Edible Landscape

- *Produces healthy, locally grown fruits and vegetables in your own front yard*
- *Reduces lawn maintenance costs and effort*
- *Provides meaningful work for children and older adults*
- *Reduces dependence on food from other countries or distant sources*
- *Increases sense of self-reliance*
- *Saves money*

6.4: Neighbors plant an orange tree in L.A. Eco-Village. It is one of 100 fruit trees that now adorn their edible landscape. Credit: L.A. Eco-Village.

Establish an Edible Landscape

Backyards at Fox Run have slowly blossomed into a play space, a secure neighborhood park for kids and adults alike, and a community garden and orchard. Not all neighbors have joined in, but there are enough participating households to make a huge difference in your lives.

But there are more changes underway now that you and your neighbors have witnessed the benefits of gardening and fruit-growing firsthand. The front yard has come under scrutiny. "What good is all that Kentucky bluegrass?" asks Marion, adding, "Besides, I think it has a drinking problem," referring to the thousands of gallons of water she and her husband must apply to the grass each year to maintain its appearance. They dig up a patch of their front yard and plant an herb garden. The basil and thyme soon produce an abundance of pungent leaves, which she shares freely with neighbors. Debra and Jackson, who live across the street and down four houses, are even more ambitious. They till half their front lawn under to grow strawberries and black raspberries. When berries begin to appear, the kids descend on their front yard (with permission) like hungry bear cubs.

Jim and Margot, formerly "the couple who live two doors down to the left," have planted a couple of apple trees and a patch of strawberries. Other neighbors are thinking of doing the same. Slowly but surely, that neatly manicured, high-maintenance grass is converted into edible landscape.

Besides providing food, the edible landscape program reduces the time and money spent on lawn maintenance and provides meaningful work for children and adults alike. Although in the grand scheme of things the contribution to global food production is insignificant, the edible landscape and community garden do help to reduce the neighborhood's dependence on food from distant sources — food that travels, on average, about 1,200 to 1,300 miles from farms where it is produced to local grocery stores. At Fox Run, food often travels less than three feet from plant to mouth.

Start a Community-supported Agriculture Program

One neighbor suggests joining a community-supported agriculture (CSA) program. "There's a local farmer," she says, "who will provide us with additional produce during the harvest season. She will either deliver it to us or we can pick it up."

CSA not only helps provide food to communities, but it also reduces the distance produce is transported and related energy costs, helps create an understanding of the importance of local farmland to the local food supply and local economy, and helps farmers stay in business, preserving the land for future generations.

Even though your neighborhood is producing lots of food, you decide to join, and you enlist neighbors from surrounding streets who have become interested in what you are doing.

Create a Van- and Truck-share Program

As your community enters the seventh year of its evolution toward Superbia! transportation comes under group scrutiny as Damion suggests buying a van and a truck for shared use. "How many times a year do you need a pickup truck or a van?" he asks. "Maybe half a dozen — to pick up lumber for a project in the case of the truck, or to take a family vacation in the case of the van.

"Despite the infrequent need," he goes on, "many people buy these gas-guzzling monsters anyway, burning excess fuel and paying higher costs year-round for the luxury of convenience." Most people know exactly what he's talking about.

"We can't buy a car together!" a neighbor chimes in.

"I know a community-owned vehicle sounds offbeat and difficult to manage, but it's already happening," Damion asserts.

"Where?"

Benefits of Sharing Vans and Trucks

• Gives individuals access to a van or truck for trips or hauling at a fraction of the cost of owning their own

• Reduces resource demand

• Saves money

"Where else but Europe?" he responds. "By one count," he continues, "there are at least 10,000 shared vehicles in European communities. Cohousing communities in the United States have begun purchasing vehicles for shared use too. At Cobb Hill in Vermont, residents share a hybrid vehicle, a Honda Insight donated by the founder of the community and a champion of sustainability, the late Dana Meadows. They share a tractor and hope to buy a truck and van for community use."

After months of research and debate, the residents of Fox Run decide to buy a used pickup truck. While some members of your community think the truck is a waste of money, you soon find that it is in constant use. The cost per household is a mere $25 per month. One neighbor agrees to manage the program, making sure the truck is well-maintained. He gets to use the vehicle free of charge in compensation for his work.

After the first year, you and your neighbors switch to a rental system, dispensing with the monthly payments and charging those who want to rent the truck a small per-mile fee. Based on the first year's usage, estimates show that rental fees will easily cover the payments as well as the insurance, gasoline, and maintenance.

Sharing vehicles means individuals have access to a van or truck for trips or hauling at a fraction of the cost of owning their own. It allows families to buy smaller, more energy-efficient vehicles for day-to-day use, reducing fuel consumption and pollution.

Retrofit Homes for Energy Efficiency

Winter comes and the cold sets in. While friends at work complain that the cost of natural gas for home heating has doubled, you haven't noticed a change in your utility bill. The reason? Last summer — the eighth year of Fox Run's evolution — while insulation contractors were offering discounts to drum up work, your neighborhood hired a contractor to beef up the insulation in all 24 homes in the community. The contractor worked for a couple of weeks on the job, and because he wasn't out hunting down work or driving all over the city to work sites, he realized significant savings. He passed them on to you and your neighbors, thanks to the friendly wrangling of one of your neighbors, a businesswoman with a knack for artful negotiation.

Besides saving money up front, you and your neighbors are enjoying substantial reductions in heating and cooling bills. Now that the snow is flying and the thermometer has dipped below zero, your house is not only more economical, but also much warmer. In a couple of years you're going to hire a contractor to upgrade windows on most of the houses. There's even talk about retrofitting foundation insulation. The developer who built your home in suburbia didn't insulate foundations at all. An energy auditor suggested that this would be an economical way of cutting fuel bills and improving comfort.

Benefits of Retrofitting Homes for Energy Efficiency

- *Saves homeowners money due to economy of scale*
- *Saves homeowners money by reducing energy and water demand*
- *Protects the environment*
- *Fosters cooperation and friendships*
- *Reduces demand for outside energy resources and promotes self-reliance*

Solarize Homes

Some neighbors are even planning to "solarize" their homes — retrofitting for passive solar heating. By adding windows on the south sides of their homes they expect to increase solar gain — that is, increase the amount of sunlight that enters their homes during the winter, when the sun cuts a lower arc in the southern sky. When sunlight streams through the south-facing windows of a passive solar home, it is converted to heat that gently warms interior spaces.

Combined with other measures — for example, higher levels of insulation and window shades that slash wintertime heat losses — a homeowner can cut fuel bills by 30 percent or more by solarizing.

"But won't the homes overheat in the summer?" one neighbor asks.

"They shouldn't," says Matt, the chief proponent of this idea. "During the summer the sun cuts a high arc through the sky, beaming down on rooftops, not streaming in through solar

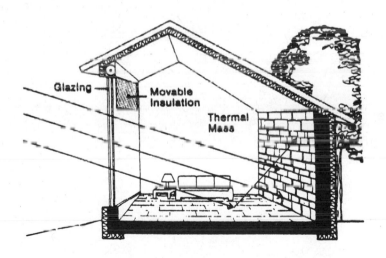

6.5: *Passive solar homes use south-facing windows to capture sunlight from the low-angled winter sun. It gently warms interiors, providing affordable comfort with little impact on the environment. Credit: U.S. Department of Energy.*

93

Benefits of Solarizing Homes

- *Reduces fossil fuel use and associated pollution*
- *Slashes fuel bills*
- *Improves comfort levels*
- *Increases natural lighting by using daylight*
- *Reduces electrical lighting*
- *Improves a home's aesthetics*

windows. This fact, combined with higher levels of insulation, will prevent a solar home from turning into an oven during the summer."

♦ ♦ ♦

As the sun sets today on Fox Run, there's a sense of unity and pride. The neighborhood is beginning to attract media attention. A local television station recently ran a short piece on community efforts, and the local recognition drew national attention. *Mother Earth News*, a national magazine that publishes articles on many of the ideas you're pursuing, is about to include a story on your changes.

Last month the neighborhood received an award from the Environmental Protection Agency. Marion is beginning to field inquiries from other neighborhoods as like-minded individuals — people who feel as dispirited by contemporary living arrangements as you did eight years ago — seek a better way to live, one that is more meaningful and conducive to building community.

Don't be afraid to take a big step if one is indicated; you can't cross a chasm in two small jumps.
LLOYD GEORGE

7

Your Neighborhood Blossoms: Boldest Steps

IN THE PAST SEVEN YEARS your community has grown from the seeds of an idea to a fruitful garden. Despite some setbacks and disappointments when, for example, one family decided it didn't want to participate and moved away, your community has begun to take form and you've got a lot to show for your efforts. You've established a joint bank account to finance neighborhood projects and have torn down many backyard privacy fences, opening up yards to make room for a community playground and a large community garden and orchard. In a grove of trees next to your flourishing garden and orchard is a small gathering place with a fountain and a koi pond, some comfortable chairs, and two hammocks in the shade. Here you and your neighbors lounge from time to time, snoozing or talking with one another or watching the children play on the nearby swings and jungle gym.

Neighbors harvest bushels of organically grown tomatoes, cucumbers, beans, corn, greens, and potatoes from the community garden each year — with excess sold at Fox Run's neighborhood market. The orchard is also beginning to supply some of your needs and promises even greater harvests in the upcoming years.

Your neighborhood composting facility is running at peak capacity, churning out humus from yard and kitchen wastes. Used to enrich the soils of the community garden and the edible landscape that now replaces many of the front lawns, it has also greatly reduced the amount of waste trucked off to the landfill each year.

Last year the recycling coordinator, Rick, opened up his garage to store reusable items such as furniture and appliances, stuff that was once hauled off to the local dump. Every month Rick distributes a list of items for sale to neighbors on Fox Run's website. He also sponsors seasonal garage sales open to the general public in the spring, summer, and fall. This empties out the stuff no one in your neighborhood wants. Goodwill and the Salvation Army pick up the leftovers.

The community-owned pickup truck has become a valuable asset, as is the community-owned van. The first year, the van was booked all summer by families taking road trips. Many parents use the van to haul kids to the local pizza place for birthday parties or to take off on weekend ski trips with their children and their friends.

The home energy-efficiency retrofits have been a colossal success. So has the water efficiency program, spurred by an ongoing drought. For both projects, neighbors banded together to hire professionals to retrofit their homes at considerable savings. A couple of government grants helped offset costs as well. As a result, you've cut energy bills by nearly half and water consumption by almost as much. The utility company liked what you were doing, so it chipped in part of the cost of the energy retrofit. As it turns out, it helps the company avoid having to build a large, expensive power plant to meet peak demands.

Boldest Steps

As your community improves, there's a feeling that you can do more, "strike out more boldly," as one neighbor put it. "More independence!" cried Marion as Ben, the neighborhood dog, rolled on the grass by her feet. What's next for a community that has already become a model of efficiency?

We have some suggestions: these boldest of the bold measures, and certainly the most challenging steps in the transition to Superbia! — a truly sustainable neighborhood — require even greater levels of creativity, cooperation, dedication, and hard work. There may be significant barriers blocking the way to some of these ideas, and the road will be steep, but then, what great achievement ever came easily?

Create a Community Energy System

"With energy supplies dwindling, energy costs up sharply, and global warming changing our daily lives, one option on the path to a truly sustainable community is to establish an alternative energy system — more precisely, a community-owned, sustainable energy system," says Jeff Hanson, a new neighbor who moved to your community to be a part of the exciting venture. "For instance, photovoltaics — solar electric panels — and wind power could be used to supply us with electricity. Costs for such systems are sure to drop, thanks to improvements in the technologies and investments by major energy producers such as British Petroleum, which has taken a leading role in the transition to a sustainable energy system. Government interest in renewable technologies will provide a boost as well."

"With energy efficiency measures in place, a neighborhood solar electric system could begin to provide clean, high-quality electricity year-round," comments Jeff's wife, Vivian, a solar architect.

"A medium-sized wind machine could provide supplemental power in areas with sufficient wind," Jeff goes on, adding to the options list. "A backup generator, run by natural gas, could provide power in times of shortage, or we could remain connected to the electrical grid for now — although our own power source could turn out to be more reliable than the grid."

"Another option is a microturbine, a small generator that burns natural gas to spin the blades of a generator large enough to supply the whole neighborhood," says Vivian. "I just installed one in a housing complex I designed.

"Microturbines," she continues, "produce electricity for a community, which can then sell surpluses to the local utility. We can capture waste heat for year-round hot water, and in the winter we can use excess heat to heat homes."

"Another energy option is a community fuel cell. That's a device that strips hydrogen from natural gas, then combines the hydrogen with oxygen in the air to produce electricity," says Jeff. "As fossil fuel supplies decline, fuel cells will be run by hydrogen derived from water.

"A community-based power system can emancipate our neighborhood from the incredible environmental damage caused by the production and consumption of fossil fuels and nuclear power. It taps into a clean, renewable source of energy that's controlled locally," he notes.

Anticipating the cost issue, Vivian adds, "Sure, it will cost more and will require community-wide cooperation, but the independence and financial stability we achieve may be well worth it.

"The efficiency measures we've implemented mean a smaller system is required ... with less cost up front. When an ice storm leaves neighbors without power for four

Benefits of a Community Energy System

- *Helps to foster independence*
- *Buffers against blackouts and brownouts*
- *Provides energy security*
- *Reduces demand for outside energy*
- *Reduces pollution and habitat destruction resulting from the production and consumption of fossil fuels*
- *Provides a model for other communities*

7.1: Photovoltaic modules convert the energy from sunlight into electricity. Although initial costs are significant, generous incentives from utility companies and state governments can make them much more affordable. Exorbitantly high electricity costs in areas like California also make them highly economical. Credit: Dan Chiras.

days, our lights will be on and our furnaces will still be running. And if electricity prices skyrocket, as they have in California in recent years, we won't be complaining about high utility bills," she says.

"Who knows, government grants and donations from solar suppliers looking to tap into the promotional value of our neighborhood experiment could help offset initial costs. Many utilities faced with rising power demands also support renewable energy to avoid having to build costly new power plants," Jeff concludes.

While many neighbors like the idea, this one will take a while. You set up a committee to research the options and come up with cost estimates and potential savings over the long run.

Establish Environmentally Friendly Water and Wastewater Systems

"While we're thinking about striking out on our own energy path, maybe we ought to think about creating more independence in water — both water supply and wastewater treatment," says Rick, who's been studying this subject for several years now, talking to neighbors privately, lobbying for support for his ideas.

"There are many ways to obtain water for domestic and outdoor uses," he goes on. "One of the easiest is to capture it from rooftops. Millions of gallons of water fall on the roofs of our homes each year, which we could use." Sensing some resistance, he adds, "People collect rainwater from their roofs all over the world."

"Rather than letting all of this valuable rainwater go to waste or cause flooding," Jennifer, Rick's wife, chimes in, "why not capture the water and store it in underground tanks? Cisterns can store thousands of gallons of water for use during the summer drought."

"Distributed through drip or root-level irrigation systems, this free water can help us keep our neighborhood green, despite city water rationing," says Rick. "Much of the system is already in place," he continues. "Roofs, gutters, and downspouts. We just need to install some underground pipes and water tanks."

"Renting a backhoe for a week might be enough to retrofit the entire neighborhood," Jennifer adds. "You'd be amazed at how much water you can collect from rain and snow melt each year."

"Catchwater can be used to irrigate vegetation, but it could also be purified and used in our homes for flushing toilets, running showers, washing dishes, washing clothes, and even for bathing, cooking, and drinking," Rick says. "But if we're going to collect water for indoor uses, we'd probably want to install metal roofs. They make a much better catchment surface than standard asphalt shingles."

You can tell by the looks on people's faces that the couple has their attention. In coming months, you and your neighbors explore the idea of collecting water, as well as different ways of treating household wastewater.

At one special meeting, Rick explains the need for such systems. "American homes produce billions of gallons of wastewater every day," he says. "Wastewater is typically divided into two categories: graywater and blackwater. Graywater comes from showers, sinks, and washing machines. It makes up about 80 percent of a household's daily wastewater production. It is dirty, but nowhere near as filthy as the water used to flush toilets, called blackwater.

"As in most environmental strategies," he explains, "the first step in dealing with a problem is conservation. Water-efficient behaviors and water-efficient fixtures, such as water-saving shower heads, washing machines, and dishwashers, reduce water demand and greatly reduce graywater production."

"But no matter how efficient you make a home, there will be some wastewater. What do you do with it?" his wife asks.

"One option is a graywater treatment system. You can install graywater systems for each and every home — or we can install a system that services our entire neighborhood. These systems produce a usable product — treated water — that can be used, along with rainwater we catch on our roofs, to irrigate gardens, lawns, trees, and shrubs.

"In some systems, graywater flows into large beds of pumice or rock lined by a waterproof barrier. Microorganisms in the rock or pumice consume organic wastes. Plants growing in the soil over the rock or pumice beds draw up nutrients and water. What's left over is fairly pure water that can be used to irrigate neighborhood crops."

"Blackwater can be treated on site as well?" a neighbor asks.

"Yes, but it's a bit more tricky," says Rick.

"However," Jennifer suggests, "we could install composting toilets."

Benefits of Environmentally Friendly Water and Wastewater Systems

- *Reduces demand on municipal water and wastewater systems*
- *Helps put waste to good use locally*
- *Reduces water pollution*
- *Enhances self-reliance*
- *Promotes efficiency*

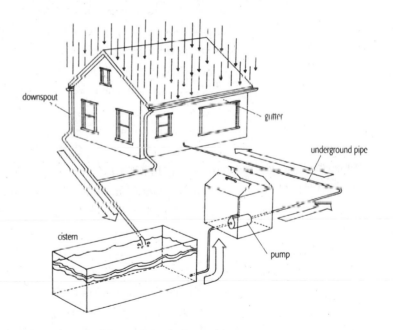

7.2: Billions of gallons of rain fall on the rooftops of the homes in our neighborhoods each year. Capturing this rainwater as well as water from melting snow can reduce our need for city water, saving money and helping the environment. Credit: Michael Middleton.

7.3: Composting toilets like this Biolet model decompose human waste rapidly and odorlessly, producing a nutrient-rich organic matter for non-edible crops. Composting toilets are easy to install, reduce water demands, and diminish the amount of waste entering septic tanks or sewage treatment systems of cities and towns. Credit: Biolet.

A few neighbors wrinkle their noses, mistaking composting toilets for those horrid outhouses they have encountered in parks. Rick sets them straight, telling them that composting toilets, installed in homes in place of standard toilets, decompose organic matter in water odorlessly, converting it to a fluffy organic material ideal for enriching soils in orchards and flowerbeds, if buried properly (usually 12 inches deep).

As the informational meeting ends, a few neighbors decide to try some of these ideas out.

Create a Common House

While you and your neighbors ponder the possibilities of creating a neighborhood energy system and your own graywater and blackwater systems, a more immediate opportunity presents itself at one of your monthly potluck dinners. Damion announces that he's been offered a job at an L.A. record company as a songwriter. He'll be moving in a couple of months.

His positive energy will be missed, but in typical fashion he suggests a way his departure can contribute to the neighborhood. "Why not buy my house?" he says.

"For what?" someone asks.

"To turn it into a community house."

Damion lays out his plan to transform his home into a common house like those found in cohousing communities (discussed in Chapter 4). The first floor, he says, could be converted to a large kitchen with a community dining area, a reading room, and a playroom for youngsters. Upstairs, there's room for guest accommodations. The finished basement, he suggests, could hold a teen room, a laundry room, and an exercise room. He even proposes that his two-car garage be remodeled to create a neighborhood library.

"The house was appraised at $225,000," Damion announces, "but if you buy it directly from me I'll deduct the real estate agent's commission. With 20 families in on the deal, the total cost would be about $10,500 each." There are a few audible gasps. "Spread over 30 years," he adds, "so the monthly mortgage payment would come to about $800 per month — or about $40 per household."

"I think he's onto something!" says Devra.

A common house offers many benefits. For example, it can provide space for a community day-care facility and gives children a safe place to play and teens a place to hang out. An exercise room offers an inexpensive and convenient place to work out, saving families expensive health club fees. A common laundry facility reduces the need for individual washers and dryers, saving money and resources.

If you select healthy, green building materials when remodeling, you can create a place that's good for people and good for the environment. You can also integrate ergonomic design, making the common house more efficient and safe by, for example, placing electrical outlets, shelves, countertops, and cupboards at more convenient heights. (We've listed many books and organizations in the Resource Guide at the end of the book that will help you learn more about these topics.)

A common house can make a community more self-reliant and more convenient.

> ### Benefits of a Common House
>
> - Promotes a sense of community and belonging
> - Reduces demand for shared resources such as washing machines
> - Provides meeting space
> - Provides space for a community day-care facility
> - Creates a safe place for kids to play or teens to hang out
> - Provides services individual households may not be able to afford, such as a weight room or a copy machine
> - Makes a community more self-reliant and convenient

Create a Community-shared Office

There are ways to make a common house even more affordable. For example, Damion makes another suggestion: "You could convert the master bedroom into an office or a couple of offices. The adjoining bedroom could house office equipment like a copy machine, fax, and laser printer. If you rent out the office spaces for $200 a month to neighbors who work at home but want more room, you could lower the monthly payment for the common house to $400 or $20 per month per household."

"I'd use it," says Janet North, a mother who's just launched a home business.

"I would, too," says another.

"I could use a nice office," says a third person. "There's just not enough room in our house for an office, and I find myself working at the kitchen table as the kids race around raising hell!"

But don't take out your checkbooks just yet. Damion's got more. He points out that several families in your neighborhood have young children, and many of them are trucked off to day-care facilities each morning as Mom and Dad head off to work. "What if you add a day-care center? Devra is looking for employment and is thinking about doing day care in her home. If she took care of seven children at $30 per day, she could save everyone a little money while earning an income. In turn, she would pay $300 to rent the space each month. The monthly mortgage payment would drop to $100 or about $10 per family per month for unlimited use of the common house.

Benefits of a Community-shared Office

- *Saves money and time for those who work at home some or all of the time*
- *Reduces resource demand*
- *Makes life in the suburbs more convenient*
- *Cuts down on trips to service providers, reducing gas consumption and pollution*

7.4: Dining at the common house once or twice a week makes life easier for busy parents and helps neighbors connect with each other. Credit: Dave Wann.

"As neighborhood children grow up and go off to school, Devra could take in children from surrounding areas, making a good living while providing a valuable service."

"We'll have to get a permit from the city, no doubt," says one neighbor. "They might frown on neighborhood offices and day-care centers. That's considered commercial activity."

"I've already talked with the planning department," says Damion. "They didn't like the idea at first, but then I talked with the mayor, who is interested in promoting people-friendly neighborhoods and reducing traffic on our highways. He is willing to work with us .... as long as we are united on this issue. He assured me that the planning department will be on our side, too, if we speak with one voice."

By now the deal is sealed.

In the next few months the community rallies behind the proposal and closes the deal. A week after Damion leaves for L.A., neighbors begin remodeling, working together rather than hiring outsiders to do the work. On the main floor you enlarge the kitchen and turn the living room and dining room into a large communal eating area. Downstairs, you create an exercise room, a laundry room, and a place where older children can hang out. Soundproofing insulation is blown into the walls and ceiling of the teen room, for reasons that require no elaboration. One family donates a TV and another donates a stereo.

Within a month, Devra starts the neighborhood day-care center, which is immediately fully booked. Parents are delighted — it's just a short walk each morning to drop off their kids, and they know they're in good hands.

Damion's bedroom is converted into a private office with a community office equipment room, complete with a fax and a copier. The remaining upstairs bedrooms are converted to private offices as well, and immediately rented out.

Within six months you are holding weekly dinners in the common house. Each week one neighbor volunteers to cook for everyone at a cost of three dollars per person. Every Monday you drive home, park the car in the garage, then saunter over to the community house for a delicious dinner. A few months later, your community is also sponsoring Friday night dinners. After the dinners, many Fox Run neighbors hang around to catch up on the news, make plans for new projects, or talk politics.

> **Benefits of a Community Entertainment Program**
>
> * *Makes a community richer and more inviting*
> * *Enhances our personal lives*
> * *Reduces the need to commute long distances to events*
> * *Cuts down on fuel consumption, air pollution, and time spent in the car*

Establish a Community Entertainment Program

In time, Damion returns to visit ... and of course he's got new ideas. He's met a number of performers who routinely tour the country, playing in small venues. "Maybe they and others like them could stop off and play for the neighbors? It won't cost much," he adds.

Before long you've got a local entertainment program that eliminates the need to hop in the car and fight traffic to attend concerts in the city. In the first year of its existence, you find that the number of trips you make to the city for entertainment have dropped dramatically, and you and your neighbors have reduced fuel use and pollution.

Narrow or Eliminate Streets

A year after the common house conversion, you and your neighbors visit a nearby cohousing community. One aspect of this community that impresses all of you is its tranquility, which is largely due to the fact that there are no streets dissecting the community. Cars are parked on the periphery in carports and garages or out in the open. Kids play freely on the central common area without fear of being struck by a car because automobiles are "banned" from the commons.

Accustomed to the drive-up convenience of modern suburbs, some folks in your group cringe at the idea of parking cars along the periphery of Fox Run. When you ask them about the inconvenience, however, most

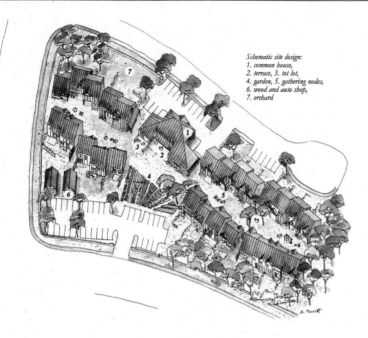

Schematic site design:
1. common house,
2. terrace, 3. tot lot,
4. garden, 5. gathering nodes,
6. wood and auto shop,
7. orchard

7.5: In cohousing, cars take a backseat to people and are relegated to peripheral parking. Although many people we've talked to fear that this arrangement will be inconvenient, most people who have tried it find the short stroll to their homes is a pleasant experience as it gives them time to connect with neighbors. Credit: Muir Commons.

of the "cohousers" have nothing but praise for the idea. Besides, they point out, parking is arranged so you're never more than a short stroll, a few hundred feet, from your car to your house. Although some cohousers found it inconvenient at first, they've grown used to the idea and most of them embrace it fully.

"When walking from my car to my home, I'm greeted not only by children at play, but by adults sitting on park benches. We often stop and chat for a few minutes, de-stressing a little. My husband tells me that when I come through the door after work I'm much more pleasant to be around," says one woman.

The cohousers shuttle groceries from cars to homes using push carts and electric golf carts, which are powered by photovoltaic panels (PVs) installed on the carports in the parking area. If residents need to carry heavier items, they can move the barrier aside and drive to their homes along the wide sidewalks.

Eliminating some or all of the paved road surfaces that slice through suburban and urban neighborhoods reduces heat buildup, road maintenance, and accidents between kids and cars. It also reduces the amount of pavement required for street construction and allows communities to devote more land to parks and edible landscape.

Could you do the same in your neighborhood?

"Although the idea may sound wildly romantic and impractical, it does have its merits," says Matt, who decides to champion the issue. Against a murmur of opposition, he notes, "Peripheral parking for those close to the end of the street means very little additional walking. For others it will be more of a hassle — but that's the problem with trying to retrofit a neighborhood built with other intentions. As a compromise, we might want to locate the parking areas more centrally. Making bicycles and golf carts available for everyone's use will make the transition to this new system more tenable for some."

"Or there are things we can do simply to quiet traffic … they call it traffic calming," his wife, Marcy, adds, sensing her husband's enthusiasm for peripheral parking is not widely shared. "Traffic circles, benches along the street, street narrowing, speed bumps ... all of these things could help us reduce the speed at which cars travel and make our neighborhood safer."

After research and considerable debate, you and your neighbors decide to give traffic calming a try. A year later, when a local newspaper reporter asks how the community managed to achieve this feat, Marion, the unofficial spokesperson, says, "It came about because we have worked together on many other ideas over the years. We have also actively recruited like-minded individuals as homes went up for sale. Through carefully placed ads, we've been able to reach out to people who want to live like us and want to be part of our little experiment."

In the future, Matt and a few other neighbors hope to reshape the community even more, removing the street entirely and replacing it with sidewalks that wend their way between gardens and benches and picnic tables.

Benefits of Narrowing and Eliminating Streets
• Creates a more parklike, aesthetically appealing neighborhood • Opens up more land for growing vegetables and fruit • Increases the chances of meeting and interacting with children and adults • Increases social contact and enriches our lives • Reduces pavement and heat buildup, reducing cooling costs

Retrofit Garages and Spare Rooms into Apartments

With private car use down — thanks to the neighborhood transportation system that encourages walking and bicycling, carpooling, and other amenities like the common house and the shared vehicles — Matt asks, "What use are our garages? What will become of them?"

The answer! "They could be converted to apartments. Students at the local college are always complaining about the lack of housing in our area. Many of them commute from downtown, where apartments are cheaper. We can help fill the housing gap and reduce commuting."

"And we can earn a little extra money, too."

"There are others who might like to live in our community. Recently divorced adults and many service workers who are shut out of the high-priced local housing market might find the renovated garages in our neighborhood to their liking."

Sure, there are barriers to overcome, including gaining approval from the city government to convert garages into living spaces or to add basement apartments. In time, working with city officials (especially zoning and planning departments), you can convert garages into economic assets. Rent will help offset renovation

7.6: *Suburbs offer many opportunities for additional housing, as shown here. This garage was retrofitted to create a small apartment for students. It provides income for the residents and a place to live in a town suffering from a chronic shortage of suitable living space. Credit: Dave Wann.*

costs, and you can use any surplus to help pay off home mortgages. Moreover, there are tax benefits to renting out space in your home. For example, a basement apartment can be depreciated, creating a nice tax deduction.

Older residents may renovate the garages as housing for live-in caretakers who can help them out with cooking, cleaning, gardening, and other chores in exchange for free living space and a monthly stipend. This means elders don't have to sell their homes and uproot themselves from their community to move into an apartment or a nursing home.

Apartment renovation isn't the only option. Some folks may want to rent out their garage space for storage. Anyone who has priced private storage knows that space isn't cheap these days; a two-car garage could easily rent for $100 to $150 per month — creating a nice stream of income.

As children grow up and head out on their own, they will free up additional living space in their parents' homes. Rather than leave their rooms vacant or move to a smaller home, homeowners can convert empty bedrooms into apartments. You'll need zoning board approval, of course, but this strategy, like converting garages into living quarters, has many clear economic benefits and numerous social benefits. It encourages financial, ethnic, and age diversity within your community, producing a richer social fabric that can make life infinitely more interesting. Diversity can also help to break down the social homogenization and cultural isolation of suburbs that often leads to insecurity and inequity.

Create a Neighborhood Coffee Shop, Market, or Other Cottage Industries

With a common house, offices, and a day-care center in place, Marion advances another proposal at the monthly meeting. "Why don't we create a corner store? A convenience store, where neighbors and their children can walk to pick up milk, bread, and other essential items ... like in the good old days?"

Images of a 7-11 come to mind and there's much head shaking.

Marion flips on the slide projector and shows a picture of a store in a traditional neighborhood designed by Andres Duany, one of America's preeminent New Urbanists. Inspired by villages in which people are within walking distance of schools, stores, doctors, and offices, these new communities are popping up all across North America. As members of your community see from the slide Marion's showing, the store's architecture blends in nicely with the housing. "It doesn't resemble a Loaf n' Jug or a Quick Stop or a 7-11 or any of the hundreds of other convenience stores that litter the landscape," she says.

Marion's husband proposes a business that he'll finance and run with their son and daughter-in-law, who, after graduating from college, recently moved back to the neighborhood. They'll build the store on an empty corner lot and it will serve Fox Run and surrounding neighborhoods.

After a few months of debate, the community gives Marion's husband the go-ahead to apply for a permit for a small convenience store with a coffee shop and a garden market where he can sell fruits and vegetables produced in Fox Run's community garden.

In time, your neighbors talk about bringing other amenities to the neighborhood. The offices in the common house are so successful that many residents are clamoring for more office space. One neighbor, who runs a small computer software design firm, says he'd jump at the opportunity to buy a house nearby and convert it into his office. He only has four employees and would love to have his office three minutes from his front door.

Benefits of Retrofitting Garages and Spare Rooms

- *Provides additional housing within your city or town without the need to convert undeveloped land*
- *Creates more social, economic, and ethnic diversity in a neighborhood*
- *Puts resources to good use*
- *Enlivens and enriches households*

7.7: Mixed-use communities provide benefits within walking distance, such as this restaurant in Dave's hometown. By using existing buildings that blend with the neighborhood, we can have the amenities we like without suffering from strip mall-like development. Credit: Dave Wann.

If we want to create community and reduce traffic, gasoline use, and pollution, our communities must provide more of what we need — as they do in traditional village designs. Changing the face of the suburbs, where functions are isolated from one another, won't be easy. But with traditional neighborhood development gaining in popularity, you may find local code officials and the planning department amenable to these ideas.

Foster Diversity

A final step in the neighborhood's transformation is the fostering of diversity through the creation of multifamily dwellings. Like the garage and spare bedroom conversions, proponents say it will foster financial, ethnic, and age diversity.

"Our options are many," says Martin, the professor who started a discussion group years ago. "Large homes in the neighborhood could be converted into duplexes or triplexes, or two or more homes could be bridged by additional living space, creating a single, large apartment complex out of two structures."

"Multifamily residences offer many benefits," Martin adds, "besides increasing diversity within homogeneous suburbs. They house more people per acre of land and require less energy to heat and cool per square foot of living space. Because they're more compact, they require less wood and other materials than single-family homes. Using environmentally friendly building materials, such as carpeting with recycled content, or non-toxic paints, stains, and finishes, could help make this a place that's good for people and the environment."

You leave the meeting to mull over this idea. Maybe it will succeed, maybe not. There's much to be considered in the months ahead.

Successes and Challenges

In Chapters 5 to 7, we've taken you on a journey of the possibilities for creating a more livable and environmentally friendly neighborhood. The ideas are relevant for suburbs and urban neighborhoods alike. This road may be more challenging than creating a cohousing community from scratch, which starts with folks already aligned by common goals. You may encounter holdouts — individuals who like the neighborhood just the way it is. Others will want too much too quickly. Along the way, compromises are inevitable. As you probably expect, government officials may balk at your ideas, even stonewall you. You may have to make friends at city hall to do what you want with your homes and your land (see Chapter 10).

Despite these and a host of other problems, considerable glory will come to those with vision and perseverance. Others will recognize the value of what you're doing and, inspired by your courage, wisdom, and foresight, will follow in your footsteps. And, of course, you will benefit directly from weekly dinners, locally grown produce, familiar smiles, helping hands, and, perhaps, a community-owned pickup truck at your disposal.

Where neighbors once lived in relative isolation, you can create security, friendship, interdependence, and meaningful social interaction. The cost of living will surely go down, over time, while the quality of your life and the lives of your loved ones soars.

The doors we open and close each day decide the lives we live.
FLORA WHITMORE

8

Suburban Revitalization I: Can This Dream Become a Reality?

I F YOU HAVE TROUBLE BELIEVING that urban and suburban neighborhoods can change as dramatically as we're suggesting, you're not alone. Many people have been skeptical. In fact, when one disgruntled reader of *Mother Earth News* read an article Dan wrote on the subject, he accused us of promoting a communist plot to ruin the suburbs, which were, in his opinion, not in need of fixing. He canceled his subscription in outrage! (His wife had mistakenly subscribed to the magazine, we were told.)

Admittedly, this has been the most extreme reaction to our ideas, and we're sorry that he missed the point of our work. We are offering suggestions on ways to improve urban and suburban neighborhoods and people's lives. We're not proposing any compulsory national laws that force neighborhoods to alter their modus operandi. If you're happy with what you have, that's fine. If you are looking for more, these ideas may be of considerable assistance. If you're a developer, we hope that you will think about these ideas and incorporate them in your next project.

So doubt is not foreign to us. We ourselves experienced periods of doubt when we started working on the Sustainable Suburbs Project through our organization, the Sustainable Futures Society, in 2001.

But then something exciting happened.

We started talking to people about our ideas. Much to our surprise, many people we talked to knew someone or had heard about a community that was pondering — or better yet, enacting — changes to create more closely knit communities, more affordable ways of living, and more environmentally friendly lifestyles. To our amazement, we found that some of the boldest steps we are suggesting — for example, buying a house and converting it to a common house — were already happening.

In this chapter we'll share some examples of people from all walks of life and from a number of different countries who are engaged in the easy and bolder steps we've presented. We'll tell you how the various suggestions work and give some advice on getting started.

Easy Steps

Suggestion 1. Sponsor Community Dinners

WHO'S DOING IT: N Street Neighborhood, Davis, California; GossGrove Neighborhood, Boulder, Colorado; cohousing communities; Staircase Dinners, Bellevue, Washington

THE WAY IT WORKS: The N Street Neighborhood began many years ago with five students living in a rental house in an older suburban neighborhood in Davis, California. Recognizing the benefits of common meals, they decided to sponsor potluck dinners. That effort has grown considerably. Today, they share meals with 17 households. They've switched from potluck dinners to meals cooked by individual members of the community. Why switch from potluck?

"The problem with potluck meals is everyone has to devote time to it," says Kevin Wolf, one of the organizers of the neighborhood. "In 1979 we realized that having a single person responsible for each meal was the way to go. That way, you come home from school, work, or other activities of the day, and you just show up." The neighbors eat on a common patio in the summertime and in a garage-turned-dining room in the winter. "If neighbors didn't know how to cook before moving in, they certainly do now," says Kevin.

The GossGrove Neighborhood in Boulder, Colorado, has established regular barbecues that accompany neighborhood meetings and garage sales. The events take place in one of three pocket parks that came into being when the city closed off the end of the street to make the neighborhood more pedestrian-friendly. One of the small parks will soon become a community garden, contributing produce for the meals.

HOW TO GET STARTED: You and your neighbors don't have to belong to a cohousing community or create a formal neighborhood association to eat together. Boulder resident Dominique Getliffe suggests making short, simple contacts with your neighbors, such as borrowing milk. From that, progress to potluck dinners. He and his neighbors set up tables on a driveway to share meals on warm summer days.

Julie Rodwell, once a resident of Winslow Cohousing in Washington, moved to Bellevue and missed having meals with neighbors, so she made a point of gradually meeting people who shared the same stairway in her condo. Then she organized "staircase dinners" that have created a sense of community in the condo.

Many neighborhoods have perfected the art of "progressive dinners," in which a small group of neighbors moves from one house to another for various courses of a meal. And the P-Patch community garden in Seattle has established a "Chefs in a Garden" tradition in which local restaurant chefs volunteer to use garden produce to cook meals that are served right in the garden!

Suggestion 2. Establish a Community Newsletter, Bulletin Board, and Roster

WHO'S DOING IT: Kinney Run Neighborhood Association, Golden, Colorado; Harmony Village, Golden, Colorado; many homeowner associations and cohousing groups

THE WAY IT WORKS: Knowing who your neighbors are and where they live is a fundamental step in creating community. Recognizing this, the Kinney Run Neighborhood Association built a durable, glass-encased bulletin board where residents can post news and notices, helping neighbors stay abreast of important activities such as proposed zoning changes and potluck dinners. At Harmony Village, a cohousing community in Golden, Colorado, a laminated map shows neighbors and visitors who lives where. *The Villager*, Harmony's quarterly newsletter, has now profiled all 27 households; neighbors learned that Ken and Nancy met on a mountaintop and that Rick once saved somebody from drowning. An entire issue of the newsletter was a memorial to the late Macon Cowles, the neighborhood's elder statesman.

Harmony's e-mail network has been extremely valuable as a support system. If you need a job, have a car for sale, or want to comment on a community activity, this is the place to do it.

HOW TO GET STARTED: The first step is easy: go door-to-door with a clipboard to obtain telephone numbers, street addresses, and e-mail addresses. Then suggest that someone in the neighborhood — a writer or editor, maybe — compile paragraph-long biographies of each neighbor on the block. Sponsor a potluck in a neighbor's yard and see if people can correctly guess which person fits which biography. You may find that the city or town you live in will print and mail out newsletters free of charge!

8.1: Keeping in touch is part of the purpose of a community bulletin board, but it can also be used to post important public notices, to sell used furniture, or to announce parties! Credit: Mike April.

There are as many ways to network as there are people in the world. Fortunately, community is hardwired into the human psyche, and first steps always seem to lead somewhere.

Suggestion 3. Establish a Neighborhood Watch Program

WHO'S DOING IT: Olde Hillcrest Neighborhood Association, Milwaukee, Wisconsin; many other communities

THE WAY IT WORKS: Thousands of communities in North America have joined the Neighborhood Crime Watch program, commonly known as block watch. A community program formed in conjunction with local police departments, a block watch requires a coordinator to recruit neighbors. The coordinator also acts as a liaison with the local police department. Once a neighborhood is organized, members of the community receive training from the police department that teaches them how to identify suspicious activities and individuals, which are reported to the police.

With neighbors watching out for neighbors, this program provides greater security and helps build community. That's what folks in the Olde Hillcrest Neighborhood, a suburb of Milwaukee, discovered. Their block watch not only provides a strategic link between citizens and the police, but also helps create a safer place to live. It has been successful at helping neighbors get to know one another, creating a friendlier community.

HOW TO GET STARTED: To learn more, check out the information we've listed in our Resource Guide or call your local police department. Residents of rural areas will likely need to call their county sheriff's office. Local authorities will provide tons of useful information and a contact person who will help you establish your program.

Suggestion 4. Start Neighborhood Clubs

WHO'S DOING IT: Boundary Street Neighborhood, Portland, Oregon; Olde Hillcrest Neighborhood Association, Milwaukee, Wisconsin; GossGrove Neighborhood, Boulder, Colorado

THE WAY IT WORKS: In the Boundary Street neighborhood, 100 neighbors routinely work in a nearby ravine to restore native plant species. "It's the best riparian area in the city," says Dick Roy, "so we've tapped into neighborhood expertise — one guy has a Ph.D. in biology — and we've taken advantage of all the good energy to make our neighborhood more environmentally stable."

Another kind of activity that can bring neighbors together is an investment club. In the Olde Hillcrest Neighborhood, 18 members gather every second Monday evening at different members' homes. "They contribute between $10 and $100 per month to a portfolio of high-growth stocks," explains Dale Tuttle, the coordinator of the group. "The last few years of the bear market have been a learning experience," he admits. "The best growth we've seen hasn't been in our investments, but in our sense of community."

HOW TO GET STARTED: More often than not, a great idea is first hatched in an informal conversation between two or three people, then gains momentum. After living with three pocket parks created by the city in Boulder's GossGrove neighborhood, residents decided to create "theme parks." One of the small parks will become a bocci ball court; bocci being a sport almost anyone can play most of the year. Another park will contain a bench where residents can visit with neighbors.

Suggestion 5. Form Discussion Groups

WHO'S DOING IT: Harmony Village, Golden, Colorado; Olde Hillcrest Neighborhood Association, Milwaukee, Wisconsin

THE WAY IT WORKS: Many of the cohousing communities we've toured sponsor discussion groups. For example, at Harmony Village, Dave's home, nearly a dozen neighbors participate in a sustainability discussion group. Members meet once a month over a simple breakfast consisting of fruit, bagels, orange juice, tea, and coffee to discuss local as well as global environmental issues. This diverse group of cohousers also addresses practical matters — instead of just sitting around and talking, they take action to help create a sustainable future. For example, they proposed that Harmony Village residents install solar panels on the roofs of their homes, and that the village use energy-efficient compact fluorescent light bulbs in outdoor light fixtures. They routinely write letters to politicians, and recently saved a nearby piece of land that was slated for development.

Olde Hillcrest Neighborhood Association in the suburbs of Milwaukee sponsors a book club where neighbors "get together with fellow book enthusiasts to converse, discuss, and debate current bestsellers and classics," according to the group's website. They've also organized a mother/daughter book club, which they describe as a "great way for mothers and daughters to share reading and discuss books."

Discussion groups may also take place in broader communities. Whole towns, for instance, have formed groups to discuss the book *Affluenza*, which Dave coauthored. When Dan was an assistant professor of biology at the University of Colorado at Denver, he formed a discussion group on contemporary issues such as workplace democracy, global climate change, and government myopia. His group consisted of a urology resident, a physics professor, two biology professors, two paralegals, a freelance writer, and Dan.

HOW TO GET STARTED: Discussion groups may form organically in tightly knit communities, especially those sharing meals, participating in work-share programs, and so on. One member may say, "Hey, why don't we get together and talk about this issue?" Or these groups may have a more formal beginning, sparked by one or two people who announce their interest at community meals or in articles in a community newsletter. Neighborhood groups can organize to discuss novels, non-fiction books, or issues with information gleaned from magazines or newspapers. In Dan's group, one individual volunteered to lead each session; that person then provided an article or two to members a few weeks before the monthly gathering.

If you are interested in environmentally oriented discussion groups, you may want to contact the Northwest Earth Institute. With the help of local volunteers, the Institute has started over 300 discussion groups throughout the United States on subjects such as voluntary simplicity, discovering a sense of place, and choices for sustainable living.

Suggestion 6. Establish a Neighborhood Babysitting Co-op

WHO'S DOING IT: Washington Street Neighborhood, Boulder, Colorado; Evergreen Meadows, Evergreen, Colorado; and most cohousing communities

THE WAY IT WORKS: Neighborhood babysitting co-ops are one of the most common forms of community participation we've uncovered in our research. In fact, we found them just about everywhere we looked: in new suburbs, older neighborhoods, and most cohousing communities.

Meeting a very basic need, neighborhood babysitting co-ops range from informal arrangements where neighbors simply help one another out without keeping tabs on who does what, to more formal programs in which participating members receive credit for each hour they babysit a child. Some programs hand out coupons — babysitting bucks.

Dominique and Vivian Getliffe, who live on Washington Street in Boulder, Colorado, share babysitting with eight families in their neighborhood. Good neighbors often take care of each others' furry and feathery friends, too. Dan's neighbors take care of his children's ferrets and parakeets when they go away, and his family watches the neighbors' chocolate Lab when they're away. Small favors like these not only provide much-needed support, especially at the last minute when it's too late to hire a babysitter; they also help to build community.

HOW TO GET STARTED: Babysitting and pet-sitting co-ops can begin informally as neighbors get to know one another. Or your may want to start out by bringing up the subject in a short piece in your neighborhood newsletter, at a community dinner, or in flyers delivered door-to-door.

Most co-ops collect names and phone numbers and create non-monetary systems for tracking participation — for example, the baby-sitting bucks mentioned above. You may also want to establish "discounts" for larger families, because watching two or three children may not be much more work than watching one.

Suggestion 7. Form an Organic Food Co-op

WHO'S DOING IT: Evergreen Food Co-op, Evergreen, Colorado; L.A. Eco-Village, Los Angeles, California

THE WAY IT WORKS: Mary Denham and four other friends in Dan's Evergreen "neighborhood" joined forces to form a community-wide organic food co-op a few years ago. Each

8.2: A baby-sitter — or two — just two doors down. Sounds like heaven to us!

Credit: Mike April.

week one member of the co-op — there are usually about a dozen participants — calls members to find out who wants a box. He or she then phones in an order to Vitamin Cottage, a locally owned retailer that offers a wide assortment of organic fruits and vegetables. The order is placed on Monday morning, and the week's coordinator picks it up the following day, takes it home, and divides it among the participants.

Vitamin Cottage sells the co-op organic produce by the case, charging cost plus ten percent, which saves each family huge amounts of money. (Dan estimates that he receives $40 worth of fruits and vegetables each week for approximately $20.) Orders typically consist of eight or more items, a mixture of fruits and vegetables, all organically grown — that is, grown without pesticides and synthetic fertilizer. It's a fantastic way to feed a family. Dan knows he and his kids eat a lot better, consuming more fruits and vegetables, since they joined the co-op. In addition, they're no longer ingesting pesticides in their food.

This system does have some drawbacks. For one, participants are never quite sure what they're going to get from one week to the next. Those who need to plan their meals ahead of time may not find this system acceptable.

Another problem is that participants sometimes receive food they don't like — or don't know how to cook. Dan's been getting a lot of pomegranates lately, and he hasn't the foggiest idea what to do with them!

To solve this problem, you might ask members to write up a list of "undesirables" — fruits and vegetables they detest. You may also want to set up your co-op so that individuals can call the weekly coordinator to make requests for specific food items. Individual members can also trade. For example, one member's onions might be traded for another's broccoli. In some co-ops, members trade recipes to make use of unfamiliar produce.

Another minor problem is that some individuals may not be able to keep up with a weekly box of produce. In the Evergreen co-op, some members order every other week or order half boxes.

HOW TO GET STARTED: If you're interested, we suggest that you start small. Contact a local organic grocery or even a regular grocery store that sells organic produce to see if it will work with you. Ask a couple of neighbors to join and give it a whirl! As you gain experience, you can recruit additional members. Dan's group has a written description of the program that is handed out to people who are interested in joining.

Suggestion 8. Create Car or Van Pools

WHO'S DOING IT: Route 2 Commuters, St. Johnsbury, Vermont; residents of Lake Forest, Illinois; Emory University, Atlanta, Georgia; Adobe Systems International, Seattle, Washington; Nike, Beaverton, Oregon

THE WAY IT WORKS: The benefits of ride-sharing are huge. One group in Vermont, the Route 2 Commuters van pool, for example, avoids the consumption of 4,000 gallons of gas very year. They calculate that the average cost of ride-sharing is approximately 7 cents per person per mile, compared to about 30 cents per person per mile for a private automobile. The group has now been in operation for close to 25 years.

Rowena Pasia of Lake Forest, Illinois, says, "My commute got a lot longer when my company moved. To save money, I started car pooling with my babysitter's daughter. About a year ago we added five more employees and started a vanpool. Using the van cuts down the wear and tear on my car."

HOW TO GET STARTED: Starting a neighborhood car pool is much easier after you know your neighbors. By asking around, you may find a handful of people going in your direction who want to cut costs, reduce the stress of driving, and help the environment. If that doesn't work, use the resources that are often available at workplaces and schools. Some companies offer incentives to car pool participants. At the Nike plant in Beaverton, Oregon, employees who arrive in car pools get reserved parking and are eligible for prize draws. Emory University offers reduced parking rates for carpoolers, largely to relieve congestion in parking lots.

Most metro areas have ride-share matching programs —
some of which resemble computerized dating services. To find
out who's car pooling in your part of town, go to the Zoomer
website (zoomer.sierraclub.org/), give your zip code, and click
on ride-sharing.

Suggestion 9. Create a Neighborhood Work-share Program

WHO'S DOING IT: L.A. Eco-Village, Los Angeles,
California; North 9th Avenue neighborhood, Tucson, Arizona;
Highlands Crossing, Littleton, Colorado

THE WAY IT WORKS: For centuries, neighbors throughout
the world have helped neighbors harvest grains, build homes and
barns, and take care of livestock. Today, however, when gardens
need to be tilled or trees have to be removed, many of us work
alone or hire high-priced "experts" to do the work for us. In the
cohousing communities we've visited and lived in (in the case of
Dave), neighbors often share in the work, chipping in on

8.3: Sharing the workload in Seattle, neighbors band together to help construct a
community garden. Credit: Jim Diers.

community projects or on projects that benefit a single household. In Highlands Crossing, a cohousing
community in Littleton, Colorado, for instance, the group schedules annual work parties to improve the
landscape or tackle other community projects. Work-sharing also appears in urban and suburban
environments.

Work parties are a time to socialize and deepen friendships. They're also a time to teach one another
useful skills. Neighbors may receive credit for every hour they work. In some groups, the house with the most
credits calls the next work party.

We've discovered informal work-sharing arrangements in other neighborhoods as well, including L.A.
Eco-Village and Tucson, Arizona. In L.A. Eco-Village, an individual who comes up with an idea for a project
— for example, converting an outdoor courtyard in their apartment building to a garden — posts a notice on
the bulletin board or on the community's listserv, calling for a meeting. Members of the community who want
to help out attend the meeting ... and they're off and running.

As informal as their work-share program is, the folks at L.A. Eco-Village have made great strides. "With almost no money," says Lois Arkin, cofounder of this neighborhood, "the community has acquired $2 million in real estate. We've converted a manicured courtyard into food production. We've built a solar water fountain and planted 100 fruit trees in the neighborhood, too."

HOW TO GET STARTED: If your community is organizing around the ideas in this book, you can mention work parties at one of your community dinners or write an article about it for your newsletter or your website. It might be useful to research work-share programs in cohousing communities and other neighborhoods. Interview folks who have experience to learn what works and what doesn't. Be sure to spread the benefits evenly — for example, make sure everyone who's interested gets a chance to sponsor a work party. You may also want to establish a system to track volunteer hours. Be patient. Don't expect everyone to be experienced or physically capable of hard work. (Some people can participate by making food!) As a starter, you might work on some projects that benefit the entire community. Take your time, have fun, and watch your community grow!

Suggestion 10. Create a Neighborhood Mission Statement

WHO'S DOING IT: West Park Neighborhood Association, Canton, Ohio; N Street Neighborhood, Davis, California; Olde Hillcrest Neighborhood Association, Milwaukee, Wisconsin

THE WAY IT WORKS: Imagine you've been meeting with your neighbors for awhile, talking about what you'd like to do, but the group doesn't yet have a clear sense of direction. You'll find that the discipline required to draft a mission statement will help create a neighborhood identity and a collective purpose. Mission statements are like haiku — short but full of content. A neighborhood in Ohio came up with this one: "The West Park Neighborhood Association is dedicated to preserving and securing our neighborhood's integrity and history, utilizing the many talents and ideas of our residents, ultimately creating a safe and desirable community for those who have chosen to make the neighborhood of West Park their home."

A Wisconsin group was even more succinct: "We are a neighborhood association dedicated and determined to make our neighborhood a friendly, fun and safe place to live."

HOW TO GET STARTED: Kick around ideas about what you'd like to create and what your values are. Then let a writer take a stab at boiling it all down. In the N Street Neighborhood (before it was cohousing), the mission statement was like a gateway to specific goals the group wanted to achieve. It included: develop a common house, become ecologically sound, encourage diversity, and develop neighborhood celebrations.

Suggestion 11. Create a Neighborhood Asset Inventory

WHO'S DOING IT: Green Park Neighborhood, Hickory, North Carolina; Seattle neighborhoods; Westwood Neighborhood, Seattle, Washington

THE WAY IT WORKS: While neighbors sometimes come together to deal with emergencies — such as plans to build a superhighway through the area or an increase in local drug traffic — veteran neighborhood activist Jim Diers from Seattle knows the advantages of exploring the positives, the neighborhood's assets. This exercise can empower a neighborhood and give it a collective identity. According to Jim, "The assets a neighborhood can build on range from natural features to school playgrounds, great stores, networks, organizations, artists, and the whole range of human and financial resources, energy, creativity, and ideas."

Diers has held workshops in many different Seattle neighborhoods to help neighbors identify neighborhood treasures. "Whether it's a restaurant with especially delicious food, a gigantic cedar tree, or a longtime resident, a neighborhood treasure is something that makes us glad we live where we do," he says.

To create their long-range neighborhood plan, residents of Green Park Neighborhood in Hickory, North Carolina, identified mature trees on the street and access to shopping, dining, entertainment, and jobs as assets. These are things that help make their neighborhood worth working on.

If you decide to create a community green map that highlights cultural and environmental assets in and around your neighborhood, including organic food stores, farmers' markets, nature centers, and hiking trails, you may want to contact Green Map System, a non-profit organization that has been helping communities since the early 1990s. It is listed in our Resource Guide.

HOW TO GET STARTED: Use your best assets to inventory other neighborhood assets. Send a neighborhood biologist out to catalog botanical treasures; encourage people who are interested in local history to work with the county historical society. Under the supervision of an adult leader, set your kids loose to explore the neighborhood, teaching them how the neighborhood fits together. The Center for Understanding the Built Environment (CUBE) offers school curricula such as "Walk Around the Block," which enables kids

8.4: Asset inventories help us identify features of our neighborhoods that are worth fighting to protect. Credit: Ginny Graves, CUBE.

to see their neighborhoods — from butterflies to brick buildings — from new perspectives. Seattle's Westwood Neighborhood discovered a unique asset when local activist Susan Harmon sought out people with developmental disabilities to get involved with her organization. Raymond and Ginger Bulch, both disabled, had in their younger days been clowns. Susan soon booked them at kids' parties, and they were back in business!

Bolder Steps

Suggestion 12. Tear Down Fences

WHO'S DOING IT: Highlands Neighborhood, Littleton, Colorado; Washington Street Neighborhood, Boulder, Colorado

THE WAY IT WORKS: "When we moved into our house," explains Highlands resident Julie Bettridge, "there was already a neighborhood tradition to have parties together in the backyards. Each house was fenced, but also had a gate. We decided to go a step further by taking down our six-foot fence and opening the space up to the neighbors, especially the kids." The Bettridges have the neighborhood swing set and playground equipment, so their yard becomes the center of activity in the summer. "Very often the adults get together too, while the kids play. Whenever we see each other out in the yard, we feel open about bringing a beer over. We miss our sense of community in the winter, when we're inside more."

For Vivian Getliffe, wife of Boulder architect Dominique Getliffe, a backyard community began when she invited a neighbor to share a garden space. "Gardening is my obsession," she says, "but it takes time, and it's more fun with other people." Soon they had a community garden going and pooled resources with a dozen families to buy an $800 garden shredder (for making mulch from yard waste) cooperatively. The neighbors began to have dinners together a few times a month, created a picnic-courtyard area in the unfenced backyard, and set up a bike rack in the side yard. "Private yards with fences allow us to push the world away," says one of the Getliffes' neighbors, Dan Diehl. "But the more you push it away, the lonelier you are."

"Converted private spaces can help develop a strong sense of community, provide safe and accessible play space for children, raise property values, cool the neighborhood, and reduce storm water runoff," says Rob Inerfield, a staff member of Community Greens, a non-profit advocacy group whose mission is to "catalyze the development of community greens in residential neighborhoods across the United States." Inerfield points to a Berkeley neighborhood that has had a common backyard since the 1970s, when a university professor bought all the houses on a large block, tore down the fences, and created a shared green area that helped him sell each of the houses. Thirty years later the common green is still intact.

Much of the rest of the world is already familiar with public courtyards and green spaces. As *Washington Post* columnist Neal Pierce pointed out in an October 2002 column, "An aerial view of Paris' choicest neighborhoods reveals patches of green in the center of block after block, matching the verdant lines of meticulously groomed trees along many of the city's chief boulevards and grand parks."

HOW TO GET STARTED: During an informal conversation with a neighbor on the sidewalk or in the alley, be bold and say you've read this book. Mention the potential benefits of creating public space out of underused backyards. Tell your neighbor about the organization called Community Greens, listed in our Resource Guide. It can help you ... or you can begin yourself, taking down fences between backyards of community members who are interested in creating both a common green space and a greater sense of community.

Suggestion 13. Plant a Community Garden and Orchard

WHO'S DOING IT: Communities across America

THE WAY IT WORKS: Neighborhood groups throughout the United States and Canada are joining together to create community gardens on what were once weed-infested and trash-filled vacant lots — and even on rooftops. Planting fruits and vegetables for local consumption reduces the distance food needs to travel, helping build a more sustainable world. In addition, community gardens bring adults and children of diverse cultures, ethnicities, ages, and abilities together, helping to knit closer alliances. Gardens also beautify run-down neighborhoods and create opportunities for city dwellers and suburbanites to work with nature. They demystify food production and help adults and children gain an appreciation for food production.

8.5a & b: You don't have to take down all fences. These neighbors in Boulder simply removed a fence between their side yards, creating a more open space for lounging, visiting, and picnicking. Credit: Dominique Getliffe.

8.6: *Converting a vacant lot to a community garden, like the P-Patch in Seattle, provides a place to grow food, but participants reap many benefits besides fruits and vegetables. Credit: Jim Diers.*

The community gardening movement began in the 1970s; today, organizations can be found in a number of cities, including Philadelphia, Detroit, Boston, New York, Chicago, Indianapolis, Kansas City, Denver, Seattle, Vancouver, and Montreal. According to the American Community Gardening Association, there are now more than 550 local programs.

We've found that schoolchildren are also establishing gardens near their schools. Lord Roberts Elementary School in urban Vancouver, British Columbia, is a great example. Working with City Farmer, a non-profit group that promotes urban food production, teachers have created a program that educates kids about food production and science. "The garden also helps teach an environmental ethic," says Gary Pennington, a professor at the University of British Columbia who coordinated the project. "The garden increases their sense of wonder. It's pretty magical."

HOW TO GET STARTED: Rather than give you pointers, we recommend that anyone interested in starting a community garden contact the American Community Gardening Association, listed in our Resource Guide. The association's website contains an excellent fact sheet entitled "Starting a Community Garden," which offers a wealth of advice. You can also contact local gardening or horticultural societies. Call a local nursery to track down this information. For teachers interested in starting a school garden, be sure to check out the National Gardening Association's kids' website, also listed in our Resource Guide.

Suggestion 14. Establish Neighborhood Composting and Recycling

WHO'S DOING IT: Harmony Village, Golden, Colorado; Gray Rock Cohousing, Fort Collins, Colorado; L.A. Eco-Village, Los Angeles, California; N Street Cohousing, Davis, California

THE WAY IT WORKS: All gardeners know that to maintain healthy soil, they need to fertilize their soil — replenish nutrients — and maintain proper levels of organic matter, typically by adding compost. Compost helps maintain essential bacteria needed to recycle plant nutrients. It also acts like a sponge, holding moisture that plants need to survive and prosper.

Increasingly, centralized programs run by cities or commercial trash haulers do the composting in urban and suburban environments. Neighbors collect yard waste and organic kitchen scraps such as potato peels, keeping them separate from recyclables and trash. The organic matter is then hauled off to a central composting facility.

Far better, because they cut down on fuel use, are backyard composting bins — simple wooden or plastic structures that receive compost from each home. With proper moisture and occasional turning, the organic matter is converted to a rich humus that can be added to flower beds and vegetable gardens.

Neighbors can also combine efforts, composting at a central location near the garden. This is a measure worth considering if you are interested in starting a community garden, because it means compost is processed only a short distance from the garden where it is used.

We've found composting facilities at a number of cohousing communities like Harmony Village, where Dave lives, and at Gray Rock Cohousing in Fort Collins, where there is a massive community garden. We've also discovered composting programs in urban and suburban neighborhoods. The folks at N Street Cohousing, for instance, maintain a group composting facility. The residents of L.A. Eco-Village collect yard waste — grass clippings and such — then grind it up and put it in their community composters. One member of the community, the "compost queen," manages the system. Individuals bring kitchen scraps to the compost bins as well.

8.7: Community compost piles, tended by the resident expert, help reduce strain on existing landfills and put a previously wasted resource to good use. Credit: Dave Wann.

HOW TO GET STARTED: Composting usually requires some training, as few people have ever engaged in this activity. You can encourage neighbors to compost on their own — starting a compost bin in their backyards or simply digging compost into their gardens as some residents of the usually warm L.A. Eco-Village do — or you can start a neighborhood composting facility. If you've established a community garden, situate the compost bins or piles near the garden for easy access. You'll probably need to appoint a composting coordinator and establish two or three bins or piles — fill the first bin, then let it sit and decompose while the second bin is filling.

Suggestion 15. Plant Trees to Produce a More Favorable Microclimate and Wildlife Habitat

WHO'S DOING IT: North 9th Avenue neighborhood, Tucson, Arizona; Village Homes, Davis, California; many cohousing communities

THE WAY IT WORKS: Shade trees beautify neighborhoods, increase property values, and provide protective habitat for birds. They also help cool homes, increasing comfort on hot summer days and dramatically reducing fuel bills. As Anne S. Moffat and Marc Schiler point out in *Energy-Efficient and Environmental Landscaping*, a single mature tree removes as much heat as five 10,000-BTU air conditioners, and it does it without burning fossil fuel or polluting our atmosphere. Trees can lower the temperature of the air surrounding a home by as much as 9°F.

We've visited many communities that have planted trees for shade, including Village Homes in Davis, California, and a number of cohousing communities. One of the best examples we've found is in Tucson Arizona, where Brad Lancaster and his brother Rodd bought an old, beat-up house in a run-down neighborhood in one of the poorest parts of the city. The yard around their home was practically barren, as were the yards of many of their neighbors. Daytime temperatures during the long, hot Arizona summers often exceed 110°F.

Shortly after moving in, the brothers began planting trees to create shade. They helped neighbors plant trees too, organizing annual tree-planting days. Brad and his brother arrange for the delivery of trees and teach neighbors how to plant them in ways that trap and conserve sparse rainwater.

Since they began, the brothers and their neighbors have planted more than 800 native trees that use little water. Over time, their neighborhood has been converted to a desert oasis, much cooler and prettier than before. "The neighborhood has been beautified, cooled, and folks are investing in the community," remarks Lancaster. "Neighbors are getting to know one another. People are regaining a sense of place with native vegetation of the Sonoran Desert, native bird populations, and diversity soaring within the inner city."

HOW TO GET STARTED: If your neighborhood could benefit from some shade — and most can — you might want to consider a community tree-planting project. You can obtain trees in bulk from a local nursery or from the state forest service if there is one in your state. You can also contact the folks at the Arbor Day

Foundation for advice and assistance. Additionally, you may want to contact state and local government officials to see if there are any incentives for planting trees. A state energy office, for instance, might be willing to partner with you, offsetting part of the cost as a means of conserving energy. A local utility might join in as well. It doesn't hurt to ask.

For maximum success, be sure that someone in the group has tree-planting expertise. If you're buying in bulk from a local nursery, it might be willing to help. Consider planting native trees, which are acclimatized to the local climate and are more resistant to diseases and insects that can wreak havoc on exotic species. (Note: Even though native species require less water, you will need to water the trees for the first couple of years to ensure a good start.) Mulching around the base of trees reduces evaporation. In dry climates you might want to install catch basins — hollowed-out areas around trees that capture rain, funneling it to their roots. You might also want to divert roof water to trees and other vegetation.

Suggestion 16. Replace Asphalt and Concrete With Porous Pavers

WHO'S DOING IT: Rozella Hall's residence, Los Angeles, California; Southface Energy Institute, Atlanta, Georgia; The Settlement, Hebron, Connecticut

THE WAY IT WORKS: Much of the suburban landscape, including streets, driveways, parking lots, and roofs, is impervious. Storm water runs off all these hard surfaces rather than soaking into the ground. Pollutants such as oil, fertilizer, and pesticides are washed into receiving waterways or into wastewater treatment plants through sewer systems, placing an additional burden on these facilities.

Research has shown that even "stubborn" pollutants, such as heavy metals, can be absorbed by microbes and roots of plants in natural landscapes, so by replacing hard surfaces with soft, pervious surfaces we can reduce toxic runoff. These measures also reduce the need to purchase water for landscaping, help to recharge groundwater, and reduce heat loads from heat-absorbing pavement.

At Rozella Hall's home in Los Angeles, a coalition of agencies worked with a non profit group called TreePeople to create a mini-watershed on the property. Slightly sunken areas, called swales, were "installed" in the front and back yards to retain storm water and let it soak into the ground. A driveway "drywell" captures engine oil drippings washing off impervious surfaces and funnels them into a filter of sand and crushed rock. Says TreePeople founder Andy Lipkis, "If city building and zoning codes are changed to require every home to be mini-watersheds, we could create thousands of 'urban watershed manager' jobs nationwide to keep these systems

unit pavers-on-sand

a.

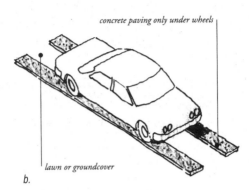

concrete paving only under wheels

lawn or groundcover

b.

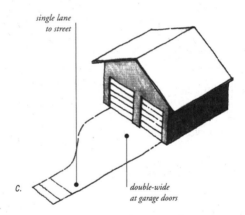

single lane to street

double-wide at garage doors

c.

8.8a, b, c: *Porous pavers provide adequate support for vehicles, yet eliminate many of the problems of conventional asphalt or concrete driveways such as heat absorption, storm water runoff, and flooding. Here are three ideas for reducing driveway pavement. Credit: Tom Richman Associates.*

working optimally. The savings in water treatment and pumping would pay their salaries."

Pervious concrete was installed at the Southface Energy Institute, which promotes sustainable building, to demonstrate its porosity and durability. "We give a lot of tours and conferences here," says Kathleen Sciole, "so there's been a lot of traffic, but the alternative pavement has held up perfectly for six years."

And at The Settlement, a suburban subdivision in Connecticut, the local planning and zoning commissions revised their road standards to allow open, grassy "swales" instead of storm sewers. The public works department mows these swales periodically (if the homeowner doesn't do the job), and also occasionally scoops out sediment (to keep the swale from filling up) with a tractor-mounted sieve device that does not damage vegetation.

HOW TO GET STARTED: Get a copy of the excellent manual *Start at the Source*, listed in the Resource Guide, and look for opportunities in your neighborhood to turn gray surfaces into green ones. One prospect is the driveway; replace it with two hard tire-path surfaces and plant ground cover (such as thyme) in between. Dig up walkways and replace them with brick or porous pavers. If your neighborhood establishes public walkways — through the backyards, for example — use crushed fines or pavers instead of concrete. Remember, since a large percentage of the potable water we use is for landscape irrigation, the water you retain on-site is water you won't have to buy.

Suggestion 17. Establish an Edible Landscape

WHO'S DOING IT: Village Homes, Davis, California; Harmony Village, Golden, Colorado; Hands-on Edible Landscaping Project (HELP), Vancouver, British Columbia

THE WAY IT WORKS: At Harmony Village, Dave deliberated several months before deciding to plant strawberries instead of grass in his front lawn. He then went out and bought about 200 bare-root, dormant strawberry plants and established a strawberry bed under the cottonwood trees in his front yard. Every fall, leaves from nearby cottonwoods collect around the plants to mulch in the moisture and warmth, and every spring for the last five years the strawberry plants emerge to form a cool-looking, green ground cover that requires less water than grass.

Occasionally, if he can get to them before the robins and the neighborhood children, Dave harvests berries for breakfast. One of his favorite sights is seeing the kids foraging for berries — he loves the idea of creating a positive experience in their memories. "I remember picking wild strawberries when I was a kid," he says. "It was kind of like an Easter egg hunt every morning in early summer." To provide a bit of variety in his edible landscape, Dave planted an irregular hedge of Nanking cherries and serviceberries, one of the sweetest native fruits in the Rocky Mountain region.

8.9: Roll up the grass and plant strawberries, as Dave has done at his home. The neighborhood children and birds love it. Now if only Dave could get a strawberry or two!
Credit: Dave Wann.

Just as sweet are the Bing cherries and oranges at Village Homes. Michael Corbett and his colleagues made sure that something edible is harvestable every day of the year along the neighborhood's walkways and in its vineyards and orchards. Surplus figs, apples, grapes, kiwis, and almonds are sold to support the daycare center and reduce homeowner dues. The grapes also yield a local wine called Village Red.

HOW TO GET STARTED: Planting an edible landscape is as easy as calling your county extension office or talking to experienced personnel at nurseries or senior gardeners in town to find out what varieties grow best in your area. Then begin the process of "un-grassing" the lawn, leaving strategic well-used areas intact. The magic word in shrinking lawn area is "mulch." You don't have to dig up unwanted lawn, just smother it.

Lay six or eight inches of grass clippings, manure, and wood chips on top of cardboard or eight layers of newspaper, cut to fit. Let nature convert your lawn into a bed for herbal ground cover, berries, and vegetables.

A group in Vancouver, the Hands-on Edible Landscaping Project (HELP), has a good idea: learn about edible landscaping by helping your neighbors do it and letting them help you. Hold design and work parties in different yards throughout the neighborhood until everyone's yard is landscaped.

Suggestion 18. Start or Join a Community-supported Agriculture Program

WHO'S DOING IT: Slack Hollow Farm, Argyle, New York; Roxbury Farm, Claverack, New York

THE WAY IT WORKS: Community-supported agriculture (CSA) "is an innovative and resourceful strategy to connect local farmers with local consumers to develop a regional food supply and strong local economy," according to the folks at the University of Massachusetts extension service, whose website contains a wealth of information on this idea.

The idea began in Japan in the early 1970s and has since spread to other parts of the globe, including North America, with well over 600 groups and 100,000 members in the United States alone. Although each group is unique, community-supported agriculture generally involves two parties: a local farmer — typically a small farmer who produces food organically — and a group of residents in a nearby city or town, the members. The members purchase produce directly from the farmer. In some groups, says author Sarah Milstein in an article in *Mother Earth News* (listed in the Resource Guide), "members pay ahead of time for a full season with the understanding that they will accept some of the risks of production." If the cucumbers grow poorly, so be it. "In other groups, members subscribe on a monthly basis and receive a predetermined amount of produce each week," she adds.

Produce is either picked up at the farm by members of the group or delivered to a central location by the farmer. Members of each group generally receive eight or more different types of vegetables each week — starting in the spring and continuing well into the fall. However, "some groups offer fruit, herbs, flowers, bread, cheese, eggs, yogurt, beef, honey, maple syrup, and most anything else you can produce on a farm," says Milstein.

CSA programs vary in size. Slack Hollow Farm in Argyle, New York, has a dozen members who cover only a small percentage of the farm's operating budget. The rest of the produce from the seven-acre farm is sold through a local food co-op. Across the Hudson River is Roxbury Farm, where growers cultivate 25 acres and sell to 700 members whose purchases cover about 90 percent of the farm's annual operating expenses.

Community-supported agriculture is a win-win-win situation. Farmers develop secure markets. By growing a diverse array of crops they reduce pest problems, increase soil fertility, and ensure a decent harvest. You, the consumer, receive an abundance of healthy food at a very good price.

The environment benefits, too. Food is produced without pesticides. The birds that frequent the hedgerows surrounding farm fields live healthy lives, gobbling down some of the insects they harvest from the field and feeding the rest to their ever-hungry offspring.

Local production also yields environmental benefits. Because food is grown only a few miles from your home, rather than on distant farms hundreds or thousands of miles from the dinner table, little energy is required to transport food to market. The less energy, the less pollution. Production at an oil well in the Middle East may decline slightly, but the billionaire sheik or American oil executives who own it won't notice the difference. They're too busy trying to decide which model Lear jet they want.

HOW TO GET STARTED: Farmers looking for a secure local market for their products initiate most, if not all, community-supported agriculture operations. They recruit members through word of mouth, brochures, flyers, media coverage, and other methods. If you're interested in such a program, ask around and do some research on the web. Attend local farmers' markets and ask the participating farmers if they also engage in CSA or know farmers in the area who do.

Americans interested in finding a local CSA program can also check with the local US Department of Agriculture extension offices in their states or can contact some of the non-profit organizations, such as the CSA Farm Network (which lists farms in the northeastern US), for listings of local CSA farms. See our Resource Guide.

If you can't find a local program, you may be able to start one yourself by contacting local farmers. You can locate potential partners by placing ads in rural newspapers, visiting local farm supply stores, or contacting organic farm organizations.

Suggestion 19. Create a Car-share Program

WHO'S DOING IT: StattAuto, Germany; Zipcar, Flexcar, City CarShare, United States

THE WAY IT WORKS: Car-sharing is an idea whose time has come. The car-share movement began in Europe in the late 1980s, and the idea was so popular that many car-share programs evolved into

8.10: *Shared vehicles are gaining in popularity. Perhaps your neighborhood could benefit from a van or pickup truck that everyone has access to. Credit: City Car Share.*

professionally run organizations that offer an efficient, flexible, short-term, neighborhood car rental. By the end of 1999 there were over 200 car clubs, with a combined membership in excess of 100,000, in Switzerland, Germany, Austria, the Netherlands, Great Britain, Denmark, Sweden, Italy, and France!

In the mid-1990s the idea of car clubs spread to Canada, and recently the idea has begun to blossom in the United States as well, where Zipcar and Flexcar offer car-share programs in more than a dozen cities, including Boston, New York, Maryland, Washington DC, Denver, Portland, and Seattle.

Zipcar and Flexcar operate fleets of vehicles in each city. Cars are available to participants at any time, for periods ranging from one hour to several days. Special arrangements can be made to rent cars for long trips. Businesses, families, and individuals can all participate.

At Zipcar, vehicles are reserved online, a process that takes about 30 seconds. The computer tells you the car's location and its license plate number. You go to the site and hold your personal Zipcard next to the windshield, where a scanner reads it. If you've reserved the car and the time is correct, the doors unlock. An electronic signal is then sent from the car's computer to company headquarters, where a billing record is activated.

"Because there are no people involved in the transaction," the company notes, "you can make your reservation for any pickup or drop-off time that is convenient to you. Our proprietary technology knows when you lock and unlock the doors and how many miles you've traveled — so there's no paperwork each time you drive." When you are done, return the car, lock it, and go about your business. Your credit card is billed monthly.

Car-share programs in Europe often offer a variety of cars — small commuters and larger cars for taking the family and the kid's friends to the country. In the United States, options are more limited — you'll find mostly small commuter cars.

In car-sharing programs, members pay a membership fee and a small hourly rate plus mileage, and the companies pay for the car, the insurance, the maintenance, and the gas. In San Francisco's City Car Share program, run by a nonprofit organization, users pay $3.50 per hour and 37 cents per mile. Cars are parked in reserved spaces, typically off-street, that are conveniently located throughout the city. This means members know where the car is and where it must be dropped off. To ensure that members return the cars on time —

so the next people can use them — Zipcar imposes a $25-per-hour late fee with a minimum charge of $25. It also prohibits smoking in the car and only allows members to transport pets if they are in appropriate carriers.

Car-share programs give people who don't own cars access to a vehicle for running personal errands, shopping, visiting a doctor, or attending business meetings. They also cater to those who have one car, but occasionally need another. Car-share programs are highly effective in urban settings with good mass-transit systems, where people have other options besides driving, but they are also found in some rural areas.

Car-share programs save money and let members avoid the hassles of car ownership; they reduce private car ownership and reduce car usage. Most people drive less when they have to pay the per-hour or per-mile fee. They'll pool trips or walk or take mass transit when it is convenient. Many people find it more convenient to ride a bus or light rail to commute to and from work; then they rent a car-share vehicle for errands. Many systems in Europe are integrated with the mass-transit system.

HOW TO GET STARTED: If your community is interested in joining Flexcar, Zipcar, or a similar program, you may be able to have a vehicle or two located within your neighborhood — provided you can generate enough local interest to justify it. For a complete listing of car-share programs in the United States, Canada, the U.K., and Europe, log on to <www.eartheasy.com/live_car_sharing.htm>.

Alternatively, you can set up your own program. In Europe, groups of friends, neighbors, and colleagues have set up their own informal car-share programs using cars already owned by individual members of the group or cars purchased jointly. You will need to establish a booking system, find a convenient location to park the vehicle, and reach agreements on buying fuel, accessing keys, servicing and insuring the vehicle, and a host of other matters. Drivers usually pay in proportion to their use by the hour and/or by the mile. In Europe, car clubs set up more informally can operate using normal insurance as long as the group or its members do not make a profit. Car clubs apply for insurance in the club's name and can list four or five people to a single policy.

Suggestion 20. Retrofit Homes for Energy Efficiency

WHO'S DOING IT: EcoTeams in Madison, Wisconsin, and Rushcliffe, Nottingham, U.K.

THE WAY IT WORKS: Since the late 1990s, neighbors have been coming together to create more efficient and environmentally sustainable lifestyles with the help of a non-profit organization, Global Action Plan. David Gershon, founder of this group, started the EcoTeams project in the early 1990s and has produced a workbook full of great ideas for homeowners and renters — and their families.

Here's how it works: Individuals and families work with other neighbors — usually five to eight households form an EcoTeam. They meet regularly over a period of six months to explore and commit to actions that will reduce garbage production, water use, home and transportation energy fuel use, and overall consumption. Members are not required to adopt any specific actions; it's up to each household to decide which steps it would like to take. EcoTeam is non-threatening. "It offers structure combined with choice," says Dr. R. Warren Flint of Five E's Unlimited, a consulting firm that can help neighborhoods set up EcoTeam programs (contact them at www.eeeee.net).

To date, more than 40,000 people in 30 U.S. states and 17 other countries have participated in EcoTeams, a project that continues today, especially in the U.K. Penney Poyzer, who coordinates EcoTeams in Rushcliffe, a borough of Nottingham, says that the "interest from around the U.K. has been extraordinary." They're even developing the program to make it more accessible to families in poorer areas.

Upon completing the EcoTeam project, families have made significant strides in creating more environmentally sustainable lifestyles, typically cutting garbage output by 40 to 50 percent through recycling and composting, water consumption by 35 percent, and gas consumption for transportation by 16 to 20 percent. Home energy consumption is typically slashed by an average of 9 to 17 percent.

These measures are not only good for the Earth and the future of humans and all other species, but they also save a fair amount of money — between $265 and $389 per year per household. EcoTeams offer many other benefits as well. Jennifer Olsen and Per Kielland-Lund, who joined an EcoTeam in Madison, Wisconsin, during the fall of 1998, note: "We were able to implement many changes in our daily lives that we, for a long time, had wanted to ... In addition to these simple, isolated actions, EcoTeam participation transformed our outlook in two ways: we have become much more aware of sustainability issues in general, and are actively seeking out and supporting ways to organize our lives in a more Earth-friendly way. In addition, we have become encouraged and more optimistic on behalf of the Earth and the future of our species.... Through our own direct experience, we see that necessary changes can be made — even by those of us that are not among the forefront ... of sustainable living. It feels good to be a part of the solution and not only the problem."

EcoTeams form a support network. Individuals can call on others for help or moral support so that new actions become lifetime habits. They also provide an opportunity for individuals to work with city government. In Madison, EcoTeams were part of the Madison Area Sustainable Lifestyle Campaign, created by a partnership of five local companies and governmental agencies including the Madison Gas and Electric Company and the Dane County Department of Recycling and Solid Waste.

HOW TO GET STARTED: Starting your own EcoTeam — either with the assistance of Global Action Plan's *Household EcoTeam Workbook* or on your own — requires little more than networking with neighbors to see who might be interested in joining. If your neighborhood has adopted some of the other suggestions we've offered, you've likely got a receptive audience. You can obtain copies of the workbook through your local bookstore or by ordering at one of the on-line book suppliers.

Suggestion 21. Solarize Homes

WHO'S DOING IT: Cobb Hill Cohousing, Hartland, Vermont; OnGoing Concerns Cohousing, Portland, Oregon; L.A. Eco-Village, Los Angeles, California; Beddington Zero Energy Development, London, U.K.

THE WAY IT WORKS: Besides reducing energy use, homeowners can also tap into solar energy to meet some portion of their annual energy demand. Even in cloudy areas, including the Pacific Northwest and the northeastern United States, there's a surprising amount of solar energy available for heating a home, providing domestic hot water, and generating electricity. Certainly solar won't provide as generously in these locations as it will at a prime solar location such as Denver, but it can still make a significant contribution.

Solar energy comes in many varieties. There's passive solar for heating homes, discussed in Chapter 6. Passive solar relies on windows or attached sunspaces (solar greenhouses) along south-facing walls to admit the low-angled winter sun. Many existing homes can be retrofitted by increasing the number of windows on south-facing walls or by adding a solar greenhouse. In the Resource Guide, we've listed an article on retrofitting that Dan published in *Natural Home* magazine, but to learn more about passive solar you might want to read Dan's book, *The Solar House: Passive Heating and Cooling*.

Many of the steps a homeowner takes to tap into solar energy — such as adding more insulation to walls and ceilings — also help to cool homes in the summer. This can lead to significant reductions in fuel bills. In many places, summer cooling costs can exceed winter heating bills.

You can install solar hot-water systems to heat water for domestic uses or for space heating. These active systems — so named because they require pumps — consist of a solar collector, usually mounted on the roof, which gathers heat from the sun. A heat-transfer liquid is pumped through the panel to remove the heat, which is then transferred to a water storage tank in the basement, and used as needed.

Modern solar hot-water systems are reliable, efficient, and make good economic sense in many areas. You can learn more about them in Dan's solar book and also his book *The Natural House*.

8.11 a & b: Passive solar can be added to existing homes either (a) by installing additional windows on south-facing walls or (b) by adding solar greenhouses. Credit: Dan Chiras.

Another system worth exploring is the solar electric system. These rely on specially designed panels that convert energy from sunlight to electricity. Dan's home in Colorado is run entirely by solar electricity generated by rooftop panels.

Because homeowners sometimes object to the aesthetics of traditional solar electric panels, also known as photovoltaic panels, sleek new systems have been devised. They consist of shingles or metal roofing containing the same material found in the solar cells of calculators, and their cost is comparable to more conventional solar electric panels.

Solar electricity, while beneficial, can also be expensive — usually around 24 to 27 cents per kilowatt-hour. Most of us pay around 8 to 10 cents per kilowatt-hour for conventionally generated energy. Even so, in some areas, such as California, where electricity is expensive and generous tax credits or rebates are available, solar electricity can be economical.

While most solarizing we're aware of has occurred on individual homes, we have discovered some communities that are implementing this strategy. Members of Cobb Hill Cohousing in rural Vermont have built their homes to take advantage of the heating potential of the sun. OnGoing Concerns Cohousing, which consists of seven homes purchased in a deteriorating inner-city neighborhood in Portland, Oregon, has added solar water heaters to three of the homes. L.A. Eco-Village is installing a solar hot-water system in a 40-unit apartment building that's part of the community. And in the Beddington Zero Energy Development, a compact, newly built community in England, all 82 homes will be equipped with solar electric panels.

HOW TO GET STARTED: If your community is interested in solarizing — and if people are keen on doing the work themselves — you will need to do a lot of research on the subject. See the books we've listed in our Resource Guide, take workshops, and talk to professionals. Local chapters of the American Solar Energy Society may prove helpful. You may want to hire a professional — a solar architect or builder — to consult on passive solar design, or hire an expert to work with you on solar hot water and solar electric systems. You can purchase solar hot water and solar electric systems directly from suppliers on the Internet — for example, Solaronsale.com or Realgoods.com — then install them yourself or with the help of a trained professional (not a bad way to go). If you're interested in installing a number of systems in your neighborhood, you may be able to hire a local installer to supply and install the equipment — and you will likely be able to negotiate a better price.

Be sure to check out rebates and other incentives from local utilities and local and state governments. You can log on to the Database of State Incentives for Renewable Energy (www.DSIREUSA.org). Some states, such as California, Illinois, New York, and New Jersey, offer extremely generous incentives for installing solar energy equipment.

8.12: *One of the newest and most efficient solar hot-water systems made by Thermomax, this rooftop collector heats water for domestic uses, even heating the home. Credit: Dan Chiras.*

♦ ♦ ♦

Converting an existing neighborhood in an older urban setting or in the suburbs requires commitment, energy, and money, but people seeking a better way of life have demonstrated that the benefits far outweigh the costs.

Every revolutionary idea seems to evoke three stages of reaction.
It's completely impossible. It's possible, but not worth doing. I said it was a good idea all along.
ARTHUR C. CLARKE

9

Suburban Revitalization II: Making Bold Dreams Come True

THROUGHOUT THE WORLD, people are uniting to work for a common goal: to create community and more socially, economically, and environmentally friendly lifestyles. Our research has shown that their efforts go far beyond what we ever imagined possible when we began this project. People are choosing dramatically different ways to provide energy, obtain water, and get rid of waste, to name a few. This chapter looks at living examples of the boldest ideas we've suggested, showing how they work and how you can get started.

Boldest Ideas

Suggestion 22. Create a Community Energy System

WHO'S DOING IT: Muir Commons, Davis, California; Cobb Hill Cohousing, Hartland, Vermont; Sun and Wind Cohousing, Beder, Denmark; Beddington Zero Energy Development, London, U.K.

THE WAY IT WORKS: Community energy systems may seem out of place in industrialized countries where central power production is the norm. On the contrary, however, more and more people recognize the value of decentralized energy production — power generated and consumed by individuals and communities right on site. Such systems not only provide power; they do it using clean, renewable resources, and they produce it close to the end user, so there's much less energy loss in transmission. These systems are also not vulnerable to system failures that routinely leave millions of households without power for long periods, often when they need power the most. Nor are they vulnerable to terrorist acts, as centralized power plants are.

9.1: *Community energy systems, like this photovoltaic system in Davis, California, provide independence and security and help build a more sustainable energy supply. Credit: Charles Ehrlich.*

Decentralized power systems designed for individuals and communities consist of wind generators, solar electric systems, micro-hydropower, and energy-efficient microturbines, which burn natural gas. These systems all produce electricity for local consumption and can feed the excess back into the power grid — the electric wires that run through most of our neighborhoods. Neighborhood energy systems can also generate heat.

Muir Commons in Davis, California, the first cohousing community in the United States, was completed in 1991. It consists of 26 homes situated on just under three acres. In 2002 the group installed a 10-kilowatt solar electric system on the roof of their common house. It supplies about three-quarters of the electrical requirements of the common house at a cost of about 8 cents per kilowatt-hour. Previously they were paying 23 cents per kWh!

On the other side of the nation is Cobb Hill Cohousing. Located in Hartland in rural Vermont, this community installed a large, central, wood-burning furnace that heats water, which is then pumped underground through insulated pipes to the homes, providing hot water for space heat and domestic uses. The homes also acquire heat directly from the sun, capitalizing on passive solar design, and each unit has a backup propane heater.

Heading farther east, to Denmark, we find Sun and Wind Cohousing, which completed construction in 1980. This group installed a 55 kW wind generator that satisfies 10 percent of the total energy requirements of the community. The wind machine is situated 1.5 miles from the community and is mounted on a 72-foot tower.

Sun and Wind also installed solar hot-water panels covering 7,000 square feet of roof surface. Most of the panels are on the common house, with the remainder on 15 houses in the 30-house community. Water heated by the panels is stored in insulated tanks located under the common house and is distributed to the homes in the community via underground pipes. The solar-heated water is used for domestic needs — such as washing dishes and showering — as well as for radiant heat to warm homes. It meets about a third of the community's total energy demand.

Across the English Channel, in the London borough of Sutton, is Beddington Zero Energy Development. This brand-new community, which has implemented many ideas we've presented in this book, consists of 82 homes — all facing south to capitalize on the sun's winter heat. Additional heat in these well-insulated buildings comes from a central furnace that burns wood chips from a local tree surgery (a company that prunes and removes trees). The chips were previously buried in a landfill. This system also generates steam that is used to produce electricity for all of the homes. However, energy demands are low as the homes were designed to use 60 percent less energy than comparable suburban homes.

HOW TO GET STARTED: If members of your community show sufficient interest in a neighborhood energy system, be sure to research your options carefully. We've included information on dozens of publications and organizations in the Resource Guide. You may want to hire a consultant or a professional installer. Be sure to look into tax incentives and rebates from local utilities and government agencies, as explained in Suggestion 21. To help fund the installation of a solar electric system, you might sponsor a hands-on workshop. The folks at Muir Commons in Davis, California, did this, and the workshop fees paid by attendees helped offset the cost of the teacher/installer.

Suggestion 23. Establish Environmentally Friendly Water and Wastewater Systems

WHO'S DOING IT: Residents in Arizona, New Mexico, and Vancouver, British Columbia; Paws, Inc., Muncie, Indiana; Darrow School, New Lebanon, New York; Hockerton Housing Project, Nottinghamshire, U.K.

THE WAY IT WORKS: Most suburban neighborhoods seem to be designed to waste water. Rain, sewage, and graywater (water from sinks and washing machines) are all channeled into pipes that carry the water away. The waste either ends up in sewage treatment plants, where it is treated and then dumped into rivers, lakes, and bays, or in septic tanks, where it seeps into the ground. States such as Arizona, California, Indiana, and New Mexico, however, are beginning to find ways to capture this water and the nutrients in household wastewater. In Arizona, for example, homeowners can use aboveground graywater systems to recover wastewater so long as the system handles less than 400 gallons per day and meets minimal requirements.

The average person generates approximately 40 gallons of graywater per day. By capturing that resource for reuse, a neighborhood could gain enough water for irrigation, helping to reduce the amount of energy and chemicals cities and towns use to treat the water.

9.2: The Living Machine is a greenhouse-contained biological waste treatment facility that uses natural methods rather than harmful chemicals to recycle human waste. Credit: Stacey Giordano.

Amy Bunting of Santa Fe captures rainwater off her roof and uses it and graywater from her washing machine to water her lush backyard garden. She washes her clothes with an "ionic ball" (available from green products suppliers like Gaiam Real Goods) so that the graywater does not upset the soil's pH balance. Rainwater from her roof also feeds into a dry streambed that waters a small grove of trees.

Even rain-rich Vancouver, B.C., acknowledges the advantages of getting full value out of each drop of rain. A thousand square feet of roof or pavement can collect 420 gallons of water from one inch of rain. To make use of this valuable resource, the city government sells rain barrels residents can use to catch water for garden irrigation. So far, more than 1,200 residents have taken advantage of the city's 50 percent subsidy of the barrels.

It is more challenging to recycle "blackwater," including sewage and kitchen wastes, than graywater, but thousands of devices that perform this task — including constructed wetlands and "Living Machines" — have already been installed in homes, schools, workplaces, parks, and neighborhoods. Constructed wetlands are shallow, gravel-filled ponds where plants like cattails, reeds, and rushes grow. The plants and microbes on their roots purify the wastewater — even in the winter. Living Machines are complete ecosystems — typically housed in greenhouses — where microbes, snails, plants, fish, and other living organisms purify domestic wastewater, essentially the way nature does it.

The Paws, Inc., facility in Muncie, Indiana, uses a Living Machine to treat the wastes of the 80-person staff responsible for creating and marketing Garfield cartoons and stuffed animals. At New York's Darrow School, a community of live-in private school students, the failure of a conventional wastewater system provided an opportunity to install a Living Machine. This system is used as a hands-on laboratory for a variety of different classes, including science, chemistry, mathematics, and even art. "Our facility is a great place for studying, writing, and drawing," says school director Lisa Riker. "It's warm. It's contained. And it's stimulating because it's so very alive."

Another approach to solid waste is the compost toilet, a waterless "water closet" that uses microbial populations to decompose human wastes quickly, as noted in Chapter 7.

One of the best examples of reliance on an alternative wastewater treatment system is the Hockerton Housing Project located in Nottinghamshire in the British Midlands. It captures rainwater off the roof and purifies it for use indoors. Water captured on the land is diverted to a small pond for outdoor use. Blackwater from toilets and graywater from sinks and showers is piped to a septic tank, but the leachate (liquid waste from the septic tank) is diverted to a biological treatment system, and the purified water is then piped to a pond in which neighbors swim. The water exceeds the European Union's water quality standard for beaches.

HOW TO GET STARTED: Catching rainwater and irrigating with graywater are relatively straightforward, as are composting toilets. Blackwater treatment is a bit more complicated. Getting approval to do these things, however, can be a challenge. Each state's codes are different. Because of water rights laws in the West, for instance, collecting rainwater that falls on the roof of your home might be against the law! Despite this, many states suffering from chronic water shortages are becoming more flexible about obtaining water for homes and treating wastewater. In Indiana, for example, the state will certify Living Machines, a technology that has been documented to be as effective as conventional treatment.

Start by doing some research on the web (see the Resource Guide) to find out about the laws in your state. Then begin by installing water-conserving fixtures (like low-flow showerheads) in your house and slowly start to make every drop of water count.

Suggestion 24. Establish an Environmentally Friendly Transportation Strategy

WHO'S DOING IT: Norwood-Quince neighborhood, Boulder, Colorado; Adobe Systems, Fremont, Washington; Beddington Zero Energy Development, London, U.K.

THE WAY IT WORKS: Neighborhood leader Graham Hill from Boulder, Colorado, refers to cars and trucks as an "alternative form of transportation" because there are a variety of other options that are routinely used by people living in his neighborhood. Out of 210 households in the area, for instance, 130 have Eco-passes for the well-managed bus system. The city provides discounts for participating neighborhoods. Neighbors also have excellent pedestrian or bike access to a shopping area and to open space in a nearby park, several bike-pedestrian walkways, and even a solar-lighted walkway that was paid for by a neighborhood mini-grant from the city. "We observed that many neighbors weren't walking to the Boulder Market at night because the street was

9.3: Neighbors in Boulder, Colorado, share this GEM electric car for running errands. The inventor, Dan Sturges, is pictured with his son. Credit: Dave Wann.

too dark and seemed unsafe," explains Hill. "So we applied for a grant to install solar-powered lights that have battery storage. More than a hundred neighbors benefit from the lights."

Forty people in the neighborhood are members in a car-share club — which essentially allows for car rental by the hour — and more than 50 have become members in an electric bike-share operation. The electric bikes are powered by solar cells incorporated into a bike locker. This project was also funded by a small grant from the city.

The neighbors are now looking into creating better access to walkways and bike paths by linking several existing pathways with easements through private yards. To demonstrate the efficiencies of muscle power versus fossil fuel power, Hill and his colleagues staged a race between the mayor, who rode a bicycle, and the county commissioner, who drove a hybrid car. They had to run several errands, and the bike-riding mayor won.

Other communities are also fostering more environmentally friendly forms of transportation, or eliminating the need for transportation At the Beddington Zero Energy Development in London, for example, work spaces were developed right in the neighborhood so many residents could work close to home, a measure that cuts down on transportation. Amenities like shops and a doctor's office are situated nearby. The developers of this 82-home complex also included an internet shopping link with a local supermarket so residents can order groceries without leaving home. The store makes regular deliveries.

But that's not all. When the community was being laid out, planners left plenty of space for storing bicycles, and roads were designed to be as pedestrian-friendly as possible. The developers purposely limited parking spaces to discourage car ownership and use and encourage the use of nearby trains, buses, and Tramlink (a light rail system). A pool of electric cars, powered by on-site generators, is available for Beddington residents' use.

HOW TO GET STARTED: Any comprehensive strategy begins with a single step. Analyze the number of trips you and your neighbors make, then work on ways to reduce each kind of trip — for example, by carpooling. Become active in your workplace, too, and help devise ways to transport more people in fewer cars.

A great example of a comprehensive strategy at work is set by Adobe Systems of Fremont, Washington. It provides bike racks, showers, and lockers for those who bike, walk, or run to work, and gives out FlexPasses, which subsidize 100 percent of transit and vanpool fares. As a result, 75 percent of the 500 employees avoid the one-car, one-driver pattern, with its many negative spin-offs.

Tom McIntire, a systems analyst, carpools to work every day in his electric Volkswagen Beetle. "I've had it about four and a half years now," he says. "Since the car recharges in the company garage, nobody has to chip in for gas." Systems analyst Joe Cornicello incorporates exercise and fun into his daily commute — he kayaks to work!

Suggestion 25. Create a Common House

WHO'S DOING IT: N Street Community, Davis, California

THE WAY IT WORKS: Common houses are a central feature of cohousing, but they are a great idea for suburban neighborhoods as well. In 1991 in Davis, California, neighbors formed a cooperative to convert a neighborhood home into a community house — complete with a community kitchen, dining room, and meeting room that houses a TV and piano. Within this building, members of the community — 17 homes and growing — dine together, play foosball, watch videos, talk, or meet to discuss plans for future projects. To keep the cost of joint ownership down, they rent out the rest of the ranch house as living space. They recently remodeled the house, adding four more rooms that are rented to generate additional income.

Now called N Street Cohousing, this community is unusual in that it arose as a result of the transformation of an existing subdivision. It's a prime example of Superbia!, although residents like to call it "retrofit cohousing." No matter what you call it, N Street Cohousing is a leading example of how to create community in existing neighborhoods.

HOW TO GET STARTED: Eating together has become a part of life in N Street Cohousing, but communal dinners didn't begin with the establishment of a common house. Rather, they started years earlier with potluck meals held at different members' houses, as described in Chapter 8. Over time, as the community evolved and grew more interdependent, the idea of establishing a common house seemed logical.

You, too, can begin the process by sponsoring potluck dinners and building community within your neighborhood (Suggestions 1 to 19). If you arrive at the point where a common house seems desirable, you may want to purchase a house in your neighborhood. As noted in Chapter 7, the economics are attractive. By renting out office and daycare space, each family's monthly share of the mortgage can be dramatically reduced. Further reductions are possible by creating a rental unit. Of course, you will need to establish a legal entity to purchase the home — but by the time you've reached this stage, that should be a snap. Each member of the neighborhood association pays a monthly fee to offset insurance, taxes, upkeep, and what's left of the mortgage.

Suggestion 26. Create a Community-shared Office

WHO'S DOING IT: Pioneer Valley Cohousing, Amherst, Massachusetts; Gray Rock Cohousing, Fort Collins, Colorado

THE WAY IT WORKS: We've found several examples of community offices in cohousing communities. In Pioneer Valley Cohousing, six members share an office building built especially for the community. According to Laura Fitch, an architect who lives in the community and owns one of the office spaces, the building contains six private offices, a conference room, and a shared general office area. The six community residents who use the private offices own the building, which is adjacent to a wood workshop and art studio, and just steps away from the common house. The shared office space houses a fax machine, copier, paper cutter, and computer for e-mail. This equipment is available to the entire community and is well used by individuals who work out of their homes.

The value of the community office, says Fitch, "is much greater than shared equipment. For me, it means being close to home, but without the isolation.… I regularly run into neighbors and fellow office owners at the copy machine, finding time to chat.… For folks at Pioneer Valley who have offices physically within their homes, the home office building creates opportunities for some fresh air and human interaction. They can use the conference room any time it is available (and it usually is) to meet with clients in a professional setting instead of bringing them into their private homes."

There are other benefits as well. Children are exposed to the work their parents, and others, do. Work is demystified. There are opportunities for cross-fertilization, as well. In Pioneer Valley, Fitch and her partner operate an architectural firm, and there's a development consultant and a builder in neighboring offices. They all bounce ideas off one another. In addition, "a home office building can make a community more of a village than just a new-fangled suburban housing complex," says Fitch.

As the folks at Gray Rock Cohousing in Fort Collins have found, shared office equipment saves money. For example, there's no need for each person who works at home to own a copier or even a laser printer.

HOW TO GET STARTED: If your neighborhood has banded together to purchase a common house, part of that building can be dedicated to offices and shared office space. Advance commitments from individuals who would like to rent or buy an office will help to offset the cost of purchasing the building, a cost borne by the rest of your neighbors. Members of your community may find it cheaper, and a heck of a lot more convenient, to rent or buy an office than to drive halfway across the city to reach their current office space. Private and community office space will also put a common house to better use. Instead of being vacant during the day, it will have occupants at all times.

Getting approval for offices may be tricky. Local officials may view it as commercial space, which is typically forbidden within residential neighborhoods. One argument that Pioneer Valley Cohousing used successfully with town officials was that the office space was not much different than home offices. Be persistent. If neighbors don't mind your establishing offices in the common house, officials are likely to acquiesce. Who knows, in areas suffering from massive gridlock and air pollution, you may start a trend!

9.4: Entertainment in your own neighborhood reduces trips to the city and enriches lives in many ways. Credit: Community Greens.

Suggestion 27. Establish a Community Entertainment Program

WHO'S DOING IT: New View Drama Group and Kids' Theater, Boston, Massachusetts, neighborhoods in Tucson, Arizona

THE WAY IT WORKS: Franny Osman of the New View cohousing community provides well-appreciated entertainment for the community by directing kids' plays. "My training in drama consists of community theater at age eleven, 30 years ago," she says. "That's it. I direct because I stepped in and said, 'It might be fun to direct a play,' called a rehearsal, and the actors came."

The challenge is to sustain a group once it's launched. To draw people to meetings, work parties, or rehearsals, there has to be an element of fun. It helps if there's a certain ingrained fortitude as well. Says

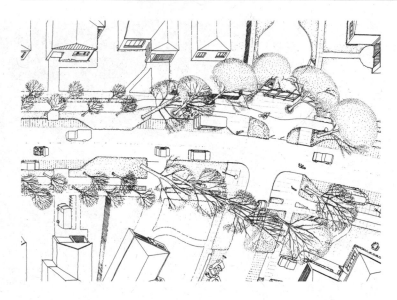

9.5: Slowing traffic in cities by narrowing streets helps residents reclaim their neighborhood, making life more pleasant and much safer. Credit: Peter Bosselman.

Osman, "Some parents have wondered how I manage the chaotic scene at rehearsals. I put myself in a zenlike mode of chaos acceptance and unfluffability. I let the leaders emerge from within the ranks and carry the day."

HOW TO GET STARTED: All it takes is a single individual with a little knowledge or passion in a given area who's willing to organize a club. Members have something to talk about and something to do together.

Suggestion 28. Narrow or Eliminate Streets

WHO'S DOING IT: Sellwood Neighborhood, Portland, Oregon; GossGrove Neighborhood, Boulder, Colorado; The Netherlands

THE WAY IT WORKS: At one time, streets were the center of our communities. People shopped at local vendors along the street, children played with one another in the street, and adults visited with friends as they passed on the street. Today, streets are the epicenter of a city's or town's vehicular community. Dissected by busy, sometimes dangerous streets, our neighborhoods have suffered tremendously. Virtually everyone's life has been diminished by excessive traffic.

Throughout the world, people are reclaiming their streets. They are finding ways to slow, reduce, even eliminate traffic. Their goal is "to turn public roads into high-quality environments that encourage walking, cycling, and social interaction," according to Living Streets Initiative, a non-profit group located in the United Kingdom.

Slowing and reducing traffic, known as *traffic calming*, began in the 1970s in the Netherlands, where streets that have been calmed are referred to as *woonerf*. (In Dutch, *woon* means "residential" and *erf* means "yard.") The Woonerf movement seeks to achieve a balance between vehicular traffic and other users of neighborhood streets, such as pedestrians, store owners, cyclists, and local residents. Today there are an estimated 6,000 *woonerf* in the Netherlands, and the idea has spread to many other countries, among them England, Germany, and the United States.

Street calming relies on simple, fairly inexpensive, physical alterations of streets and roads. These include intentional narrowing of streets or placing traffic circles at intersections to slow traffic. Traffic circles often add beauty by including flowers and shrubs. These and numerous other alterations of the streetscape subtly compel motorists to drive more carefully and at much lower speeds, an effort supported by many local and national laws. Many measures, such as flowers in a traffic circle, can also alter the psychology of drivers, making them less aggressive and hurried.

In the Sellwood neighborhood of Portland, Oregon, residents reclaimed a local street intersection as their own public square — Share-it Square — with government approval. They've installed a Tea Station, where people can get a free cup of tea 24 hours a day; they built a kid's playhouse; and they constructed a Produce Station, where neighbors can buy or exchange food. Neighbors have even painted a huge, colorful design on the road in the intersection.

9.6: Traffic circles, such as this one in Seattle, provide a splash of color and help to slow traffic. Two neighbors whose passion is gardening proudly take care of it. Credit: City of Seattle.

"On a daily basis, intersection repairs such as these are places that people can run into other people in their community," says Daniel Lerch, co-director of the City Repair Project, a Portland non-profit organization that helps neighborhoods reclaim their intersections. He adds, "Many people make a point of traveling through the square on their way to the store to check out the kiosk where neighborhood news is posted. Or they bring friends, kids, or simply go alone to enjoy the beauty of the place." The intersection is still open to traffic most of the time, but the square is closed off two or three times a year for neighborhood block parties.

Intersection reclaiming has helped neighbors get to know one another. "Anecdotes abound of neighbors who had lived next to each other for years, yet never knew each other, becoming friends as a result of working on the project or simply meeting at the square," says Lerch. The square has created community identity, and 90 percent of the residents believe that it has slowed traffic speed, while over 80 percent believe it has made their streets safer. Other reclamation projects in this progressive city report similar results.

9.7: *Three women from Boulder chat in one of three "theme" parks created when the city closed off part of their street. This little park is for talking and meditation; a second will be a community garden, and the third a bocci ball court. Credit: Doug Crigler.*

In Boulder, Colorado, the GossGrove Neighborhood was dramatically altered when the city blocked some of its streets. Parts of the closed-off intersections were converted to pocket parks, discussed in Suggestion 4. Although such measures have greatly reduced traffic and made the neighborhood more pleasant, city officials say they have also increased traffic on nearby roads and made navigating through the community a bit frustrating. The city council and the planning department have voted not to repeat the experiment, and now favor other measures to slow traffic rather than prevent it. Another area of confusion is whether the parks department or the traffic department should maintain the pocket parks.

HOW TO GET STARTED: "Living streets give priority to pedestrians and cyclists, and create safe places for people to walk, cycle, play, and meet friends," according to the Living Streets Initiative. "Cars and other motor vehicles are not excluded, but the street is designed to make drivers aware that they are driving in an area where pedestrians and other users have priority. Any street that is not a motorway or expressway can become a living street."

The success of street reclaiming depends on effective and well-conceived plans, but also requires that a community buy in to the idea and cooperate, according to Home Zone, a non-profit organization that promotes street reclaiming in Europe. If you and your neighbors are interested in tackling this challenge, read David Engwicht's book *Street Reclaiming* or log on to websites of the Living Streets Initiative, the City Repair Project, and others. These sites will provide you with a wealth of information on how to get started — and how to succeed.

Suggestion 29. Retrofit Garages and Spare Rooms into Apartments

WHO'S DOING IT: N Street Community, Davis, California; City of Golden, Colorado

THE WAY IT WORKS: In our research, we've found that the building departments in a number of cities and towns are starting to ease up on restrictions in urban and suburban neighborhoods, allowing some infill development. In Golden, Colorado, for example, code officials now permit local residents to convert garages to apartments or add apartments on top of garages. This simple measure greatly increases available housing in a community hard-pressed to meet the needs of its large student population. (It is home to the Colorado School of Mines.)

In Davis, California, city officials also changed building codes to assist members of the N Street Community. According to Kevin Wolf, an N Street pioneer, "the neighborhood largely consists of 1,000-square-foot homes on 6,000-square-foot lots." Because of escalating prices, homes are becoming unaffordable for many people. To make it feasible for individuals to buy homes in their neighborhood, N Street members lobbied the city for permission to rezone and add larger attached granny flats than had previously been permitted by code. Their efforts paid off. The city changed the neighborhood's zoning status, allowing locals to build larger attached units that added more living space in their neighborhood without building on the precious common area they'd established behind their homes.

9.8: *Garage conversions, like conversions of unused rooms into apartments, provide living space and also enhance neighborhood diversity. More and more cities and towns are changing building codes to allow such development. Credit: Dave Wann.*

So how does this legal wrangling help? Instead of buying a costly house alone, a family can partner with another individual or family. They (families and/or individuals) buy the existing house with the agreement that a second unit will be added. In one instance, two single women bought a home; then one applied for a construction loan to build a 1,125-square-foot granny flat. The existing house was completely remodeled.

Individual houses can also be remodeled. We learned about a frugal family in the Pacific Northwest that remodeled a 1,300-square-foot home to create a 450-square-foot apartment where one of the family's grandmothers now lives.

Suggestion 30. Create a Mixed-use Neighborhood

WHO'S DOING IT: Seaside, Florida; Depot East, Minneapolis, Minnesota; Centennial Place, Atlanta, Georgia

THE WAY IT WORKS: The idea of incorporating retail space for coffee shops, grocery stores, garden markets, barbers, and other activities is not a new one. It is, however, an idea developers abandoned in their rush to house our growing population after World War II, in large part because zoning regulations required a separation of activities — housing and schools were to be separated from factories, municipal government, and shopping.

Today, New Urbanists are promoting mixed-use communities — communities based on the traditional neighborhood model with shops, schools, civic places, offices, and homes all within a short walking distance of each other. Encouragingly, there are hundreds of these communities in various stages of development in the United States. Seaside is one of the earliest examples. Situated in Florida's panhandle, a stone's throw from the Gulf of Mexico, this community was built to resemble a quaint southern town — with dozens of amenities located a short distance from the homes.

Mixed-use development is also occurring in urbanized areas during infill development and redevelopment of certain areas. Slated for completion in December 2004, Depot East is an infill development in Minneapolis. The developer, CSM Corporation, is converting a parking lot into a four-story building that houses offices, retail space, a restaurant, and 22 owner-occupied residences. Parking for residents and shoppers is underground or hidden by the buildings. A new center for the arts was also built on-site. When complete, the facility will bring people to work, play, learn, and live in the historic Mills District.

Centennial Place is a mixed-use, mixed-income community in Atlanta, forged from an existing public housing project. This 60-acre community is home to 900 families. A new school was built on the site, along with a new YMCA and a police substation. The renovated community center, grocery stores, and retail outlets make the neighborhood nearly self-contained. "What we're talking about here is re-creating the kind of communities many of us grew up in years ago," says Egbert Perry, principal of the Integral Group, the managing partner of Centennial Place.

Lorrie Hammond, who lived in the housing project and now lives in Centennial Place, says, "It's a different atmosphere. Students, lawyers, doctors, white and black, live here. It's a lot better. Cleaner. Nicer school. Makes you want to keep it up."

Having businesses in our communities not only makes our lives more convenient, but can also have a positive social influence on youth. One extraordinary example is Bike Works, a bike repair shop in Seattle. This business occupies a formerly vacant and blighted storefront that was renovated by community volunteers. It benefits local youth in a variety of ways. First, it's the only bicycle repair shop in southeast Seattle, and it charges low rates. Second, and most important, the business gives young people a positive place to spend time, opportunities for exercise, and a way to build self-esteem. It also exposes youth to community service and provides important skills. How?

Any child between the ages of 9 and 17 is eligible to participate in the Earn-a-Bike program. The kids attend eight classes in bicycle repair. Then they repair used bicycles that have been donated to Bike Works. After completing 24 hours of work, each is given a refurbished bicycle, a helmet, and a bike lock.

So far, more than 150 children have earned bicycles. So many bicycles have been refurbished that they are donated to organizations supporting foster children and homeless adults. Recently, 300 recycled bicycles were shipped to Ghana. Bike Works also manages an annual Kid's Bike Swap, where children can trade up for a bicycle that fits their growing bodies. All of this is made possible by a small staff and about 100 adult volunteers.

0.0: Inviting businesses into our communities fosters diversity and enhances convenience. More and more cities and towns are looking favorably on such schemes to help reduce traffic and create more people-friendly neighborhoods. Credit: Dave Wann.

HOW TO GET STARTED: Mixed-use development — or, in the case of an existing neighborhood, redevelopment — encourages a variety of community activities and services in a neighborhood. It reduces our need for extensive automobile travel and is, as the folks at the Smart Communities Network point out, "an antidote to the widely separated life and work centers that are conducive to urban sprawl." It helps build community and saves resources, time, and money.

If living, working, shopping, and playing in your community appeals to you, you may want to include a small convenience store — perhaps by converting an existing house into a store and an apartment for the owner, manager, or a student. You could add a coffee shop or a café, or encourage a dentist to open up shop in your neighborhood. You could buy a house and convert it into office spaces for those who are self-employed and would like to work closer to home.

You can do all this without changing the character of the neighborhood and without increasing traffic very much. But there will be obstacles. Zoning regulations in many parts of the country currently prohibit mixed-used communities. By working with your planning office — as well as the mayor's office — you can prevail. Because of its many environmental and social benefits, mixed-use development is becoming an easier sell with local officials.

Suggestion 31. Foster Diversity

WHO'S DOING IT: Monterey Cohousing, Saint Louis Park, Minnesota; L.A. Eco-Village, Los Angeles, California

THE WAY IT WORKS: Our final suggestion involves measures you can take to create diversity in communities. While many of us feel more comfortable when surrounded by people of like mind, the suburbs can become sterile if they are populated solely by people cut from the same cloth. More diverse neighborhoods can be vibrant and instructive. Diversity helps us open our minds to different viewpoints and lifestyles. This fact has not escaped modern neighborhood designers like Andres Duany. He and other New Urbanists are designing neighborhoods that will draw a mix of people.

One feature of these neighborhoods is mixed housing. Rather than building a bland assortment of similar four-bedroom suburban homes, they're including tastefully done apartments and duplexes nestled among the rest of the homes. If the architectural style is consistent with that of neighboring houses, as it usually is, the results can be stunning.

We have found examples of the mixed-neighborhood model in some cohousing communities, too. For instance, in Saint Louis Park, Minnesota, a group of eight families — all cohousing aspirants — bought a mansion to remodel. This building, which had been a retirement home in earlier days, soon contained eight independent apartments, ranging from two-room suites of less than 500 square feet to a three-bedroom unit that's more than 1,500 square feet. The community is diverse in age, ranging from 4 year olds to folks over 70. It's also socially diverse. Residents seem to appreciate the learning that's achieved by considering issues from another's perspective.

Many other communities encourage or celebrate diversity. For example, residents of L.A. Eco-Village come from a variety of ethnic backgrounds. The group recently purchased a 40-unit apartment complex in the neighborhood, creating an opportunity for even further ethnic diversity. (Currently, some of the residents participate in the Eco-Village and others do not.) This is their second apartment building, and there are nearly a dozen more in the area that they hope to purchase and remodel.

HOW TO GET STARTED: If you have completed many of the steps described in previous pages of this chapter, chances are you're not too far ideologically from steps that could enhance the diversity of the social fabric of your community. While buying a house and converting it to a duplex or triplex may have seemed difficult when you first started your quest for Superbia!, after implementing earlier suggestions we've made, you may find your neighbors open to the idea of enhancing the diversity of your community's social fabric.

If you live in an older neighborhood, there may be an apartment dwelling in your midst already — or you may be able to tear down a couple of older dilapidated homes and build your own. To promote environmental values, be sure to remodel using green building materials that are earth- and people-friendly. This is what the folks at L.A. Eco-Village are doing with apartments and homes in their neighborhood.

Putting it All Together

"Okay," you say, "I'm convinced. These ideas are doable. But surely not the whole ball of wax. You can't convert an entire community. That seems too far out there, too grandiose."

Think again.

In time, anything's possible.

And you don't have to be wealthy to make the transition.

Consider the case of Brad Lancaster. When he was 27, Brad and his brother Rodd purchased a dilapidated home in a run-down neighborhood in Tucson, Arizona. Most people would have razed the house and started over, but not these two. Over the years the brothers have devoted their energy to fixing up the house and breathing life back into the weed-infested, arid lot, turning the grounds into an oasis and the house into a stellar example of urban self-sufficiency.

To reduce heat gain in the hot Arizona summers, they painted the house white so it reflects sunlight and reduces heat absorption and discomfort. They also increased the length of the overhang (eaves), providing additional shade. They constructed trellises from salvaged rebar and steel mesh, then planted vegetables that grow on vines. During the summer, squash adorn the trellises, providing food as well as shade. In the winter, snow peas grow there. Because they only grow to a height of three to four feet, they don't block the low-angled winter sun, which heats the house.

Over the years, these two remarkable men have planted trees to shade their home and a vegetable garden that's fed by rainwater collected from their small roof. To protect against overheating in the summer, they often cook food outdoors in a solar oven. Because the desert air cools down substantially at night, they open a few windows each evening to permit the chilly desert air to purge heat that has accumulated inside the house during the day.

In the winter they heat their home with solar energy entering through south-facing windows. A small woodstove provides backup heat, using wood from the trees that grow in their yard as fuel. All year round, hot water comes from a solar water heater.

They get their electricity from a solar electric panel with battery storage. In the summer, solar electricity powers a small ceiling fan that helps keep the place cool. "As the fan is powered by the panel, we literally cool the house with the sun," remarks Lancaster.

Slowly but surely, these advocates of environmentally friendly lifestyles have become more and more self-sufficient. They've also organized the creation of an organic community garden and orchard. Thirty-five members participate in the community garden, growing an assortment of vegetables including tomatoes, chilies, herbs, eggplants, snow peas, lettuce, broccoli, and watermelon. The community orchard, located in the middle of the neighborhood near the playground, produces peaches, plums, almonds, dates, citrus fruits, dates, and apricots. This has brought more neighbors together, stressed a more sustainable system of local food production, created a gathering place (there are weekly potlucks and regular work parties), and become a news and gossip hub with a community bulletin board.

The Lancasters have even created a small nature park in the inner city. "We grow native species once common around Tucson, but now lost to blading (bulldozers) and development," says Brad. "It brings a piece of the desert back to the inner city."

These energetic visionaries have also established a monthly neighborhood newsletter, mailed out to everyone in the neighborhood. "The City pays for printing and mailing," says Lancaster, "which is a great service, because the newsletter keeps everyone current and connected. Anyone can submit articles, art, or stories." The newsletter reaped other benefits as well. For example, it "greatly reduced ridiculous rumors, speculation, and backstabbing, as folks know what is going on. It has also enabled us to mobilize volunteers for projects and push city and county officials to recognize our issues and positions."

But there's still more. In recent years the neighbors have established an artists' cooperative in a nearby abandoned warehouse. "These low-cost live/work spaces and the creativity of those within them has created an unofficial and vibrant community center with ongoing classes, concerts, workshops, services, art shows, theater, bike repair/rental/sales, and more. Nothing had to be built, it only had to be opened and made affordable."

When asked about the motivation for his efforts, Brad is eloquent. "I want to live in a vibrant community," he says. "I want to live where people know each other, wave to one another, talk to and help each other, work to make things better, and play together. I want to live in a community that encourages and celebrates diversity and creativity. I want to live in a community with a sense of place connected to the local cultures, history, and bioregion. I want to live in a community that leaves the car behind to welcome leisurely strolls and bike rides. I want to live in a community where we grow much of our food and share it through potluck dinners. I want to live in a community that creates rather than extracts resources. As I want such a community, I work to create it and support it."

It's hard to argue with success.

• • •

The Lancasters and their Tucson neighbors are just one among many examples we've found. Be sure to read more about N Street Cohousing and L.A. Eco-Village on the web; they are superb illustrations of what can happen in existing communities.

Given time, we can transform our neighborhoods dramatically, creating vibrant communities we're proud to belong to. All we need is the vision, the tools, and the willpower ... and a little cooperation from city hall.

The community stagnates without the impulse of the individual. The impulse dies away without the sympathy of the community.

WILLIAM JAMES

10

Taking Care in the Neighborhood

S OMETIMES WE SAY THE WORDS "take care" without much thought as we proceed through our daily routines. "Who's going to take care of the kids?" we ask. "Who's going to take care of the dog, or the lawn?" "Take care," we say as a quick farewell as we start up the car.

Ideally, there's more to it than that, and we hope this book gives you ideas that will bring more meaning and intention to these two small words. Certainly a neighborhood that has become more sustainable takes care in many different ways.

For example, in one Seattle neighborhood a man offered to watch his neighbors' house while they were on vacation. When he checked on the house after a heavy rainstorm, he discovered that the basement had flooded. This is the kind of guy you want to trust your house with because he pumped the water out of the basement, dried the items that had gotten wet, cleaned the carpet, and repainted the walls! In another Seattle neighborhood a resident observed that fallen apples created a rodent problem each year, so he organized his neighbors to make cider using a press he rented with a small grant from the city.

These stories and many more come from Jim Diers, a neighborhood activist who directed Seattle's cutting-edge Department of Neighborhoods for several decades. With a staff that grew steadily from four people and a shoestring budget in 1988 to a hundred people and a $12 million budget in 2002, Diers helped maintain a balance of power between community and government. Under three different mayors, his role was, in his words, to "preserve and enhance Seattle's diverse neighborhoods, empower people to make positive contributions, and bring government closer to the people."

Now he focuses on building community in one particular neighborhood and spends lots of time on the road, giving talks about what makes Seattle's program successful. "Since 1989," says Diers, "the city's

Neighborhood Matching Fund has backed more than 2,000 projects. Community groups have contributed thousands of hours to create new parks, reforest open space, plant street trees, develop community gardens, restore streams and wetlands, install information kiosks, build traffic circles, pilot community school programs, document community histories, develop neighborhood plans, create murals and banners and sculpture, and much, much more. These projects are visible in every neighborhood of Seattle."

He tells the story of a mural artist who was hired by a neighborhood association to brighten up a blank wall on the side of a building. When the artist came back to touch up the mural, a policeman stopped to ask what he was doing. Because the neighborhood valued the mural, a resident who thought it was being defaced asked the police to check into it — another example of taking care in the neighborhood.

Talking with Jim was one of the highlights of our research because his neighborhood success stories dramatically verified our conviction that when neighbors become active, they can really make something happen. "Taking care" (and being taken care of) becomes a way of life. If neighborhoods are like flowering plants that blossom when they are well-tended, they can also be thought of as seed producers. The lessons learned in one neighborhood can germinate in another neighborhood a thousand miles or more away. For example, Diers put us in touch with Cherie Murphy, the neighborhood liaison in the Chicago suburb of Elgin.

We asked her what the City of Elgin was doing to promote Superbia!-type neighborhoods. "Quite a lot," she responded. "We're working with citizens to bring in the kind of retail they want, for one thing. We're trying to provide better public transportation for the neighborhoods, to reduce some of the congestion on our roads. And we're building zoning flexibility into our comprehensive plan, which will be updated this year."

Having Fun

Cherie also told us about the "Popcorn and Planning" events she helps facilitate in Elgin. City officials sit down with neighborhood leaders to watch video programs about sustainable communities and then discuss creative options for their own neighborhoods. It was Cherie's story about the Blue Tulip that caught our imagination, however. In one of Elgin's neighborhoods, someone had scavenged a four-foot-tall wooden tulip at a garage sale and "transplanted it" in a friend's lawn as a prank. The tulip passed from lawn to lawn and gradually came to be a symbol for a party. "It would appear mysteriously on someone's lawn, which meant that person had to host a Friday night party," Cherie said. "People from all over town now go looking for the

Blue Tulip, and everyone's welcome to come to the party. Even for political foes, Blue Tulip parties are a safe space — a place of inherent equality."

The Blue Tulip is a symbol of another trend in municipal government — the need to have a sense of humor and celebrate daily life. One Seattle example is the Fremont Troll, which guards a neighborhood park under the Aurora Bridge. Proposed by the neighborhood as publicly funded art, the Troll fought his way through the application process, ultimately becoming an offbeat tourist attraction. In one hand he clutches an actual Volkswagen Bug, as if he's just snatched it off the bridge.

In these times of transition, we believe fun needs to be a high priority in all neighborhood efforts. Seattle's neighborhood groups celebrate just about any occasion, asking, "Why have a meeting when you can have a party?" As a result, meetings are typically potlucks, where neighbors can socialize. Even "grunt work," like turning the compost pile, is referred to as a "compost social." One couple decided to get married in their community garden, where they had met. Jim Diers recalls, "In lieu of traditional wedding gifts, they asked all their guests to bring something for the compost pile, which Kate and Jon would mix in as part of the wedding. Wedding compost ingredients came from all over, among them a banana peel from Julia Child, buffalo droppings, and even something (indirectly) from George W. Bush: a tax refund check."

On the official Seattle holiday, Neighbor Appreciation Day (celebrated in the doldrums of February), neighborhood festivals

10.1: The Blue Tulip became an Elgin, Illinois, symbol for "open house." Now another Elgin neighborhood has begun a similar tradition: "Painted Lady" parties are announced by a brightly colored mannequin. Credit: Cherie Murphy

10.2: One Blue Tulip party was a White Elephant sale that raised several hundred dollars to help pay a neighbor's medical expenses. A more formal party that followed raised $30,000 for the family. Credit: Cherie Murphy.

are held all over the city, and cards designed by kids are available free from city hall. In 2001, 18,000 cards were not enough to fill all the requests.

Why shouldn't we have fun in the places we live? Why shouldn't we show movies on the side of a neighborhood building, post Worm Crossing signs at community gardens, and sponsor paper airplane contests off the roof of the school (the kid whose plane makes the longest flight doesn't have to help clean up)?

Learning to be Resourceful

Another aspect of "taking care" involves the wise use of resources. Here again, the city of Seattle is an example, as it made resourcefulness a mission. Its comprehensive plan, "Towards a Sustainable Seattle," emphasizes getting the greatest value out of each resource.

After the September 11, 2001, terrorist attacks, about a million flowers — 80 cubic yards — encircled Seattle's International Fountain. Instead of taking the wilting flowers to the dump, though, gardeners from the Interbay community garden volunteered to compost them. They separated flowers from poignant messages, children's drawings, stuffed animals, flags, and candle stubs; then 80 gardeners spent a whole day hauling, chopping, and mixing — creating compost for a peace garden.

Other projects are designed to make full use of a locally abundant resource — rain. In the Cascade neighborhood, a downspout carries roof runoff down the side of a commercial building and into a second-story window for use by a glass studio. The rest of the water continues down to street level, where it enters a cistern adjacent to the sidewalk. Gravity carries water from the cistern through a hose to holding tanks that release the water into a series of planter boxes that run the length of the sidewalk.

At the neighborhood's community garden, rainwater from the roof of the community center flows into four dozen 55-gallon barrels and an underground cistern with a capacity of 5,000 gallons. This "captured water" supplies 40 percent of the water used by the garden, and it will soon flush the toilets in the community center.

Seattle's Tree Fund pays for thousands of trees that are planted by volunteers every year. According to Diers, "A person simply recruits five or more neighbors who would like to plant trees in front of their houses or in a nearby park and notifies the Department of Neighborhoods. In 2001 the Tree Fund was used by 134 neighborhood groups to plant 4,400 trees throughout Seattle."

There are many non-profit and for-profit organizations that help neighborhoods become more resourceful and sustainable. For example, Denver's Neighborhood Resource Center stimulates activism in both urban and suburban neighborhoods. NRC's Jane Hanley sees neighbors becoming empowered and energetic through neighborhood problem-solving projects. One project in Longmont, Colorado, focused on high school students who created a nuisance by loitering at the local strip mall. "They simply had no place to go," says Jane. "As part of our problem-solving process, in which the kids participated, the idea of a café for the students emerged. A church donated space, and local businesses and organizations helped with the funding. The neighborhood provided its own solution."

Sowing the Seeds of Superbia!

Neighborhoods are the flesh and bones of cities, towns, and even large, amorphous subdivisions. It makes sense for local governments to fund neighborhood efforts, because neighborhoods *are* the town or city. The good news is that

10.3, 10.4 and 10.5: A scenario for creating a village square around what was once a vacant lot. Sometimes it just takes a good idea ...
Credit: Urban Advantage, Berkeley, California.

neighborhood matching-fund programs like Seattle's — in which volunteer labor and private contributions match municipal capital — now exist in Victoria, B.C.; Shoreline, Washington; Eugene, Oregon; Santa Monica, California; Salt Lake City, Utah; Las Vegas, Nevada; Wichita, Kansas; Houston, Texas; Madison, Wisconsin; Detroit, Michigan; Cleveland, Ohio; Buffalo, New York; Sarasota, Florida, and dozens of other towns and cities.

These programs will help create the right "seedbed" for the germination of Superbia! Flexibility tops the list of conditions: zoning codes, traffic patterns, and comprehensive plans need to be flexible enough to allow innovations like street narrowing, neighborhood stores, and "outbuildings" such as rentals, granny flats, and late-teen apartments. Residents need to be flexible in their thinking, too, and willing to try out new ideas at the grassroots level, where cultural change is born. Lenders need to be flexible because the New Suburbanism we're hoping to spark will require capital. In many cases, getting past the first cost of an innovative design or device will return a steady stream of savings — at a better rate than stocks or bonds. For example, home improvement loans can put cost-saving solar panels on suburban roofs, front-loading washing machines in the laundry rooms, and hybrid cars in garages, making each neighborhood stronger.

We believe Thomas Jefferson was right on the mark a few centuries ago when he wrote, "I am not an advocate for frequent changes in laws and constitution, but laws and institutions go hand in hand with the progress of the human mind... We might as well require a man to wear the same coat that fitted him when he was a boy...." We advocate revisions in certain zoning, planning, and traffic engineering rules so that neighborhoods can become more sustainable.

Planners in Burlington, Vermont, and Belmont, North Carolina, would likely agree. Innovative ordinances there provide guidelines for sustainable subdivisions, encouraging narrow streets to slow traffic, narrow setbacks to bring houses closer to sidewalks, and stores and shops in residential areas. City councilors in Port Arthur, Texas, and Boulder, Colorado, implemented ordinances for preserving solar access. This means one neighbor can't build or plant trees in such a way that it might block another neighbor's potential solar energy. In Carpenteria, California, there are regulations governing the planting, care, and maintenance of trees. The states of Maryland, Oregon, Wisconsin, Minnesota, Illinois, and Arizona have created particularly innovative planning regulations that prescribe "smart growth," New Urbanism, and many of the Superbia! steps from this book.

In conversations with municipal officials across the country, we heard about dozens of other innovations. Like a huge ocean liner making a 90-degree turn, planning and zoning regulations are beginning to change course to enable neighborhood retail, work/live arrangements, and resident-requested changes in both streets and landscapes. We're not claiming that every town council will be wildly enthusiastic about Superbia!, but at least they will have to listen if a neighborhood group speaks with one voice.

Citizen Planning

Another way to sow the seeds of Superbia! is to become a "citizen planner." There are now many courses available (do a web search for "citizen planner") that educate residents about the key features of their neighborhoods and how they might be improved. Some offer certificates so graduates are qualified to serve on citizen-staffed planning commissions. Harrison Rue, a citizen-planning guru, says, "The habit of looking at the built environment through a windshield has led our public decision-making processes for more than two generations."

Rue's central thesis is that citizens can take control of reshaping their communities and lives. "We've handed over to professionals all the decisions about how and where our communities should grow and what they should look like. We're stuck living with the consequences. For example, our roads are designed by traffic engineers unconcerned with life on the streets."

Rue has observed that solutions are born when citizens become educated. "As a builder/developer for twenty-something years, I've come to view the connections among people, businesses, towns, and natural systems from the standpoint of urban design — the physical relationship of buildings, blocks, streets, parks, civic and commercial structures. I believe average citizens and public officials can learn to look at their communities in a similar fashion and be motivated to act on this knowledge."[1]

In New York, Florida, Hawaii, and Virginia, Rue has worked with existing neighborhoods to help create "real towns for real people." His philosophy is a very green and grassroots one. "If I can learn to make sense of appropriate building siting, street widths and turning radii, street tree placement and sustainable building technology, identifying neighborhood centers and edges, and maximizing scarce resources, then so can almost everyone.

"Time and again I've seen average citizens 'get' and embrace sophisticated concepts far quicker than educated professionals stuck in 'the way we've always done it' mode. Obtaining zoning approvals and funding often requires educating local officials, bankers, builders, and neighborhood activists about how historically based, human-scaled design can generate comprehensive solutions."

He cites the example of rising taxes to pay for aging suburban infrastructure. "The costs of building and repairing sewage infrastructure could be reduced with a little creativity. For example, we wouldn't have to worry about where to put sewer pumping stations or how long large main pipes would last if we created a network of neighborhood-based, self-contained, wetland-habitat, mini-treatment plants like the one John Todd designed to take care of the restrooms at the National Audubon Society's Corkscrew Swamp Sanctuary near Immokalee, Florida."

As I (Dave) was writing this last chapter, my neighbors and I were actively proposing that our town acquire a small, elevated parcel of land near our property in order to create a small neighborhood park that would preserve the great views of the foothills. A developer had already submitted a plan, but we managed to persuade him that he could make just as much money by selling the lot for open space.

We arranged an appointment with the planning office; formed an official-sounding Coalition to Preserve Open Space; designed letterhead with that title; wrote letters and e-mails to city council members; took photographs of the site and drew several scenarios of the possible size and shape of the park; put together fact sheets and information packets; got 400 neighbors to sign a petition of support and pledge about $2,000 of personal money; then finally presented our proposal to the citizens' advisory board and city council.

Our campaign lasted several months, and we learned many things along the way. For example, we discovered that the phrase "pocket park" was not popular with city officials or advisory boards because small parks are inconvenient to maintain and are thought to be underused. We began to call the land an "overlook" instead. We also discovered the great value of inviting the mayor, council members, and advisory board members out to the property, one by one, to personally offer them our perspectives on why this land was a great investment. As we stood shoulder to shoulder with them, looking out over the vista, we'd point out all the potential users, from dog walkers and cyclists to sunrise lovers and moms with strollers. Instead of saying, "Not in my backyard," we said, "Here's an idea."

To our great delight, our efforts paid off. Most of the decision makers complimented our neighborhood's advocacy and agreed to use $120,000 of bond revenues to buy the land. The mayor made a point of saying that our effort was "democracy at its best." We felt like we were taking care of all future residents of our neighborhood, whose view will be the foothills rather than the back walls of townhouses.

Getting It Right to Begin With

A *Newsweek* article I tucked away a few years ago is titled "15 Ways to Fix the Suburbs." It focuses on the New Urbanism, an architectural and town-planning movement that brings people back into the picture in suburban and urban developments. The article includes fixes like Give Up Big Lawns, Bring Back the Corner Store, Make the Streets Skinny, Mix Housing Types, Link Work to Home, Think Green, Make a Town Center.[2]

In other words, the New Urbanism espouses many of the same principles we've proposed in this book, except it sees them happening in *new* developments. Before writing this book, we interviewed most of the founders of New Urbanism in person, asking them what can be done in *existing* suburbs. Peter Calthorpe told us about projects at the edges of suburbia, like The Crossings, his transit-oriented development in Mountain View, California, that successfully replaced an extinct mall with a diverse, compact neighborhood. For many years Calthorpe has been an advocate of Pedestrian Pockets, small communities attached to a railway like leaves on a stem.

When we talked to author James Kunstler, who presents the principles of New Urbanism in *Home from Nowhere*, he predicted that in 20 or 30 years the prairie castles and McMansions of posh suburban developments "will be occupied by six or eight families, and where the juniper bushes now are, there will be tidy, productive rows of tomatoes and squash."

Victor Dover, Elizabeth Plater-Zyberk, Jonathan Rose, Andres Duany, Elizabeth Moule, and other innovative architects and designers we interviewed all agreed that something needs to happen in existing neighborhoods, but they didn't seem to know exactly what. After all, their work typically begins when a neighborhood needs to be built or rebuilt. We realized that it wasn't architects and town builders who will reinvent existing urban and suburban neighborhoods, but the residents themselves — people like you and me. That's why we decided to write this book, to prepare the seedbed for the germination of "New Suburbanism."

But we are very much in favor of getting it right in the design phase. Why not offer homebuyers something new on the menu that can enrich their lives? If we think back to the 1970s, we remember how smug American

10.6: A mixed-use light-rail stop within walking distance of many homes is a true community asset. Credit: Lyle Grant

car manufacturers were about the automobile market. They believed that all Americans wanted big, powerful cars, or at least could be trained to want them. But then the compact, fuel-efficient designs of Toyota, Subaru, BMW, and Saab convinced them they were missing a full quarter of the market.

It's the same with houses and neighborhoods in the 2000s. Books with titles like *The Not So Big House*, *The Natural House* (Dan's book), and *Cohousing* are selling well, and developers like Richard Holt and Jim Soules are finding a niche by essentially creating Superbia! from scratch. Holt and his colleagues built Fairview Village, a New Urbanist-type village on the outskirts of Portland, Oregon. Says Holt, "Because Fairview Village is an expansion of an existing suburban community, we knew we had to engage the public and key decision makers in creating a consensus-based village plan. More than 75 stakeholders participated in our three-day design workshop, which produced a regulating plan, a new zoning code, and architectural guidelines."

"We moved away from the traditional approach of putting up solitary structures on individual lots and concentrated instead on building a cohesive community," he continues. "To avoid the mistakes of post-World War II suburban sprawl, we looked at notable historic garden suburbs — Mariemont in Cincinnati, Shaker Heights in Cleveland, and Country Club District in Kansas City — famous for blending residences with neighborhood shops."[3]

In Fairview Village, the town center is within a quarter mile of 95 percent of the village's houses, so residents can walk to the library, the post office, or the coffee shop. This gives the new development an award-winning sense of place and a high degree of resident satisfaction. It was municipal flexibility that made it happen. Innovative zoning codes allowed houses to be closer to the street, common green parks to substitute for expansive yards, and retail to be located right in the neighborhood.

The Cottage Company, which builds compact neighborhoods in the suburbs of Seattle, is another great example of what might be called "zonesmithing." The builders have convinced a handful of suburban governments to adopt the "Cottage Code." This flexible zoning allows small (e.g., 1,200 to 1,500 square feet), well-built homes to be arranged around a commons at densities twice as high as normal. In Kirkland, for example, not-so-big houses are allowed in conjunction with amenities such as mandatory porches — which in Washington are three-season outdoor rooms — a maximum house height of 25 feet, clustered parking, and a common courtyard.

According to Jim Soules, "We've seen a high level of satisfaction among the people who now occupy our neighborhoods. For example, not a single resident has complained about the parking, which typically is 100 to 140 feet from a house. They like what they get for the minor inconvenience — a quiet, car-free courtyard and the sense of an outdoor room. They also like the common buildings in our projects and the quality construction we insist on, with lots of details like tile insets on front porches and hardwood floors inside. These homes won't be tear-downs."

Soules believes the cottages, sometimes half the national average of 2,200 square feet — meet a growing demand for single-occupancy, low-maintenance, detached homes. "We call it 're-sizing' rather than 'downsizing,'" he says. "Each cottage has a private yard as well as the common area that includes perennial flower borders, lawn, fruit trees, and a tool shed." Because fewer tons of building materials are used in each cottage, and because they are 15 percent above the strict Washington insulation standards, the houses are more sustainable than conventional homes. Soules adds. "People like the 'resized' energy bills they get living in our cottages, that's for sure."

10.7, 10.8, & 10.9: A scenario for sustainable growth on the Colfax Avenue "strip" in Lakewood, Colorado. Credit: Urban Advantage, Berkeley, California.

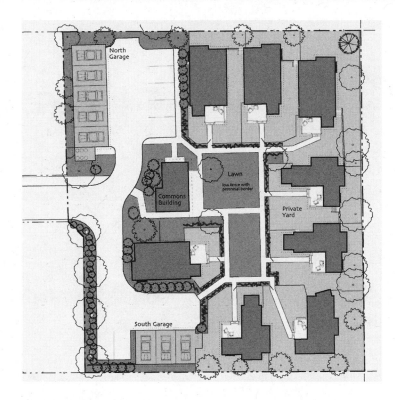

10.10: The Cottage Company's Greenwood Avenue cottage development includes clustered parking, a central courtyard, and a common building with a dining room and workshop. Credit: <www.rosschapin.com>.

Whether we're talking New Urbanism or New Suburbanism, changes in architecture as well as attitude can help create a more sustainable way of life and an enduring human presence — a goal many people now strive to achieve.

Good-bye for Now

We hope this book helps readers become planners and activists in their own neighborhoods and then reach out to the wider community. Creating sustainable suburbs will require coordination with adjacent neighborhoods, with regional transportation officials, watershed experts, zoning and planning departments, and elected officials, among others. The result will be neighborhoods that come to life! Our research shows that creating more sustainable neighborhoods can also create a stronger sense of community, save money, preserve resources, and make life more enjoyable. It shouldn't surprise anyone if Superbia! begins to spread across the North American landscape like a sunrise. We sincerely hope it comes soon to the neighborhood you live in. Take care!

Dan Chiras   *Dave Wann*

Chapter 1

1. Adam Rome, *The Bulldozer in the Countryside: Suburban Sprawl and the Rise of American Environmentalism*, Cambridge University Press, 1995, p. 19.
2. Bruce Katz, "The Exit Ramp Economy," *Boston Globe*, May 13, 2001.
3. Ibid.
4. "Paving the Planet: Cars and Crops Competing for Land," Earth Policy Institute [online], [cited February 14, 2001] <www.earth-policy.org/Alerts/Alert12.htm>
5. Cynthia Girling and Kenneth Helphand, *Yard Street Park: The Design of Suburban Open Space*, John Wiley & Sons, 1994, p. 38.
6. Chad Kimmel, "Revisiting Levittown, Pennsylvania: Changes within a Postwar Planned Community," *Proteus: A Journal of Ideas*, Vol. 18, No. 2, Fall 2001, pp. 89–96.
7. Victor Lebow quoted in Michael F. Jacobson and Laurie Ann Mazur, *Marketing Madness: A Survival Guide for a Consumer Society*, Westview Press, 1995, p. 191.

Chapter 2

1. Gans, Herbert. *The Levittowners*, Columbia University Press, 1982.
2. Donald Appleyard, *Livable Streets*, University of California Press, 1981, p. 22.
3. Personal conversation with Dr. Richard Jackson, October 2002.
4. Richard Kordesh "Community for Children," *National Civic Review*, Fall 1991.
5. James Hibberd, "Home Sweet Clone," *Westword*, October 18–24, 2001, p. 25.

Chapter 3

1. Andres Duany, Elizabeth Plater-Zyberk, and Jeff Speck, *Suburban Nation*, North Point Press, 2001, p. 63.
2. Ibid, p. 64.
3. Donald Chen, "The Science of Smart Growth," *Scientific American*, December 2000, p. 84.
4. Peter Calthorpe and Sim Van der Ryn, *Sustainable Communities: A New Design Synthesis for Cities, Suburbs, and Towns*, Sierra Club Books, 1986, p. 42.
5. Jon Schulz, "The Sustainable Suburb: Characteristics Based on Basic Principles," Integrated Living Systems, May 2001, p. 5.
6. Anton C. Nelessen, and James Constantine, "Understanding and Making Use of People's Visual Use Preferences," *Planning Commissioner's Journal* 9, March/April 1993. A reprint of this article is available as part of the Design and Aesthetics reprint set from *Planning Commissioner's Journal*, Box 4295, Burlington VT 05406. <www.plannersweb.com>
7. "15 Ways to Fix the Suburbs," *Newsweek*, May 15, 1995, p. 46.

Chapter 4

1. Cynthia Girling and Kenneth Helphand, *Yard Street Park: The Design of Suburban Open Space*, John Wiley & Sons, 1994, p. 36.
2. Ibid.
3. Adam Rome, *The Bulldozer in the Countryside: Suburban Sprawl and the Rise of American Environmentalism*, Cambridge University Press, 1995, p. 46.
4. Ibid., p. 61.
5. F. Herbert Bormann, Diana Balmori, and Gordon T. Geballe, *Redesigning the American Lawn: A Search for Environmental Harmony*, Yale University Press, 1993, pp. 56–60.
6. Karen Schell, "Virtual Village Homes," <www.sustainablepetaluma.net/fieldtrips/villagehomes.html, 2002>
7. Bill Browning and Kim Hamilton, "Village Homes: A Model Solar Community Proves Its Worth," *In Context: A Quarterly of Humane Sustainable Culture*, Spring 1993, p. 33.

8. Personal interview with Judy and Michael Corbett, 1996, for "Building Connections," a video teleconference produced for the American Institute of Architects.

Chapter 10

1. Harrison Rue, "Real Towns for Real People," *Terra Nova: A Journal of Nature and Culture*, Vol. 1, No. 4, 1997.
2. "15 Ways to Fix the Suburbs," *Newsweek*, May 15, 1995, p. 46.
3. For more on Fairview Village, visit the website

Resource Guide

THIS RESOURCE GUIDE CONTAINS lists of books, articles, videos, magazines, newsletters, and organizations that will help you and your neighbors learn more about creating sustainable neighborhoods. We have included general references on subjects such as cohousing and ecovillages at the beginning of the guide, then listed the remainder of the resources by Suggestion Number. Because addresses, phone numbers, and websites change from time to time, we have tried to provide multiple access points for each listing. If a website or phone number is no longer in service, you may want to try writing.

Cohousing, Ecovillages, New Towns, and Suburbs

Publications

Alexander, Christopher, Sara Ishikawa, and Merry Silverstein, *A Pattern Language: Towns, Buildings, Construction*, Oxford University Press, 1977. A classic with great insights on people-friendly design.

Arendt, Randall G., *Conservation Design for Subdivisions*, Island Press, 1996. An interesting look at ways to create more environmentally sensitive subdivisions.

Baxandall, Rosalyn, and Elizabeth Ewen, *Picture Windows: How the Suburbs Happened*, Basic Books, 2000. Interesting look at the history of suburban development.

Beldon, Russonello and Stewart, *Choices Between Asphalt and Nature: Americans Discuss Sprawl*, The Biodiversity Project and The Nature Conservancy, 1998. Findings of 20 focus groups across the United States that show how Americans feel about life in the suburbs.

Boehland, Jessica, "Cohousing: How Green is My Village?" *Environmental Building News* 11, no. 9, 2002, 1, pp. 10–17. Available from BuildingGreen, Inc. <www.BuildingGreen.com>. Great overview with loads of valuable information.

Chiras, Daniel D., "Cohousing: A Model for the Suburbs" *Mother Earth News*, June/July 2002, p. 57. A brief look at cohousing that explains what cohousing communities are and how we can benefit from them.

Chiras, Daniel D., "From Suburbia to Superbia!" *Mother Earth News*, June/July 2002, pp. 54–56. An overview of ways to make suburbs more people-friendly and environmentally sustainable.

Communities Directory: A Guide To Intentional Communities and Cooperative Living, Fellowship for Intentional Community, 2000. Includes cohousing and other intentional communities.

Corbett, Judy, and Michael Corbett, *Designing Sustainable Communities: Learning from Village Homes*, Island Press, 2000. Learn from two pioneers of the movement.

Duany, Andres, Elizabeth Plater-Zyberk, and Jeff Speck, *Suburban Nation: The Rise of Sprawl and the Decline of the American Dream*, North Point Press, 2000. A must-read.

Christian, Diane L., *Creating a Life Together: Practical Tools to Grow Ecovillages and Intentional Communities*, New Society Publishers, 2003. Great resource.

Hanson, Chris, *The Cohousing Handbook*, Hartley and Marks, 1996. A great book for people who want to learn more about cohousing or start their own cohousing community.

Hildur, Jackson, and Karen Svensson, eds., *Ecovillage Living; Restoring the Earth and Her People*, Green Books, 2002. A full-color guide to ecovillages around the world.

McCamant, Kathryn, Charles Durrett, and Ellen Hertzman, *Cohousing: A Contemporary Approach to Housing Ourselves*, 2nd ed., Ten Speed Press, 1994. Very thorough examination of cohousing communities and the steps needed to establish one.

Norwood, Ken, and Kathleen Smith, *Rebuilding Community in America: Housing for Ecological Living, Personal Empowerment, and the New Extended Family*, Shared Living Resource Center, 1995. A valuable discussion of what it means to live cooperatively.

Roseland, Mark, Maureen Cureton, Heather Wornell, and Hazel Henderson, *Toward Sustainable Communities: Resources for Citizens and Their Governments*, New Society Publishers, 1998. One of the best resources for creating livable, sustainable communities.

Organizations

Beddington Zero Energy Development, c/o Peabody Trust, 45 Westminster Bridge Road, London, UK, SE1 7JB. Phone: 020 7922 0239. Website. <www.bedzed.org.uk>. For information on a truly inspiring ecovillage in the United Kingdom.

Center for a New American Dream, 6930 Carroll Avenue, Suite 900, Takoma Park, MD 20912. Phone: (301) 891•3683 or 1 (877) 68•DREAM. Website: <www.newdream.org/contact.html>. Great site for resources and ideas on sustainable living.

The Cohousing Network, P.O. Box 2584, Berkeley, CA 94702. Phone: (510) 486•2656. Website: <www.cohousing.org>. Offers a wealth of information on cohousing, including a list of cohousing communities in various stages of development, with contact information. It also provides a connection to consultants and developers. Check out the Cohousing Network's web page for a list of cohousing organizations in other countries and various regions, and for Organizational Resources.

Congress for a New Urbanism, The Hearst Building, 5 Third Street, Suite 725, San Francisco, CA 94103-3296. Phone: (415) 495•2555. Website: <www@cnu.org>. This non-profit group actively promotes New Urbanism, development based on the neighborhood model.

Global Ecovillage Network Website: <www.gaia.org/>. U.S. Contact: EcoVillage Network of the Americas, EarthArt Village/Institute, 64001 County Road DD, Moffat, CO 81143. Phone: (719) 256•4221. Website: <http://ena.ecovillages.org>. Provides a wealth of information on ecovillages in your area and around the world.

Hockerton Housing Project Trading Ltd., The Watershed, Gables Drive, Hockerton, Southwell, Nottinghamshire, U.K., NG25 0QU. For information on a small housing development that incorporated many of the environmental aspects of Superbia!

The Trust for Public Land, 116 New Montgomery Street, Fourth floor, San Francisco, CA 94105. Phone: (415) 495•4014. Website: <www.tpl.org>. Provides a wealth of information on the protection of land for parks, gardens, greenbelts, and riverways, all vital to successful and livable communities.

Urban Land Institute, 1025 Thomas Jefferson Street NW, Suite 500 West, Washington DC 20007. Phone: (800) 321•5011. Website: <www.uli.org>. Provides information on urban revitalization, smart growth to limit sprawl and its impacts, and sensible transportation.

Cohousing Consultants

Abraham and Associates, 1460 Quince Avenue, Suite 102, Boulder, CO 80304. Phone: (303) 413•8066. Website: <www.abrahampaiss.com/>. Provides public relations and community-building expertise.

The Cohousing Company (Charles Durrett and Kathryn McCamant), 1250 Addison Street #113, Berkeley, CA 94702. Phone: (510) 549•9980. Website: <www.cohousingco.com>. Pioneers of the cohousing movement, this firm works with resident groups and developers to form, facilitate, design, and build cohousing communities.

Cohousing Resources, LLC, 9813 NE Murden Cove Drive, Bainbridge Island, WA 98110. Phone: (206) 842•9160. Website: <www.cohousingresources.com>. Has assisted more than 35 cohousing groups across the country with all aspects of the cohousing development process.

Kraus-Fitch Architects, Inc., Environmentally Inspired Design, 110 Pulpit Hill Road, Amherst, MA 01002. Phone: (413) 549•5799. Website: <www.krausfitch.com/>. Integrates architecture with community, environment, and quality of life. Offers a full range of services with an emphasis on ecologically sound and socially responsible design.

Shared Living Resource Center, Parker Street #9, Berkeley, CA 94704•2841. Phone: (510) 548•6608. Website: <www.sharedliving.org/>. Focuses on ecologically sustainable villages.

Wonderland Hill Development Company, 745 Poplar Avenue, Boulder, CO 80304. Phone: (303) 449•3232. Website: <www.whdc.com/>. Largest cohousing developers in the U.S.

New Urbanist/ New Suburbanist Builders

The Cottage Company, LLC, 8215 41st Avenue NE, Seattle, WA 98115. Phone: (206) 525•0835. E-mail jim@cottagecompany.com. A development and construction company based in Seattle, Washington, and focused on the implementation of "pocket neighborhoods" of cottages and "not-so-big" homes.

Holt & Haugh, Inc., 1200 NW Naito Parkway, Portland, OR 97209. Phone: (503) 222•5522. This company has been nationally recognized for the development of Fairview Village.

Superbia! Consultants

The Sustainable Suburbs Project at the Sustainable Futures Society. Contact Dave Wann at (303) 216•1281 or Wanndavejr@cs.com or Dan Chiras at (303) 674•9688 or danchiras@msn.com. We offer workshops, seminars, speeches, slide shows, and consultation on creating sustainable suburbs. We're looking for neighborhoods that are interested in partnering with us to obtain funding to pursue the ideas discussed in this book.

Suggestion 1. Sponsor Community Dinners

Magazines

Cohousing Journal, available from The Cohousing Network, P.O. Box 2584, Berkeley, CA 94702. Phone: (510) 486•2656. Website: <www.cohousing.org>. The best source for seeing the day-to-day life in cohousing. Regularly has articles on common meals

Communities Magazine 96 (Fall 1997). This issue contains a number of articles on common meals in cohousing communities. To obtain this issue, contact Diana Christian, 52 Willow Street, Marion, NC 28752•4840. Phone: (828) 652•8517. E-mail: communities@ic.org.

On-line Resources

The Slow Food Movement. Website: <www.slowfood.com>. For information on thinking about food as a way to create community.

For creative ideas on how to get community dinners started, do a search on the web for the phrases "community meals," "common meals," "progressive dinner," and "communal dining."

Suggestion 2. Establish a Community Newsletter, Bulletin Board, and Roster

On-line Resources

Neighbors Aware of Their Environment (NATE) website: <www.geocities.com/neighborsaware/about.html>. This website is a free service designed to allow neighbors to create a free on-line neighborhood bulletin board.

Suggestion 3. Establish a Neighborhood Watch Program

To establish a Neighborhood Crime Watch Program, contact your local police office or county sheriff's office.

On-line Resources

National Sheriff's Association Neighborhood Watch website: <www.usaonwatch.org>. This valuable website offers much useful information on Neighborhood Watch programs. Be sure to check out "Other Resources" for a list of articles and success stories, law enforcement links, federal agency links, and more.

Neighbors Aware of Their Environment (NATE) website: <www.geocities.com/neighborsaware/about.html>. This website is a free service designed to give individuals a chance to inform neighbors of what is going on around their community — for example, to alert one another to potential dangers or crimes.

Suggestion 4. Start Neighborhood Clubs

Organizations

For information on backyard wildlife programs, see resources listed under Suggestion 15.

Suggestion 5. Form Discussion Groups

Publications

Wheatley, Margaret J., *Turning to One Another: Simple Conversations to Restore Hope to the Future*, Berrett-Koehler, 2002. A great book for examining why communication is at the core of community.

Study Circles

Northwest Earth Institute, *Discussion Course on Choices for Sustainable Living: Guidebook*, Northwest Earth Institute (506 SW Sixth Avenue, Suite 1100, Portland, OR 97204. Phone: (503) 227•2807. Website: <www.nwei.org/>, 1999. These discussion courses will build bridges between you and your neighbors. Seven to twelve people meet weekly for about an hour to discuss readings from a course book. Course books, each about 100 to 150 pages in length, contain a diverse collection of essays, articles, and book excerpts organized around weekly themes to create lively discussion.

Seeds of Simplicity, P.O. Box 9955, Glendale, CA 91226. Phone/Fax: (818) 247•4332 or 1 (877)•UNSTUFF. Founder Cecille Andrews says, "Being happier with less focus on trappings is easy when it saves you money, benefits the environment, teaches children meaningful values and helps others in need." Her study circles can help you find this path.

Suggestion 6. Establish a Neighborhood Babysitting Co-op

On-line Resources

Two good websites for setting up a babysitting co-op in your area are: <http://mt.essortment.com/babysittingcoop_rvzh.htm> and <www.geocities.com/babysitting_coop/>.

Suggestion 7. Form an Organic Food Co-op

On-line Resources

Food Co-op Directory website: <www.prairienet.org/co-op/directory/>. A listing of food co-ops in the U.S. and Canada.

Jim Williams' listing of food co-ops website: www.columbia.edu/~jw157/food.coop.html. Includes links to co-ops with web pages.

National Cooperative Business Association website: <www.ncba.coop/ntlfood.cfm>. Listing of food co-op web pages.

University of Wisconsin Center for Cooperatives website: <www.wisc.edu/uwcc/links/foodlinks.html>. Listing of links to food cooperatives: retails, distributors, other lists, and pet food co-ops.

Suggestion 8. Create Car or Van Pools

Publications

Oakland Metro Planning Commission, *Moving Towards More Community-Oriented Transportation Strategies in the Bay Area: A Guide to Getting the Information*, Metropolitan Planning Commission, 1996. This guide discusses improving streetscapes and transit stop designs, and using infill development, mixed-use development, and networks of streets and paths for cyclists and pedestrians.

Organizations

Building Livable Communities through Transportation website: <www.pps.org/Transportation/livable_transportation.htm>. This is an initiative of the Project for Public Spaces, with information on streets, transit, national and regional programs, and publications on transportation and livable communities.

Community Transportation Association of America, 1341 G Street NW, 10th Floor, Washington DC 20005. Phone: (202) 628•1480. Website: <www.ctaa.org/>. Great source of information on environmentally friendly transportation alternatives.

Energy Efficiency and Renewable Energy Network (EREN) transportation website: <www.eere.energy.gov/EE/transportation.html>. Offers information on transportation technologies including alternative fuel infrastructure and reducing miles traveled.

Transportation Alternatives, 115 West 30th Street, Suite 1207, New York, NY 10001. Phone: (212) 629•8080. Website: <www.transalt.org/>. Promotes walking and environmentally sensible transportation.

On-line Resources

Carfree.com. This website provides background information on the concept of car-free cities, discusses related issues, and offers links and lists of print resources on alternatives to automobile transportation.

Suggestion 9. Create a Neighborhood Work-Share Program

Publications

Brandt, Barbara, *Whole Life Economics: Revaluing Daily Life*, New Society Publishers, 1995. An important discussion of values.

Cahn, Edgar S., *No More Throw-Away People: The Co-Production Imperative*, Essential Books, 2000. A discussion of how Time Dollars were developed into a practical and powerful tool for community transformation.

Suggestion 10. Create a Neighborhood Mission Statement

Publications

Kretzman, John P., and John L. McKnight, *Building Communities from the Inside Out: A Path Toward Finding and Mobilizing Community Assets*, ACTA Publications, 1997. Great resource for those wishing to revamp their neighborhood.

Shaffer, Carolyn R., Kristin Anundsen, M. Scott Peck, and Patricia Backlar, *Creating Community Anywhere: Finding Support and Connection in a Fragmented World*, Perigee, 1993.

Suggestion 11. Create a Neighborhood Asset Inventory

Publications

Berman, Morris, *The Reenchantment of the World*, Bantam Books, 1984. Discusses how to become re-connected with one's immediate surroundings.

Sobel, David, *Map-Making with Children: Sense-of-Place Education for the Elementary School Years*, Heineman, 1998. Good introduction to map-making by children, which helps them discover community assets.

Organizations

Center for Understanding the Built Environment (CUBE), 5328 West 67 Street, Prairie Village, KS 66208. Phone: (913) 262•8222. Website: <cubekc.org>. Brings together educators and community partners to effect change that will lead to a quality built and natural environment.

Green Map System, P.O. Box 249, New York, NY 10002. Phone: (212) 674•1631. Website: <www.greenmap.org>. Provides assistance in developing asset inventories, specifically "green" assets in a community.

Suggestion 12. Tear Down Fences

Publications

Cooper Marcus, Clare, "The Neighborhood Approach to Building Community: A Different Perspective on Smart Growth," *Western City Magazine* <westerncity.com>, March 2001. How to create cooperative spaces in your neighborhood.

Drayton, Bill, "Secret Gardens," *The Atlantic Monthly*, June 2000. <www.theatlantic.com/issues/2000/06/drayton.htm>. An excellent article that describes the many benefits of creating community greens.

Organizations

Community Greens, 1700 N Moore Street, Suite 2000, Arlington, VA 22209-1939. Phone: (703) 527•8300. Website: <www.communitygreens.org/>. A non-profit organization that facilitates the development of community greens in residential neighborhoods in the United States.

Suggestion 13. Plant a Community Garden and Orchard

Publications

Abi-Nader, Jeanette, David Buckley, Kendall Dunnigan, and Kristen Markley, "Growing Communities: How to Build Community Through Community Gardening," [online] <www.communitygarden. org/>. Terrific resource for those interested in the social aspects of community gardening.

Ableman, Michael, *On Good Land: The Autobiography of an Urban Farm*, Chronicle Books, 1998. How Ableman preserved a farm that was totally surrounded by suburban development.

Ambler, Wayne, Carol Landa Christensen, Larry Hodgson, Peter Loewer, and Ted Marston, *Treasury of Gardening*, Publications International, 1997. Contains a wealth of information on landscape design that will be useful as you transform your yard into an edible landscape.

Bartholomew, Mel, *Square Foot Gardening*, Rodale Press, 1981. How to optimize your yield on small plots of land.

Bradley, Fern Marshall, ed., *Rodale's All-New Encyclopedia of Organic Gardening*, Rodale Press, 1992. A compendium of organic gardening techniques — a classic.

Butler, Karan Davis, *The Complete Vegetable and Herb Gardener*, Macmillan, 1997. An accessible, comprehensive resource with lots of lists and high-yield approaches.

Chotzinoff, Robin, *People With Dirty Hands*, John Wiley & Sons, 1997. A book that celebrates the passion of gardening: ordinary folks who can't stop growing.

Denckla, Tanya, *The Organic Gardener's Home Reference*, Storey Communications, Inc., 1994. Contains a wealth of information on fruits, nuts, vegetables, herbs, and pest control. A nice book to have on your potting bench or the arm of your easy chair in the winter.

Hemenway, Toby, *Gaia's Garden: A Guide to Home-Scale Permaculture*, Chelsea Green, 2001. A whole-systems approach to gardening.

Jeavons, John, *How to Grow More Vegetables*, 10 Speed Press, 1991. Excellent reference, compiles 30 years of meticulous research on bio-intensive growing.

Payne, Karen, and Deborah Fryman, *Cultivating Community: Principles and Practices for Community Gardening as a Community-Building Tool*, [online] <www.communitygarden.org/>. Discusses how to structure and manage a community garden.

Shapiro, Howard-Yana, and John Harrisson, *Gardening for the Future of the Earth*, Bantam, 2000. Literally grounded in the principles of sustainability.

Smith, Shane, *The Greenhouse Gardener's Companion*, Fulcrum Publishers, 2000. How to operate a solar greenhouse, from planting to harvesting.

Wann, David, *The Zen of Gardening in the High and Arid West*, Fulcrum Publishers, 2003. Tips, tools, and techniques for growing everything from peanuts to poppies.

Organizations

American Community Gardening Association, 100 N 20th Street, 5th Floor, Philadelphia, PA 19103-1495. Phone: (215) 988-8785. Website: <http://aggie-horticulture.tamu.edu>. A non-profit organization that offers a wealth of information on community gardens. Be sure to check out their website for tips on starting a community garden.

City Farmer, Canada's Office of Urban Agriculture, 801 – 318 Homer Street, Vancouver, BC V6B 2V3 Phone: (604) 685-5832. Website: <www.cityfarmer.org>. This site contains information on many topics, and offers resources, including lesson plans, for starting a garden at a local school. Great resource for teachers and interested community members.

National Gardening Association, 1100 Dorset Street, South Burlington, VT 05403. Phone: (800) 538-7476. For information on gardening for kids, log on to their site at <www.kidsgardening.com>.

Suggestion 14. Establish Neighborhood Composting and Recycling

Publications

Martin, Deborah L., *The Rodale Book of Composting*, Rodale Press, 1992. Contains all the fundamental wisdom from half a century of experience.

Stell, Elizabeth, *Secrets to Great Soil: A Grower's Guide to Composting, Mulching, and Creating Healthy, Fertile Soil*, Dimensions Press, 1998. A good, basic resource for learning how to compost.

Organizations

Ecological Engineering and Design, 152 Commonwealth Avenue, Concord, MA 01742-2968. Phone: (978) 369•9440. Website: <www.oldgrowth.org/compost/products/large>. (The Compost Resource Page). Good source of information on composting, among other topics.

Suggestion 15. Plant Trees to Produce a More Favorable Microclimate and Wildlife Habitat

Publications

Damstad, Wenche E., James D. Olson, and Richard T. Forman, *Landscape Ecology: Principles in Landscape Architecture and Land-Use Planning*, Island Press, 1996. A useful textbook on the subject.

Lipkis, Andy, and Katie Lipkis, *The Simple Act of Planting a Tree: Healing Your Neighborhoods, Your City, and Your World*, Tarcher, 1990. A great book from the founder of Tree People, an organization that knows the value of trees.

Moffat, Anne S., Marc Schiler, and the Staff of Green Living, *Energy-Efficient and Environmental Landscaping*, Appropriate Solutions Press, 1994. An excellent reference (though now out of print), with an abundance of information on landscaping strategies and plant varieties suitable for your climate zone.

National Renewable Energy Lab, *Landscaping for Energy Efficiency*, DOE/GO-10095-046, Washington DC: Department of Energy Office of Energy Efficiency and Renewable Energy, 1995. Provides a decent, though somewhat disorganized overview of the topic.

Stein, Sara Bonnett, *Noah's Garden: Restoring the Ecology of Our Own Backyards*, Houghton Mifflin, 1995. Explains how urban and suburban lawns wipe out entire communities of plants and animals, and what we can do about it.

Stein, Sara Bonnett, *Planting Noah's Garden*, Houghton Mifflin, 1997. Shows how people are helping to restore backyard ecosystems.

Striefel, Jan, and Wesley A. Groesbeck, *The Resource Guide to Sustainable Landscapes*, Environmental Resources, Inc., 1995. Excellent resource.

Vivian, John, "The Working Lawn: A Step Beyond an Expanse of Green," *Mother Earth News*, June/July 2001, pp. 66–74. A guide to converting lawn to a productive landscape.

Organizations

Lady Bird Johnson Wildflower Center, 4801 LaCrosse Avenue, Austin, TX 78739. Phone: (512) 292·4200. Website: <www.wildflower.org>. Offers a wealth of information and assistance on planting native wildflowers.

National Arbor Day Foundation, 100 Arbor Avenue, Nebraska City, NE 68410. Website: <www. arborday. org>. Promotes tree-planting efforts in the U.S. and gives free trees to new members

National Wildlife Federation's Backyard Wildlife Habitat Program, 11100 Wildlife Center Drive, Reston, VA 20190-5362. Phone: (703) 438·6000. Website: <nwf.org/backyardwidlifehabitat>. Superb source of information on establishing backyard wildlife habitat program. See the NWF's newsletter, *Habitats*.

Suggestion 16. Replace Asphalt and Concrete With Porous Pavers

Publication

Bay Area Stormwater Management Agencies Association and Tom Richman Associates, *Start at the Source: Design Guidance Manual for Stormwater Quality Protection*, Forbes Custom Publishing, 1997. Although this is designed for the Bay Area, there's much useful advice for other regions as well.

Organizations

Low Impact Development Center, 5010 Sunnyside Avenue, Suite 200, Beltsville, MD 20705. Phone: (301) 982·5559. Website: <http://lowimpactdevelopment.org/>. A non-profit organization dedicated to maintaining and enhancing pre-development hydrologic regime in urban and developing watersheds.

Middlesex County Extension Center, 1066 Saybrook Road, Box 70, Haddam, CT 06438. Phone: (860) 345•4511. Website: <http://nemo.uconn.edu/about.htm>. Good resource with case studies of alternative pavements and surfaces.

Suggestion 17. Establish an Edible Landscape

Publications

Bruchklackher, Ann E., "Mind Your Mulch," *Natural Home*, March/April 2003, pp. 70–71. Available from 201 Fourth Street, Loveland, CO 80537. Website: <www.naturalhomemagazine.com>. A short but informative article on eco-friendly mulches.

Creasy, Rosalind, and Marcia Kier-Hawthorne, *The Complete Book of Edible Landscaping*, Sierra Club Books, 1982. Considered a basic resource on this subject.

Glickman, Marshall, "Xeriscaping for Everyone," *Natural Home*, March/April 2003, pp. 66–69. Great introduction to the topic.

Kourik, Robert, *Designing and Maintaining Your Edible Landscape Naturally*, Metamorphic Press, 1986. Getting started with herbs, berries, and fruits in your yard.

Mollison, B., *Perma-Culture Two: Practical Design for Town and Country in Permanent Agriculture*, Tagari Books, 1979. A seminal work in the field of permaculture.

Also see resources listed under Suggestions 13 and 14.

Suggestion 18. Start or Join a Community-supported Agriculture Program

Publications

BioDynamic Association, *Community Related Agriculture*, BioDynamic Association, n.d. Available from the BioDynamic Association, P.O. Box 550, Kimberton, PA 19422. Phone: (800) 516•7797. A brochure that outlines the organization and planning of community farms, CSA, and subscription farms.

DeMuth, Suzanne, *Community Supported Agriculture (CSA): An Annotated Bibliography and Resource Guide*, Alternative Farming Systems Information Center, 1993. Available from the Alternative Farming Systems Information Center (AFSIC), National Agricultural Library, Beltsville, MD 20705-2351. Phone: (301) 504-6559.

Groh, Trauger, and Steven McFadden, *Farms of Tomorrow: Community Supported Farms, Farm Supported Communities*, BioDynamic Association, 1990; and *Farms of Tomorrow: Revisited*, BioDynamic Association, 1997. Available from the BioDynamic Association, listed above. Basic text and updated version on CSA in general and on several BioDynamic farms in particular.

Henderson, Elizabeth, and Robyn Van En, *Sharing the Harvest: A Guide to Community-Supported Agriculture*, Chelsea Green, 1999. Good introduction to this important subject.

Iowa State University Extension Service, *Community Supported Agriculture: Local Food Systems for Iowa*. (PM 1692). ISU Extension Agency, n.d. Available from ISU Extension Distribution, 119 Printing and Publisher, ISU, Ames, IA 50011-3171. Phone: (515) 294-2945.

Iowa State University Extension Service. *Iowa Community Supported Agriculture Resource Book for Producers and Organizers* (PM 1694). ISU Extension Agency, n.d. Available from ISU Extension Distribution, listed above.

Kane, Deborah, *Maximizing Shareholder Retention in Southeastern CSAs: A Step Toward Long-Term Stability*, Institute of Ecology, 1997. Available from the Institute of Ecology, University of Georgia, Athens, GA 30602-2202.

Milstein, Sarah, "Creating a Market: Community Supported Agriculture," *Mother Earth News*, February 1999. This article is geared to farmers but contains a lot of useful information for members of CSAs.

Towley, Tamsyn, and Chris Beeman, *Our Field: A Manual for Community Shared Agriculture*, University of Guelph, 1994. Available from Tamsyn Towley, University of Guelph, Guelph, ON, Canada N1G 2W1. Phone: (519) 824-4120 ext. 8480. Fax: (519) 763-4686. Covers many important topics.

University of California Cooperative Extension, *Community Supported Agriculture: Making the Connection*, UC Cooperative Extension, n.d. Available from UC Cooperative Extension, Attn: CSA Handbook, 11477 E. Avenue, Auburn, CA 95603. This guidebook covers designing a CSA program, recruiting members, creating production and harvest plans, setting share prices, and dealing with legal issues. Incorporates ideas and strategies of successful CSA farms.

Van En, Robyn, *Basic Formula to Create Community Supported Agriculture*, Van En Center For Community Supported Agriculture, 1992. Available from Van En Center For Community Supported Agriculture, listed under Organizations. An 80-page handbook/start-up manual including sample budgets, job descriptions, community outreach tactics, bibliography, and more.

Van En, Robyn, and Cathy Roth, *Community Supported Agriculture*, Cooperative Extension Publication C-212, University of Massachusetts, n.d. Available from Bulletin Center, Cottage A, Thatcher Way, U of M, Amherst, MA 01003. Phone: (413) 545•2717. A basic introduction to CSA.

Magazines and Newsletters

Biodynamics: A Bimonthly Magazine Centered on Health and Wholeness, BioDynamic Association, P.O. Box 550, Kimberton, PA 19442. Phone: (800) 516•7797. Classifieds offer lists of positions for CSA growers, etc.

The Community Farm: A Voice for Community Supported Agriculture, 3480 Potter Road, Bear Lake, MI 49614. Phone: (616) 889•3216. Contains a lot of practical information on CSA.

Growing for Market: News and Ideas for Market Gardeners, Fairplain Publications, P.O. Box 3747, Lawrence, KS 66046. Phone: (913) 841•2259. Regular stories on CSA.

Videos

CSA: Making a Difference, Van En Center for CSA, c/o Wilson College, 1997. Available from Center for Sustainable Living, 1015 Philadelphia Avenue, Chambersburg, PA 17201. Phone: (717) 264•4141, ext. 3247.

It's Not Just About Vegetables, Downtown Productions and Jan Vandertuin, 1986. Available from Downtown Productions, 22 Railroad Street, Great Barrington, MA 01230. Phone: (413) 528•9395.

Shared Farming: Towards a Sustainable Community, CSA Canada. Available from CSA Canada, Box 353, St. Adolphe, MB, Canada R5A 1A2.

Organizations

Alternative Farming Systems Information Center website: <www.nal.usda.gov/afsic/csa>. This website offers a wealth of information on community supported agriculture, including a link to a site you can use to locate a farm near you.

BioDynamic Association, P.O. Box 550, Kimberton, PA 19442. Phone: (800) 516•7797. Website: <www.his.com/-claymont/bd/assoc.html>. This major proponent of CSA in North America publishes a bimonthly newsletter, sponsors conferences, provides a catalog of resources, and maintains a large CSA database.

CSA Center website: <www.csacenter.org/csastate.htm>. For a list of community-supported agriculture farms in your area, check out this site.

CSA Farm Network, Steve Gilman, 130 Ruckytucks Road, Stillwater, NY 12170. Phone: (518) 583•4613. Promotes CSA in the northeast.

CSA Farm Network West, P.O. Box 363, Davis, CA 95617. Phone: (916) 756•8518. Website: <www.caff.org>. CSA information on the West Coast.

Community Supported Agriculture of North America at the University of Massachusetts Extension website: <www.umass.edu/umext/csa/>. Check out this website for a wealth of information, including an extensive list of resources.

CSA Works, 115 Bay Road, Hadley, MA 01035. Phone: (413)586•5133. Provides assistance to the farmers needed to run efficient CSA enterprises.

Just Food, 625 Broadway, Suite 9C, New York, NY 10012. Phone: (212) 677•1602. Fax: (212) 505•8613. E-mail: justfood@igc.org. Helps connect northeast CSA farmers and New Yorkers; provides start-up and ongoing support to farmers and core group members.

Madison Area Community Supported Agricultural Coalition (MACSAC), 4915 Monona Drive, Suite 304, Monona, WI 53716. Phone: (608) 226•0300. Website: <www.wisc.edu/cias/macsac>. Coalition of community activists, representatives of organizations supporting sustainable agriculture, and farmers in the Madison area that educates the public about CSA; publishes an annual CSA directory; and provides support and networking opportunities to CSA farms.

Robyn Van En Center for Community Supported Agriculture, c/o Wilson College, Center for Sustainable Living, 1015 Philadelphia Avenue, Chambersburg, PA 17201. Phone: (717) 264•4141, ext. 3247.

Provides information, handbook, video, slide show, and information on CSA development and promotion, research compilations, etc.

Suggestion 19. Create a Car-share Program

Organizations

Car Plus, The Studio, 32 The Calls, Leeds, UK, LS2 7EW. Phone: 0113 234 9299. Website: <www.carclubs.org.uk/carplus/index.htm>. A European non-profit organization that works with communities, local authorities, and partner associations to promote and support development of car clubs — car-sharing programs in the United Kingdom. The website contains a wealth of valuable information.

City CarShare. Phone: (415) 995•8588. Website: <www.cityshare.org/about>. A non-profit organization that promotes car-sharing in and around San Francisco.

Flexcar website: <www.flexcar.com>. A company that operates car-share programs in California, Maryland, Oregon, Virginia, Washington DC, and the state of Washington.

Zipcar. Phone: (800) 494•7227. Website: <www.zipcar.com>. A company that operates car-share programs in Boston, New York City, Washington DC, and Denver.

Suggestion 20. Retrofit Homes for Energy Efficiency: Creating Energy-Efficient Buildings

Publications

Carmody, John, Stephen Selkowitz, and Lisa Heschong, *Residential Windows: A Guide to New Technologies and Energy Performance*, Norton, 1996. Extremely important reading for creating energy-efficient homes.

Chiras, Dan, "Retrofitting a Foundation for Energy Efficiency," *The Last Straw* 38, Summer 2002, 10 <www.strawhomes.com>. Describes ways to retrofit foundations to reduce heat loss.

Fine Homebuilding, *The Best of Fine Homebuilding: Energy-Efficient Building*, Taunton Press, 1999. A collection of detailed, somewhat technical, articles on a wide assortment of topics related to energy efficiency including insulation, energy-saving details, windows, housewraps, skylights, and heating systems.

Hurst-Wajszczuk, Joe, "Save Energy and Money — Now," *Mother Earth News*, October/November 2001, pp. 24–33. Useful tips on saving energy in new and existing homes.

Lstiburek, Joe, and Betsy Pettit, *EEBA Builder's Guide — Cold Climate*, Energy Efficient Building Association, 1999. Superb resource for advice on building in cold climates.

Lstiburek, Joe, and Betsy Pettit, *EEBA Builder's Guide — Mixed Humid Climate*, Energy Efficient Building Association, 1999. Superb resource for advice on building in a mixed humid climate

Lstiburek, Joe, and Betsy Pettit, *EEBA Builder's Guide — Hot-Arid Climate*, Energy Efficient Building Association, 1999. Superb resource for advice on building in hot arid climates.

Mumma, Tracy, *Guide to Resource Efficient Building Elements*, National Center for Appropriate Technology, Center for Resourceful Building Technology, 1997. Updated versions are available free online at www.crbt.org. A handy guide to materials that help improve the efficiency of homes and other buildings.

National Association of Home Builders Research Center, *Design Guide for Frost-Protected Shallow Foundations*, NAHB Research Center, 1996. Technical but essential resource on this topic.

Pahl, Greg, *Home Heating Basics*, Chelsea Green, 2003. A useful overview of home heating.

Wilson, Alex, "Windows: Looking through the Options," *Solar Today*, May/June 2001, pp. 36–39. Available from 2400 Central Avenue, Suite G-1, Boulder, CO 80301 <www.ases.org/solar/>. A great overview of windows with a useful checklist for those in the market to buy new windows.

Wilson, Alex, Jennifer Thorne, and John Morrill, *Consumer Guide to Home Energy Savings*, 7th ed., American Council for an Energy-Efficient Economy, 1999. Excellent book, full of information on energy-saving appliances. This book is updated every few years, so be sure to obtain the most recent edition to acquire the most up-to-date data on appliances and other devices.

Yost, Harry, *Home Insulation: Do It Yourself and Save as Much as 40%*, Storey Communications, 1991. Extremely useful book for anyone building his or her own home.

Organizations

American Council for an Energy-Efficient Economy, 1001 Connecticut Avenue NW, Suite 801, Washington DC, 20036. Phone: (202) 429•0063. Website: <www.aceee.org>. Numerous excellent publications on energy efficiency, including *Consumer Guide to Home Energy Savings*.

Building America Program, U.S. Department of Energy, Office of Building Systems, EE-41, 1000 Independence Avenue SW, Washington DC, 20585. Phone: (202) 586•9472. Leaders in promoting energy efficiency and renewable energy to achieve zero energy buildings.

Energy Efficiency and Renewable Energy Clearinghouse, P.O. Box 3048, Merrifield, VA 22116. Phone: (800) 363•3732. Great source of a variety of useful information on energy efficiency.

Energy Efficient Building Association, 490 Concordia Avenue, P.O. Box 22307, Eagen, MN 55122. Phone: (651) 268•7585. Website: <www.eeba.org/>. Offers conferences, workshops, publications and an on-line bookstore.

Global Action Plan, 8 Fulwood Place, London, UK, WC1V 6HG. Phone (020) 7405 5633. Website: www.globalactionplan.org.uk. For information on creating an environmentally friendly household.

Southface Energy Institute, 241 Pine Street, Atlanta, GA 30308. Phone: (404) 872•3549. Website: <www.southface.org/>. Promotes sustainable homes, workplaces, and communities through education, research, advocacy, and technical assistance.

U.S. Department of Energy and Environmental Protection Agency's ENERGY STAR program. Phone: (888) 782•7937. Website: <www.energystar.gov>. Provides information on energy-efficient houses and energy-efficient appliances.

Suggestion 20. Retrofit Homes for Energy Efficiency: Energy-Efficient Heating Systems

Publications

Chiras, Daniel D., *The Solar House: Passive Heating and Cooling*, Chelsea Green, 2002. See Chapter 4 for a discussion of energy-efficient heating systems.

Gulland, John, "Woodstove Buyer's Guide," *Mother Earth News*, December/January 2002, pp. 32–43. Superb overview of woodstoves with a useful table to help you select a model that meets your needs.

Lyle, David, *The Book of Masonry Stoves: Rediscovering an Old Way of Warming*, Chelsea Green, 1984. This book contains a wealth of information on the history, function, design, and construction of masonry stoves.

Malin, Nadav, and Alex Wilson, "Ground-Source Heat Pumps: Are They Green?" *Environmental Building News* 9, July/August 2000, 1, pp. 16–22. Available from BuildingGreen, Inc. <www.BuildingGreen.com>. Detailed overview of the operation and pros and cons of ground-source heat pumps.

National Renewable Energy Lab. "Geothermal Heat Pumps," [online], <www.eren.doe.gov/erec/fact sheets/geo_heatpumps.html>. Great overview of ground-source heat pumps.

Siegenthaler, John, "Hydronic Radiant-Floor Heating," *Fine Homebuilding*, October/November 1996, pp. 58–63. Available from Taunton Press <www.taunton.com/finehomebuilding/index.asp>. Extremely useful reference. Well-written, thorough, and well-illustrated.

Wilson, Alex, "A Primer on Heating Systems," *Fine Homebuilding*, February/March 1997, pp. 50–55. Available from Taunton Press (see above). Superb overview of furnaces, boilers, and heat systems.

Wilson, A, "Radiant-Floor Heating: When It Does — and Doesn't — Make Sense," *Environmental Building News*, January 2002, 1, pp. 9–14. Available from BuildingGreen, listed above. Valuable reading.

Organizations

Geo-Heat Center, Oregon Institute of Technology, 3201 Campus Drive, Klamath, OR 97601. Phone: (541) 885-1750. Website: <www.oit.osshe.edu/~geoheat/>. Technical information on heat pumps.

Geothermal Heat Pump Consortium, Inc., 701 Pennsylvania Avenue NW, Washington DC, 20004-2696. Phone: (888) 333-4472. Website: <www.ghpc.org>. General and technical information on heat pumps.

Hearth, Patio, and Barbecue Association (formerly the Hearth Products Association), 1601 North Kent Street, Suite 1001, Arlington, VA 22209. Website: <http://hpba.org>. International trade association that promotes the interests of the hearth products industry. Offers lots of valuable information.

Masonry Heater Association of North America, 1252 Stock Farm Road, Randolph, VT 05060. Phone: (802) 728•5896. Website: <www.mha-net.org>. Publishes a valuable newsletter and has a website with links to dealers and masons who design and build masonry stoves.

Radiant Panel Association, 1433 West 29 Street, Loveland, CO 80539. Phone: (970) 613•0100. Website: <www.radiantpanelassociation.org>. Professional organization consisting of radiant heating and cooling contractors, wholesalers, manufacturers, and professionals.

U.S. Department of Energy, Office of Geothermal Technologies, EE-12, 1000 Independence Avenue SW, Washington DC, 20585-0121. Phone: (202) 586•5340. Carries out research on ground source heat pumps and works closely with industry to implement new ideas.

Suggestion 21. Solarize Homes

Publications

Chiras, Daniel D., *The Solar House: Passive Heating and Cooling*, Chelsea Green, 2002. A comprehensive guide to heating and cooling homes naturally.

Chiras, Daniel D., "Build a Solar Home and Let the Sunshine In," *Mother Earth News*, August/September 2002, pp. 74–81. A survey of passive solar design principles and a case study showing the economics of passive solar heating.

Chiras, Dan, "Tapping into the Sun," *Natural Home*, March/April 2003, pp. 78–81. Available from 201 Fourth Street, Loveland, CO 80537 <www.naturalhomemagazine.com>. A brief introduction to passive solar heating with ideas on retrofitting homes for passive solar.

Energy Division, North Carolina Department of Commerce, *Solar Homes for North Carolina: A Guide to Building and Planning Solar Homes*, North Carolina Solar Center, 1999. Available on-line at the North Carolina Solar Center's website, listed under Organizations.

Miller, Burke, *Solar Energy: Today's Technologies for a Sustainable Future*, American Solar Energy Society, 1997. Available from American Solar Energy Society, listed under Organizations. An extremely valuable resource with numerous case studies showing how passive solar heating can be used in different climates, even some fairly solar-deprived places.

Olson, Ken, and Joe Schwartz, "Home Sweet Solar Home: A Passive Solar Design Primer," *Home Power*, August/September 2002, pp. 86–94. Available from P.O. Box 520, Ashland, OR 97520 <www.homepower.com>. Superb introduction to passive solar design principles.

Sustainable Buildings Industry Council. *Designing Low-Energy Buildings: Passive Solar Strategies and Energy-10 Software*, SBIC, 1996. Available from Sustainable Buildings Industry Council, listed under Organizations. A superb resource! This book of design guidelines and the Energy-10 software that comes with it enable builders to analyze the energy and cost savings in building designs. Helps permit region-specific design.

Magazines and Newsletters

Backwoods Home Magazine, P.O. Box 712, Gold Beach, OR 97444. Phone: (800) 835-2418. Website: <www.backhome.com>. Publishes articles on all aspects of self-reliant living, including renewable energy strategies such as solar.

Home Energy Magazine, 2124 Kittredge Street, No. 95, Berkeley, CA 94704. Great resource for those who want to learn more about ways to save energy in conventional home construction.

Home Power, P.O. Box 520, Ashland, OR 97520. Phone: (800) 707-6585. Website: <www.homepower. com>. Publishes numerous articles on photovoltaics, wind energy, and micro-hydroelectric and occasionally an article or two on passive solar heating and cooling.

Solar Today, 2400 Central Avenue, Suite G-1, Boulder, CO 80301. Phone: (303) 443-3130. Website: <www.ases.org/solar/>. This magazine, published by the American Solar Energy Society, contains a wealth of information on passive solar, solar thermal, photovoltaics, hydrogen, and other topics. Also lists names of engineers, builders, and installers and lists workshops and conferences

Videos

Buildings for a Sustainable America. Available from the Sustainable Buildings Industry Council (SBIC), 1331 H Street NW, Suite 1000, Washington DC, 20005. Phone: (202) 628-7400. Website: www. sbicouncil.org. A concise overview of passive solar buildings and their benefits.

The Solar-Powered Home with Rob Roy. Can be purchased from the Earthwood Building School, 366 Murtagh Hill Road, West Chazy, NY 12992. Phone: (518) 493•7744. Website: <www.interlog.com/~ewood>. An 84-minute video that examines basic principles, components, set-up, and system planning for an off-grid home, featuring tips from America's leading experts in the field of home power.

Organizations

American Solar Energy Society, 2400 Central Avenue, Suite G-1, Boulder, CO 80301. Website: <www.ases.org/solar/>. Publishes *Solar Today* magazine and sponsors an annual national meeting. Also publishes an on-line catalog of publications and sponsors the National Tour of Solar Homes. Contact this organization to find out about an ASES chapter in your area.

Center for Buildings and Thermal Systems of the National Renewable Energy Lab (NREL), 1617 Cole Boulevard, Golden, CO 80401. Phone: (303) 384•7349. Website: <www.nrel.gov/buildings/high performance>. Key players in research and education on energy efficiency and passive solar heating and cooling.

Center for Renewable Energy and Sustainable Technologies (CREST), 1612 K Street NW, Suite 410, Washington DC, 20006. Phone: (202) 293•2898. Website: <http://solstice.crest.org>. Non-profit organization dedicated to renewable energy, energy efficiency, and sustainable living.

Energy Efficiency and Renewable Energy Clearinghouse, P.O. Box 3048, Merrifield, VA 22116. Phone: (800) 363•3732. Great source of a variety of useful information on renewable energy.

North Carolina Solar Center, Box 7401, Raleigh, NC 27695. Phone: (919) 51•3480. Website: <www.ncsc.ncsu.edu>. Offers workshops, tours, publications, and much more.

Solar Energy International, P.O. Box 715, Carbondale, CO 81623. Phone: (970) 963•8855. Website: <www.solarenergy.org>. Offers a wide range of workshops on solar energy, wind energy, and natural building.

Sustainable Buildings Industries Council (SBIC), 331 H Street NW, Suite 1000, Washington DC, 20005. Phone: (202) 628•7400. Website: <www.psic.org/>. This organization has a terrific website with information on workshops, books, and publications, and links to many other international, national, and state solar energy organizations. Publishes a newsletter, *Buildings Inside and Out*.

Suggestion 22. Create a Community Energy System

See resources listed under Suggestions 20 and 21.

Publications

Gipe, Paul, *Wind Power: For Homes and Business. Renewable Energy for the 1990s and Beyond*, Chelsea Green, 1993. Comprehensive, technical coverage of home wind power.

Hackleman, Michael, and Claire Anderson, "Harvest the Wind," *Mother Earth News*, June/July 2002, pp. 70–81. A wonderful introduction to wind power.

Jeffrey, Kevin, *Independent Energy Guide: Electrical Power for Home, Boat, and RV*, Orwell Cove Press, 1995. Contains a wealth of information on solar electric systems and wind generators — and it is fairly easy to read.

Komp, Richard J., *Practical Photovoltaics: Electricity from Solar Cells*, 3rd ed., aatec Publications, 1999. Fairly popular book on PVs.

Peavy, Michael A., *Fuel from Water: Energy Independence with Hydrogen*, 8th ed., Merit, Inc., 1998. Technical analysis for engineers and chemists.

Potts, Michael, *The New Independent Home: People and Houses that Harvest the Sun, Wind, and Water*, Chelsea Green, 1999. Looks at a variety of ways to achieve energy independence in one's home.

Sagrillo, Mick, "Apples and Oranges 2002: Choosing a Home-Sized Wind Generator," *Home Power*, August/September 2002, 50–66. Available from P.O. Box 520, Ashland, OR 97520 <www.home power.com>. An extremely useful comparison of popular wind generators with lots of good advice on choosing a wind machine that works best for you. A must read for anyone interested in buying a wind generator.

Schaeffer, John, and the Real Goods Staff, *Solar Living Source Book*, 10th ed., Real Goods, 1999. Contains an enormous amount of background information on wind, solar, and micro-hydroelectric.

Seuss, Terri, and Cheryl Long, "Eliminate Your Electric Bill: Go Solar, Be Secure," *Mother Earth News*, February/March 2002, pp. 72–82. An excellent discussion of solar roofing materials.

Videos

An Introduction to Residential Microhydro Power with Don Harris, produced by Scott S. Andrews, P.O. Box 3027, Sausalito, CA 94965. Phone: (415) 332•5191. Outstanding video packed with lots of useful information.

An Introduction to Residential Solar Electricity with Johnny Weiss. Source: listed above. Good basic introduction to solar electricity.

An Introduction to Residential Wind Power with Mick Sagrillo. Source: listed above. A very informative video, especially for those wishing to install a medium-sized system.

An Introduction to Solar Water Pumping with Windy Dankoff. Source: listed above. A very useful introduction to the subject.

An Introduction to Storage Batteries for Renewable Energy Systems with Richard Perez. Source: listed above. This is one of the best videos in the series. It's full of great information.

Newsletters and Magazines

Home Power Magazine, P.O. Box 520, Ashland, OR 97520. Phone: (800) 707•6585. Website: <www.homepower.com>. See description under Suggestion 21.

Solar Today, 2400 Central Avenue, Suite G-1, Boulder, CO 80301. Phone: (303) 443•3130. Website: <www.ases.org/solar/> See description under Suggestion 21.

Wind Energy Weekly, 122 C Street NW, Suite 380, Washington DC, 20001. Phone: (202) 383•2500. Website: <www.ogc.apc.org/awea/>. Newsletter published by the American Wind Energy Association.

Organizations

American Solar Energy Society, 2400 Central Avenue, Suite G-1, Boulder, CO 80301. Website: <www.ases.org/solar/>. See description under Suggestion 21.

American Wind Energy Association, 122 C Street NW, Suite 380, Washington DC, 20001. Phone: (202) 383•2500. Website: <www.ogc.apc.org/awea/>. This organization sponsors an annual conference on wind energy. Check out the website, which contains a list of publications, an on-line newsletter, frequently asked questions, news releases, and links to companies and organizations.

Beddington Zero Energy Development, c/o Peabody Trust, 45 Westminster Bridge Road, London, UK, SE1 7JB. Phone: 020 7922 0239. Website: <www.bedzed.org.uk>. For information on a truly inspiring ecovillage in the United Kingdom.

Hockerton Housing Project Trading Ltd., The Watershed, Gables Drive, Hockerton, Southwell, Nottinghamshire, U.K., NG25 0QU. For information on a small housing development that incorporated many of the environmental aspects of Superbia!

National Wind Technology Center of The National Renewable Energy Laboratory, 1617 Cole Boulevard, Golden, CO 80401-3393. Phone: (303) 275-3000. Website: <www.nrel.gov/wind/index.html>. Website provides a search mode so you can check out the site, which provides a great deal of information on wind energy, including a wind resource database.

Solar Living Institute, P.O. Box 836, Hopland, CA 95449. Phone: (707) 744-2017. Website: <www.solarliving.org>. A non-profit organization that offers frequent hands-on workshops on solar and wind energy and many other topics.

Suggestion 23. Establish Environmentally Friendly Water and Wastewater Systems

Publications

Banks, Suzy, and Richard Heinichen, *Rainwater Collection for the Mechanically Challenged*, Tank Town Publishing, 1997. Humorous and informative guide to aboveground rainwater catchment systems.

Campbell, Stu, *The Home Water Supply: How to Find, Filter, Store, and Conserve It*, Storey Communications, Inc., 1983. Good resource on water supply systems, although it is dated. Unfortunately, it has very little about catchwater or graywater systems.

Del Porto, David, and Carol Steinfeld, *The Composting Toilet System Book*, Center for Ecological Pollution Prevention, 1999. Contains detailed information on composting toilets and graywater systems.

Jenkins, Joseph, *The Humanure Handbook: A Guide to Composting Human Manure*, 2nd ed., Jenkins Publishing, 1999. Excellent resource. Well worth your time.

Ludwig, Art, *Creating an Oasis with Greywater: Your Complete Guide to Managing Greywater in the Landscape*, Oasis Design, 1994. Fairly detailed discussion of the various types of graywater systems.

Ludwig, Art, *Building Professional's Supplement: Your Complete Guide to Professional Installation of Greywater Systems*, Oasis Design, 1995. Contains a wealth of information on graywater systems, including important information on safety and chemical contents of detergents.

Solar Survival Architecture, "Catchwater," In *Earthship Chronicles* series, Solar Survival Press, 1998. Focuses primarily on catchwater systems for Earthships, but has ideas that are relevant to all homes.

Solar Survival Architecture, "Greywater," In *Earthship Chronicles* series, Solar Survival Press, 1998. Focuses primarily on graywater systems for Earthships, but has ideas that are relevant to all homes.

Solar Survival Architecture, "Black Water." In *Earthship Chronicles* series, Solar Survival Press, 1998. Provides an introduction to the black water systems under development by SSA.

U.S. Environmental Protection Agency, *US EPA Guidelines for Water Reuse*, Publication USEPA/USAID EPA625/R-92/004, Washington DC: U.S. EPA, 1992. You can obtain a copy of this document from the U.S. EPA National Center for Environmental Publications, P.O. Box 42419, Cincinnati, OH 45242. Phone: (800) 489•9198. Website: <www.epa.gov/epahome/publications.htm>.

Videos

Rainwater Collection Systems, available from Garden-Ville Nursery, 8648 Old Bee Cave Road, Austin, TX 78735. Phone: (512) 288•6113. This brief, informative video comes with a 50-page booklet that provides more details on systems and provide information on equipment and suppliers.

Organizations

American Water Works Association, 6666 West Quincy Avenue, Denver, CO 80235. Phone: (303) 794•7711. Website: <www.awwa.org>. Concerned with many aspects of water, including water reuse. Publishes proceedings from its water-reuse conferences.

Rocky Mountain Institute, 1739 Snowmass Creek Road, Snowmass, CO 81654. Phone: (970) 927•3851. Website: <www.rmi.org>. Check out the catalog of this outstanding organization for publications on water efficiency and water reuse.

Suggestion 24. Establish an Environmentally Friendly Transportation Strategy

Organizations

Neighborhood Transportation Planning Resources website: <www.ar.utexas.edu/cadlab/handyweb/ NTransPlanLinks.html>. Provides great links to a wealth of resources for rethinking neighborhood transportation.

Transportation Alternatives, 115 West 30 Street, Suite 1207, New York, NY 10001. Phone: 212-629-8080. Website: <www.transalt.org/>. Promotes walking and environmentally sensible transportation.

Suggestion 25. Create a Common House

See cohousing resources listed earlier, such as *Cohousing Journal*, available from The Cohousing Network, listed above.

Fitch, Laura, "Home Officing at Pioneer Valley Cohousing," *Cohousing Journal*, Winter 2001. Excellent article on the benefits of community offices.

Suggestion 26. Create a Community-shared Office

See cohousing resources such as *Cohousing Journal*, available from The Cohousing Network, listed above.

Suggestion 27. Establish a Community Entertainment Program

Publications

Burnham, Linda Frye, and Steven Durland, *The Citizen Artist: 20 Years of Art in the Public Arena*, Critical Press, 1998. An anthology on performance art, art for activists, and art for building community.

Cleveland, William. *Art in Other Places: Artists at Work in America's Community and Social Institutions*, University of Massachusetts Arts Extension Service, 2000. Describes how community arts programs have been used to address some of our most pressing issues.

Communities Magazine 107 (Summer 2000), "Song, Dance, & Celebration," contact: Diana Christian, 52 Willow Street, Marion, NC 28752-4840. Phone: (828) 652•8517. E-mail: communities@ic.org. A good issue from a magazine with 30 years of reporting about intentional communities from urban co-ops to cohousing groups to ecovillages to rural communes.

Organizations

Community Arts Network (CAN), PB 308, Virginia Tech, Blackburg, VA 24061. Phone: (540) 231•6594. Website: <www.communityarts.net>. Promotes art as part of education, political life, health recovery, and community regeneration.

Ecoartspace website: <www.ecoartspace.org>. Supports art that raises environmental awareness, provides links to other organizations.

Suggestion 28. Narrow or Eliminate Streets

Publications

Appleyard, Donald, *Livable Streets*, University of California Press, 1981. A good source of information from the pioneer in street reclamation.

Beatley, Timothy, *Green Urbanism: Learning from European Cities*, Island Press, 2000. Worthwhile reading.

Burden, David. *Street Design Guidelines for Healthy Neighborhoods*, Center for Livable Communities, 1999. A publication from the folks at Local Government Commission, an excellent organization (see listing under Suggestion 30).

Burrington, Stephen, and Veronika Thiebach, *Take Back Your Streets: How to Protect Communities from Asphalt and Traffic*, Conservation Law Foundation, 1995. Good reference on street calming.

Engwicht, David, *Street Reclaiming: Creating Livable Streets and Vibrant Communities*, New Society Publishers, 1999. Offers valuable insights on the changes that have occurred in our cities and suburbs with the rise of the automobile's popularity, and ways to reverse them, regaining streets and creating more livable communities.

Organizations

Better Environmentally Sound Transportation, 510 West Hastings Street, Suite 822, Vancouver, BC, Canada V6B 1L8. Phone: (604) 669-3869. Provides information on environmentally friendly transportation alternatives.

The City Repair Project, P.O. Box 42615, Portland, OR 97242. Phone: (503) 235-8946. Helps facilitate intersection repair and much more.

Creative Communities International, 7 Fletcher Parade, Bardon Queensland 4065, Australia. Phone: (617) 3366-7748. Visit all three of their websites: <www.lesstraffic.com> for resources on street reclaiming; www.traffictamers.com to encourage kids to walk to school; <www.playforchange.com>, which invites people to change the world by playing a range of simple games.

Home Zone website: <www.homezones.org>. Provides assistance on street calming efforts in the U.K. and other European countries.

Living Streets Initiative, Pedestrians Association, 3rd Floor, 31–33 Bondway, London, UK, SW8 1SJ. Phone: 020 7820 1010. Website: <www.livingstreets.org.uk>. Promotes the safety of the walking public and the comfort of and general amenities for pedestrians.

Walkable Communities, 320 S. Main Street, High Springs, FL 32643. Phone: (386) 454-3304. Website: <www.walkable.org>. Dedicated to helping whole communities, from large cities to small towns, or parts of communities, become more walkable and pedestrian friendly.

Suggestion 29. Retrofit Garages and Spare Rooms into Apartments

The references in this section will help you create a healthy, environmentally friendly structure.

Publications

Baker-Laporte, Paula, Erica Elliot, and John Banta, *Prescriptions for a Healthy House: A Practical Guide for Architects, Builders, and Homeowners*. 2nd ed., New Society Publishers, 2001. Contains a great amount of useful information.

Bower, John, *The Healthy House: How to Buy One, How to Build One, How to Cure a Sick One*, 3rd ed., The Healthy House Institute, 1997. A detailed guide to all aspects of home construction.

Bower, John, and Lynn Marie Bower, *The Healthy House Answer Book: Answers to the 133 Most Commonly Asked Questions*, The Healthy House Institute, 1997. Great resource.

Center for Resourceful Building Technology Staff, *Reducing Construction and Demolition Waste*, National Center for Appropriate Technology, Center for Resourceful Building Technology, 1995. A guide for builders and homeowners on jobsite recycling.

Chiras, Daniel D., *The Natural House: A Complete Guide to Healthy, Energy-efficient, Environmental Homes*, Chelsea Green, 2000. Contains a wealth of information on natural building materials with discussions of the pros and cons of each one.

Chiras, Dan, "Green Remodeling: Keeping it Clean," *Solar Today*, May/June 2001, pp. 24–27. Available from 2400 Central Avenue, Suite G-1, Boulder, CO 80301 <www.ases.org/solar/>. Describes a strategy for remodeling a home to prevent indoor air pollution.

Chiras, Daniel, *Green Building*, Chelsea Green, 2004. A highly readable book that describes the steps needed to create environmentally friendly homes.

Edminster, Ann, and Sami Yassa, *Efficient Wood Use in Residential Construction: A Practical Guide to Saving Wood, Money, and Forests*, Natural Resources Defense Council, 1998. Available in print and on-line at <www.nrdc.org/cities/building/rwoodus.asp>. Describes how to reduce lumber use by 30 percent without compromising the structural integrity of a home.

Hermannsson, John. *Green Building Resource Guide*, Taunton Press, 1997. A goldmine of information on environmentally friendly building materials.

Holmes, Dwight, Larry Strain, Alex Wilson, and Sandra Leibowitz, *GreenSpec: The Environmental Building News Product Directory and Guideline Specifications*, BuildingGreen, Inc., 1999. Guideline specifications make this a valuable resource for commercial builders and architects.

Magwood, Chris, and Peter Mack, *Straw Bale Building: How to Plan, Design, and Build Straw Bale*, New Society Publishers, 2000. A wonderfully written book on building straw bale in a variety of climates, especially northern ones. Contains a fair amount of information on plastering.

Myhrman, Matts, and S.O. Myhrman, *Build It with Bales (Version 2.0): A Step-by-Step Guide to Straw-bale Construction*, Out on Bale, 1998. A superbly illustrated and recently updated manual on straw bale construction. Contains a fair amount of information on wall preparation, plasters, and plastering.

Oblensky, Kira, *Garage: Reinventing the Place We Park*, Taunton Press, 2001. A fun look at ways to convert garages to living spaces.

Steen, Athena S., Bill Steen, David Bainbridge, and David Eisenberg, *The Straw Bale House*, Chelsea Green, 1994. Contains a wealth of information on straw bale construction, wall preparation, and plasters.

Sustainable Buildings Industry Council, *Green Building Guidelines: Meeting the Demand for Low-Energy, Resource-Efficient Homes*, SBIC, 2002. General guide to green building, covering many important topics.

U.S. Environmental Protection Agency, *A Citizen's Guide to Radon: The Guide to Protecting Yourself and Your Family from Radon*, 2nd ed., U.S. EPA, 1992. A very basic on-line introduction to radon. Available at: <www.epa.gov/iaq/radon/pubs/citguide.html>.

U.S. Environmental Protection Agency, *What You Should Know About Combustion Appliances and Indoor Air Quality*, U.S. EPA, undated. A great introduction to the effects of indoor air pollutants from combustion sources. Available at: <www.epa/iaq/pubs/combust.html>.

U.S. Environmental Protection Agency and the U.S. Consumer Product Safety Commission, *The Inside Story: A Guide to Indoor Air Quality*. EPA Document No. 402-K-93-007, U.S. Government Printing Office, 1995. Also available online at <www.epa.gov/iaq/insidest.html>. Helpful publication for those interested in learning more about indoor air quality issues and solutions.

Wells, Malcolm, *How to Build an Underground House*, self-published, 1994. To obtain a copy, contact the author at Box 1149, 673 Satucket Road, Brewster, MA 02631. Overview of earth-sheltered building.

Wells, Malcolm, *The Earth-Sheltered House: An Architect's Sketchbook*, Chelsea Green, 1998. Great little book on earth-sheltered design.

Magazines and Newsletters

Environmental Building News, BuildingGreen, Inc., 122 Birge Street, Suite 30, Brattleboro, VT 05301. Phone: (803) 257•7300. Website: <www.BuildingGreen.com>. The nation's leading source of objective information on green building, including alternative energy and backup heating systems. Archives containing all issues published from 1992 to 2001 are available on a CD-ROM.

Environmental Design and Construction, 81 Landers Street, San Francisco, CA 94114. Phone: (415) 863•2614. Website: <www.EDCmag.com>. Publishes numerous articles on green building; geared more toward commercial buildings.

Mother Earth News, 1503 SW 42 Street, Topeka, KS 66609. Phone: (800) 678•5779. Website: <www.motherearthnews.com>. Publishes a wide assortment of stories on green building, from natural building to solar and wind energy to natural swimming pools to green building materials.

Natural Home, 201 Fourth Street, Loveland, CO 80537. Website: <www.naturalhomemagazine.com>. Publishes numerous articles on green building, especially natural building and healthy building products, with lots of inspiring photographs.

Online Sources

Austin's Green Building program at <www.greenbuilder.com/sourcebook/>. Provides on-line information on manufacturers.

Center for Resourceful Building Technology's e-Guide: <www.crbt.org>. Provides a searchable database on green building materials and their manufacturers.

National Park Service Sustainable Design and Construction Database website: <www.nps.gov/dsc/dsgncnstr/gpsd>. Provides brief reviews of over 1,300 products from over 550 manufacturers.

Oikos Green Building Product Information website: <www.oikos.com/products>. Yet another on-line source of information.

Wholesale and Retail Outlets

Building for Health Materials Center, P.O. Box 113, Carbondale, CO 81623. Phone: (970) 963•0437. Website: <www.buildingforhealth.com>. Offers a complete line of healthy, environmentally safe building materials and home appliances including straw bale construction products; natural plastering products; flooring; natural paints, oils, stains, and finishes; sealants; and construction materials. Offers special pricing for owner-builders and contractors.

EcoBuild, P.O. Box 4655, Boulder, CO 80306. Phone: (303) 545•6255 Website: <www.eco-build.com>. This company located in Boulder, Colorado, works specifically with builders and general contractors, providing consultation and green building materials at competitive prices.

Eco-Products, Inc., 1780 – 55th Street, Boulder, CO 80301. Phone: (303) 449•1876. Website: <www.ecoproducts.com>. Offers a variety of green building products including plastic lumber.

Eco-Wise, 110 W Elizabeth, Austin, TX 78704. Phone: (512) 326•4474. Website: <www.ecowise.com>. Carries a wide range of environmental building materials, including non-toxic natural finishes and adhesives.

Environmental Building Supplies, 1331 NW Kearney Street, Portland, OR 97209. Phone: (503) 222•3881. Website: <www.ecohaus.com>. Green building materials outlet for the Pacific Northwest.

Environmental Construction Outfitters, 44 Crosby Street, New York, NY 10012. Phone: (800) 238•5008. Website: <www.environproducts.com>. Sells an assortment of green building materials.

Environmental Home Center, 1724 Fourth Avenue South, Seattle, WA 98134. Phone: (800) 281•9785. Website: <www.built-e.com>. Offers a variety of green building materials.

Planetary Solutions, 2030 17th Street, Boulder, CO 80302. Phone: (303) 442•6228. Website: <www.planetearth.com>. Long-time green building material supplier. Offers paints, flooring, tile, and much more.

Real Goods, 13771 S. Highway 101, Hopland, CA 95449. Phone: (800) 919•2400. Website: <www.realgoods.com>. Sells a wide range of environmentally responsible products for homes from solar and wind energy equipment to water efficiency products to air filters and environmentally responsible furnishings.

Organizations

American Institute of Architects, 1735 New York Avenue NW, Washington DC, 20006. Phone: (800) 242•3837. Website: <www.aia.org>. Their national and state committees on the environment are actively promoting green building practices and have been for many years.

BuildingGreen, Inc., 122 Birge Street, Suite 30, Brattleboro, VT 05301. Phone (800) 861•0954. Website: <www.BuildingGreen.com>. Publishes *Environmental Building News*, *GreenSpec Directory* (a comprehensive listing of green building materials, *Green Building Advisor* (a CD-ROM that provides advice on incorporating green building materials and techniques in residential and commercial applications), and Premium Online Resources (a website containing an electronic version of its newsletter).

Building Industry Professionals for Environmental Responsibility, 5245 College Avenue, #225, Oakland, CA 94618. Website: <www.biperusa.biz>. A national non-profit organization that promotes environmentally sustainable building.

Center for Resourceful Building Technology, P.O. Box 100, Missoula, MT 59806. Phone: (406) 549•7678. Web: <www.crbt.org>. A project of the National Center for Appropriate Technology. Promotes environmentally responsible construction.

Ecological Building Network, 209 Caledonia Street, Sausalito, CA 94965-1926. Phone: (415) 331•7360. Website: <www.ecobuildnetwork>. Seeks ways to build environmentally sustainable shelter in wealthy industrial and non-industrial nations.

The Healthy House Institute, 430 N. Sewell Road, Bloomington, IN 47408. Phone: (812) 332•5073. Website: <http://hhinst.com/index.html>. Offers books and videos on healthy building.

National Association of Home Builders Research Center, 400 Prince George's Boulevard, Upper Marlboro, MD 20744. Phone: (301) 249•4000. Website: <www.nahbrc.org>. A leader in green building, including energy efficiency. Sponsors important conferences, research, and publications. For a listing of their books visit <www.builderbooks.com>.

National Radon Hotline: (800) SOS•RADON. Website: <www.epa.gov/iaq/contacts.html>. Calling this number or contacting the website will give you access to local contacts who can answer radon questions.

Suggestion 30. Create a Mixed-use Neighborhood

Publications

Calthorpe, Peter, *The Next American Metropolis: Ecology, Community, and the American Dream*, Princeton Architectural Press, 1993. A great and very thorough look at how the pieces of the metropolitan fabric fit together.

Calthorpe, Peter, William Fulton, and Robert Fishman, *The Regional City: Planning for the End of Sprawl*, Island Press, 2001. An update of *The Next American Metropolis* with additional analysis and design ideas.

Duany, Andres, Elizabeth Plater-Zyberk, and Jeff Speck, *Suburban Nation: The Rise of Sprawl and the Decline of the American Dream*, North Point Press, 2000. Examines creative ways to alter the course of urban and suburban development primarily through neighborhood development.

Hall, Kenneth B., and Gerald A. Porterfield, *Community by Design: New Urbanism for Suburbs and Small Communities*, McGraw-Hill, 1995.

Organizations

Local Government Commission, 909 12th Street, Suite 205, Sacramento, CA 95814. Phone: (800) 290-8202 or (916) 448-1198. Website: <www.cnt.org/>. This organization keeps track of innovations in land use, New Urbanism, Smart Growth, and livable communities. Its newsletter is well worth receiving.

Suggestion 31. Foster Diversity

Organizations

Center of Excellence for Sustainable Development, U.S. Department of Energy, Office of Energy Efficiency and Renewable Energy, 1617 Cole Boulevard, Golden, CO 80401. Phone: (303) 275•4826. Website: <www.sustainable.doe.gov>. Promotes mixed-use, diverse communities.

Rocky Mountain Institute, 1739 Snowmass Creek Road, Snowmass, CO 81654. Phone: (970) 927•3420. Website: <www.rmi.org/>. A non-profit organization whose mission is to create a sustainable society. RMI's Green Development staff promotes diverse neighborhoods.

Index

About the authors

Dan Chiras is a freelance writer, consultant, and educator. The author of 19 books, including *The Natural Plaster Book*, with New Society Publishes, and over 200 articles in publications such as *Natural Home*, *Home Power Journal* and *The Last Straw*. He is also a contributing editor and advisor to *Mother Earth News*; an adjunct professor at two universities in Denver; and currently teaches courses on ecological design and renewable energy at Colorado College. Chiras is a member of the Colorado Renewable Energy Society and the American Solar Energy Society.

Dave Wann worked with the EPA for a decade and is now a writer and video producer. Widely published in magazines such as *Organic Gardening*, *Mother Earth News* and *Sierra*, he is also the coauthor of the successful book, *Affluenza: The All-Consuming Epidemic* and two other books about design, as well as six video programs on community. He is the 2002 winner of the Timothy Wirth Award for Sustainability and us the Vice President of the Sustainable Future Society.

If you have enjoyed *Superbia!* you might also enjoy other

BOOKS TO BUILD A NEW SOCIETY

Our books provide positive solutions for people who want to make a difference. We specialize in:

**Sustainable Living • Ecological Design and Planning • Natural Building & Appropriate Technology
New Forestry • Environment and Justice • Conscientious Commerce • Progressive Leadership
Educational and Parenting Resources • Resistance and Community • Nonviolence**

For a full list of NSP's titles, please call 1-800-567-6772 or check out our web site at: **www.newsociety.com**

New Society Publishers

ENVIRONMENTAL BENEFITS STATEMENT

New Society Publishers has chosen to produce this book on Enviro, recycled paper made with 100% post consumer waste, processed chlorine free, and old growth free.

For every 5,000 books printed, New Society saves the following resources:[1]

46	Trees
4,147	Pounds of Solid Waste
4,563	Gallons of Water
5,951	Kilowatt Hours of Electricity
7,538	Pounds of Greenhouse Gases
32	Pounds of HAPs, VOCs, and AOX Combined
11	Cubic Yards of Landfill Space

[1]Environmental benefits are calculated based on research done by the Environmental Defense Fund and other members of the Paper Task Force who study the environmental impacts of the paper industry.

NEW SOCIETY PUBLISHERS